PENGUIN BOOKS

MIDSTREAM

Le Anne Schreiber was born in Evanston, Illinois. She received her B.A. from Rice University, her M.A. from Stanford on a Woodrow Wilson Fellowship, and accepted a Harvard Prize Fellowship for five more years of graduate study and teaching. She worked at *Time* Magazine, writing on foreign affairs, then covered the 1976 Olympics, and began a meteoric rise in sports journalism, first becoming editor-in-chief of *WomenSports*, then editor of *The New York Times* sports section. In 1980 she left sports coverage to serve as the deputy editor of *The New York Times Book Review*, and four years later left New York altogether to fish, tend to her garden, and write. She lives in Ancrum, New York.

LE ANNE SCHREIBER
MIDSTREAM

PENGUIN BOOKS

PENGUIN BOOKS
Published by the Penguin Group
Viking Penguin, a division of Penguin Books USA Inc.,
375 Hudson Street, New York, New York 10014, U.S.A.
Penguin Books Ltd, 27 Wrights Lane, London W8 5TZ, England
Penguin Books Australia Ltd, Ringwood, Victoria, Australia
Penguin Books Canada Ltd, 2801 John Street,
Markham, Ontario, Canada L3R 1B4
Penguin Books (N.Z.) Ltd, 182–190 Wairau Road,
Auckland 10, New Zealand

Penguin Books Ltd, Registered Offices:
Harmondsworth, Middlesex, England

First published in the United States of America by Viking Penguin, a division of
Penguin Books USA Inc., 1990
Published in Penguin Books 1991

10   9   8   7   6   5   4   3   2   1

LIBRARY OF CONGRESS CATALOGING IN PUBLICATION DATA
Schreiber, Le Anne, 1945–
Midstream/Le Anne Schreiber.
p.   cm.
1. Schreiber, Le Anne, 1945—Diaries.   2. Pancreas—Cancer—
Patients—United States—Biography.   3. Mothers and daughters—
United States—Biography.   I. Title.
ISBN 0 14 01.2187 0
[RC280.P25S37   1991]
362.1′9699437′0092—dc20   90–43838

Printed in the United States of America
Set in Garamond Number 3
Designed by Fritz Metsch

For Beatrice and Newton,
in sickness and in health

CONTENTS

MIDSTREAM

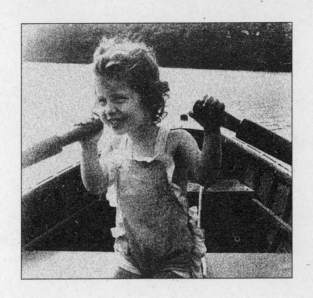

I had just turned forty and was feeling very pleased with myself. Earlier in the week, I had returned to New York from a summer in Italy, and I was eager to take up the life I had left behind in the spring. I had seen forty coming and was prepared for it. After ten hard-working years as a journalist in Manhattan, I had resigned my position at *The New York Times* in May 1984 and had moved into a drafty old house in a rural hamlet two hours north of the city. In the past year, my first as a country woman, I had created a life full of pleasure and freedom, and I was determined to make it permanent. The perfect life, my version of it anyway, seemed within reach: a life of reading, writing, trout fishing and tending my garden; a solitary life made civilized by occasional trips to the city and frequent visits from city friends who wanted a taste of rural delights.

It was a second childhood of sorts, this one in the setting of my choice. For thirty-nine years, I had lived in big cities or their nearest suburbs, my settings chosen for their schools or jobs. For thirty-nine years, I had satisfied a yearning for landscape with city parks or precious snatches of vacation spent gazing out car windows at other people's countryside. I learned to count in a park across the street from my first address in Evanston, Illinois, the desire for knowledge fueled by a need to boast how many fireflies I caught there one summer evening in 1948. I learned proportion there as well; as I grew bigger, the park grew smaller. When my mother stuck her head out the window of our third-floor apartment and hollered me home, I no longer felt I was being called to safety from the wild.

My second home, our first house, was set among weed fields on the undeveloped, western edge of town, where I could search for pheasant nests and rabbit holes and play at being Gunga Din. But within two years, the fields had turned to lawns; footpaths stomped through head-high weeds by children tracking tigers had been paved over by streets bearing the names of American presidents. I no longer lived at the edge of the known world. I lived on Cleveland Street, between Dewey and Monroe.

Those two years of roaming through weed lots in Evanston were the closest I had come to country living until August 1983, when I spent a month's vacation on a hilltop in Tuscany. It was not my first trip to Italy, but it was the first time I was able to enter the landscape that beckoned from train windows as I sped, *diretto,* between Rome and Florence. For a month, I lived in a centuries-old farmhouse, its cellar stocked with wine from its own vineyards, with olive oil from its orchards. Mornings, I combed the woods for chanterelles and fungi porcini, the most prized of local mushrooms. I plucked heads of garlic from the garden and shelled peas among the lizards on the patio. On a moonless August 12, I saw my first shooting stars. Every day I watched the sun rise over the Pratomagno, southern foothills of the Apennines, and set over the Chianti Mountains. In the valley between the two ranges flowed the Arno, linking my adopted piece of rural Tuscany to the enticements of Florence, only forty kilometers north. I did not want to leave.

Sitting in the open arches of the loggia, my back nestled against a graceful curve of warm stone, I decided to reclaim my life, to give birth not to a new self but to a new set of circumstances. My situation at the brink of forty was not onerous by any standard; I was well rewarded for working at a job I liked, I relished the intimacy of long-standing friendships and the stimulation of the wide, diverse acquaintanceship that Manhattan provides. I had neither drifted into my situation nor been compelled there by harsh necessities; like most people, I had arrived at my post by continually shifting proportions of choice and accident. The accidents had mostly been lucky ones; without them, I would never have won the privilege of choice I was about to exercise.

Mine had been a curiously well-timed life. I was born the week they dropped the atom bomb, a fact whose implications are so vast that I am only slightly better equipped to unravel them now than I was during those August days in 1945. I do know I was spared much, and given much. By parents, who loved and protected their children in the sheltered garden of postwar suburbia. By a booming postwar economy that placed even the highest education within reach of modest incomes. I came of majority in such a grant-happy time that I reaped nine years of higher education without paying a cent of tuition.

Strange as it now seems, I reached my mid-twenties without giving any sustained thought to questions of career or economic survival. I was a woman formed by the experience of a 1950s Catholic girlhood. Growing up, I knew only two kinds of adult women—nuns and mothers—and I simply presumed I would enter one of their ranks. It seemed a hard choice—poverty, chastity and obedience versus love, honor and obey. Even as a child, the obedience clause in both stations (the word *role* was never used) gave me pause, but I suspected some mysterious

3

hormonal change overcame women in their young adulthood, probably on their twenty-first birthday, making them compliant and content in their choice of lot.

My twenty-first birthday came and went, without the onset of any noticeable personality change. I married at twenty-two, thinking the ceremony itself might alter my chemistry. I didn't worry too much about my vows; my young husband faced four years of Navy duty, much of it at sea, so I could still postpone the time of domesticity and childbearing. In the meantime I would gladly accept the latest grant offer, this one for five years of graduate study in the English department at Harvard. Years hence, I thought, when my children were of school age, perhaps I could get a part-time college teaching job.

In 1972, when my husband returned to civilian life, his body and expectations intact, I was a member of a consciousness-raising group. The women's movement had arrived, just in the nick of time. Within two years, we divorced, without children, without alimony, without rancor. I was also without a job, an income or a direction. I had $100 to my name, a very fancy education, a resurgent curiosity and no practical skills. In August 1974, taking the time-honored path for people in my circumstances, I went to New York to seek my fortune.

Within a week I was offered a job as a writer for *Time* magazine, a plum more often tendered to tall, handsome, well-born men who had edited their Ivy League yearbooks. I was not the only woman on *Time*'s writing staff in 1974, but I was one of a very few, the youngest and, to understate the case, by far the least experienced. I was to be their experiment in seeing what these newly liberated, clamorous young women could do.

For the next ten years I rode a rocket of unprecedented opportunity. Without seeking them, I was offered jobs better suited to someone of far greater years and experience. In each job, I acquitted myself well, but at the stage I might begin to relax into a sense of comfortable mastery, I would be catapulted into a position as improbably outside my experience as the last. I was exhilarated by the adventure of it all, but also exhausted by the constant strain of overreaching.

The pinnacle of miscasting was achieved in 1978 when I was named sports editor of *The New York Times*. I say miscasting, because at the age of thirty-three, there was nothing I wanted to do less than spend eighty hours a week administering a staff of fifty-nine men and one woman in producing three editions a day and two special sections a week of sports coverage. I accepted the job in the spirit of a military conscript. If *The New York Times* was ready to appoint a female head of a hugely male department for the first time in its history, I had no right to refuse the position.

I signed on for a two-year stint as pioneer, knowing I was forfeiting my claims to privacy, a personal life or the indulgence of any interests other than those that might find expression in the sports pages. My identity was no longer my own; I was, depending on one's point of view, the bitch, the saint, the amazon, the token, the recipient of awards and death threats and, ultimately, the ingrate, for insisting upon my pre-agreed release after two excruciating years. I was transferred to The Book Review section, which felt like a homecoming of sorts, and for three years I enjoyed just enough tranquillity to want more.

In August 1983, sitting on the loggia in Italy, my gaze falling on the silvery ruffling of the olive orchard below, I did not regret any of my years in Manhattan, but I was eager to redress certain imbalances. After such a decade, I was ready for a life of my own invention, a life more contemplative, more pastoral. Above all I wanted a life under my own control.

Back in New York I made plans. I would quit my job at The Book Review the following spring and give myself the present of an entire summer in Italy. Between now and then I would find an American landscape satisfying enough to lure me back across the Atlantic, where I could remain close to friends and the English language. I didn't have to look far. Two hours north of New York City, in rural Columbia County, I found my American Tuscany. The Hudson River would be my Arno, the Catskills to the west and the Berkshires to the east my Pratomagno and Chianti Mountains. On the hillsides at twilight, orderly rows of apple trees made the same black silhouette against the same blue sky as the olive trees a continent away. The same stars shot overhead on the same August nights.

So in September 1984, after my promised summer in Italy, I sublet my city apartment, moved into an imposing if ramshackle white clapboard house, vintage 1860s, and began to explore the trout stream whose steep bank formed its back boundary. And, after several months of settling in, I began to write, not for hire, as I had for ten years, but for pleasure.

My friends in New York believed that was the true reason I had removed myself from Manhattan and the perquisites of a well-established career. I was less sure. Days without deadlines seemed their own reward. That first spring, though, after long days spent wading in the stream, I found myself writing, sporadically to be sure, and not with much purpose, but with stirrings of pleasure I had never felt before. That was one of the reasons I was ready to return home after my second long summer in Italy.

In another few days I would be back in my rented house in Glenco Mills, angling for the last trout of the season and looking for a house to call my own. In the meantime I was staying in a borrowed apartment on the Lower East Side. It was a warm, mild Tuesday night—August 27, 1985—and I had arranged to meet a friend at a restaurant on Avenue A. Over dinner she told tales of her summer, working on a film in Africa, and I boasted of long, sunny days and star-filled nights spent among Italians in the hill towns of Tuscany. Wine and balmy night breezes made us even more giddy with self-satisfaction.

Walking home at midnight, I was brimming with well-being, delighted with life and my place in it. I had no idea that I was being stalked, that something had been lying in wait for me ever since that week in August 1945 when my parents, doubly grateful for the end of a war and the birth of a child, made plans to raise her in the immortal innocence that would now be possible.

When I entered the apartment on East Eleventh Street, I saw the red light blinking on the answering machine. My brother, Michael, who lives in Pennsylvania, had called and wanted me to call him back. Despite a four-year age difference, my older brother and I had been very close during the days of Evanston weed lots and pickup softball games, but our adulthoods had taken very different turns, and the distances between us went untraversed. We seldom called each other, and it would have taken some effort for him to find me at this number so despite the late hour I returned the call.

"What's wrong?" I asked, without preface.

"It's Mom," Mike answered. "She has cancer."

I felt something in me collapse, and then, just as suddenly, collect itself. Cancer is not the grim reaper. It's a disease and there are treatments and lots of people survive.

"What kind?" I asked.

"Pancreatic," he said.

"What does that mean?" I asked without breathing.

"It means Mom has two to six months to live," he said. "More likely two than six."

In a subdued, even tone, Mike explained that surgery and chemotherapy are sometimes used to treat this cancer, but the treatments are extremely arduous and the five-year survival rates abysmally low, less than one in fifty. The diagnosis is usually presented as a death sentence and treatment limited to pain control.

My brother is a doctor, a diagnostic radiologist. Everything in me wanted to reject the finality of what he was saying, but I had no ground to stand on to issue my challenge. At this moment, he was authority to my ignorance.

"How is she taking it?" I asked.

"She's scared," Mike answered.

Suddenly there was nothing more to say. It was after 1:00 and we decided it would be better for me to call Mom in the morning than to wake her now from the escape of sleep. We said good-night and made plans to talk again tomorrow.

As soon as I hung up, I began to feel the impact of what I had been told. I've read that people who experience near-death feel themselves being drawn into a tunnel of white light. What I felt at that moment was the opposite; the contemplation of certain death felt like confrontation with a solid black wall so high and wide and thick it filled the universe. There was no way to get over, around or under it and there was nothing else. My mind refused to fix its gaze on this impasse, and so began the process of what is called either hope or denial, and the mental anguish of not knowing which is which.

That night my mind raced backward and forward in time, trying to find a place to rest, a prospect that was tolerable. Superstition offered its consolations. Mom was lucky. She was the one who could sit down on any patch of lawn, run her hand gently through the grass and come up with a four-leafed clover every time. She saw more shooting stars than anyone else. She taught me that the things you worry about most never happen. She couldn't die.

But what if she did? What would happen to Dad? Alone, bereft, his uncertain health strained by grief, he would have to leave Minnesota and come live with me. What would happen to me? Would I be able to sacrifice the freedom I had worked so hard to secure for myself? Only hours ago the future seemed so limitless. And now I can see only the short arc of a pendulum swinging between guilt and sacrifice.

I pull back from the future to the present. Awaiting me there is the thought of my mother, asleep now but soon to wake and remember, her mind frantic with fear, that black wall bearing down on her.

Finally, I remember what I have been told by friends who

have endured long periods of suffering. Take it day by day. Don't anticipate.

I begin to learn the wisdom of that lesson the next morning when I call my mother. She is scared, tearful, but not shattered. She is not contemplating certain death. She is contemplating a biopsy. Maybe the tumor isn't malignant.

I get off the phone feeling reprieved.

Later in the day Mike calls and tells me he now thinks there are more possibilities for treatment than he realized. He has talked to several specialists and arranged appointments for Mom on Friday at a prestigious medical center in Minnesota.

By Friday I am in Glenco Mills making preparations to vacate my country life. In the evening my parents call to say the results of the day's needle biopsy were inconclusive and they have to return to the medical center next Tuesday for more tests. There is no panic in their voices. They are calm, matter-of-fact, as if equilibrium had been restored after a false crisis. For every problem there is a solution, and in a few days they will settle upon the solution of their choice. In the meantime there is no need for me to fly out.

Between Friday and Tuesday I busy myself sorting through a summer's worth of mail, paying bills, unpacking, packing, ordering a season's worth of home heating oil, finding neighbors who can be caretakers for house and car and mail. I call my parents several times over the weekend, mostly to be reassured by the calm in their voices. There is fright below the surface, but it is kept in check by the feeling that Mike and the nice doctors at the medical center have come to Mom's rescue.

Tuesday afternoon, I go fishing rather than sit and wait for the phone to ring. I realize that no matter what news this day brings, I am glad for the past few days' reprieve from certainty. It has given us time to accept the loss of normalcy, time to brace ourselves for whatever is ahead.

The call comes at 7:00 P.M. The tumor is malignant and inoperable. The medical center is advising an experimental radiation treatment. The alternative is very imminent death. My father's voice is low, without affect, stunned. My mother wants me there, now. "I want my daughter," she says, as if she means, "I want my mother."

My only thought now is of getting there. I make a reservation on an early-morning flight out of Newark and pack my bags for a Minnesota fall. I look through my bookshelves for a novel to read on the plane, but nothing will do, nothing promises to hold my attention. For the first time in my life, I pack no fiction. Instead I stuff two notebooks in my bags.

I had been keeping what I called my "trout-fishing journal" since the previous spring, when days in the stream were followed by nights of recording what I had seen there. I took the journal on the plane knowing that I was as ignorant about what I would face in Minnesota as I was about the natural world of my new setting. I knew the entries I would make there, like my trout-fishing entries, would be full of error and misperception, that earlier entries would be contradicted by later ones, that one day's wisdom would be the next day's folly. I did not seek consummate understanding. I just wanted to record day by day, hoping that would help me live day by day.

It did help, in more ways than I ever could have anticipated. In the pages of the notebooks I recorded the beginnings of my new life and the ending of my mother's, never imagining that, placed side by side, they might come to coexist with less painful discordance. I wrote in this journal the day I found the old house that I would restore as my new home. And I wrote in it minutes before my mother died, knowing that she was going to die in minutes. The juxtapositions of beginnings and endings were shattering as I recorded them, but ultimately, it was through them that I found points of contact between my living and her dying. I also found the points of separation.

During the last month of my mother's life, this journal was

my means of survival. In part it gave me a saving distance, reminded me that I was a witness to dying, not the one dying. The journal was also my weapon against denial, my way of looking in the presence of so many averted eyes, my way of remembering in the face of so much forgetting.

I learned many things during the time I kept this journal. I learned that much living goes on in the course of dying, I learned that there are as many ways of dying as of living, and I learned that unless we want to consign one another to the profoundest loneliness, we must find a way of looking into eyes that have nowhere left to look. I learned that denial does not stop with death. It never stops.

Those of us born after the war were raised in an era of mass forgetfulness. Death was put behind us. Our well-intentioned parents, with exceptions, wished this for their children. But suddenly, as a generation, we are being reminded of what we were spared. Age is claiming our parents and AIDS our peers. Unless we accept the knowledge of death, not as a mistake, a form of bad luck or malpractice, but death as an ordinary event, we face a great divide, between generations, between peers, against ourselves.

This journal takes you toward death as certainly as a nineteenth century British novel takes you toward marriage, and many readers will be as reluctant to enter into its experience as I was to return to it. But I don't want to be alone on either side of the divide. Healthy, I don't want to be divided from the sick. Alive I want to make peace with the dead.

G L I N T S

GLENCO MILLS, N.Y.
TUESDAY, APRIL 16, 1985 :

I am beginning to notice different things now. The softness of
Midnight's fur, the pale green of his eyes and how the blackness
opens from a vertical slit in his pupil to a full roundness in fright,
overwhelming the inquiring green. The whiteness that edges a
brook trout's mouth and fins, the signal that something alive is
nestled among the stones at the bottom of the stream. The gray-
brown of their bodies blends so completely with the color of
the stones that until I see the strip of slightly undulating white,
I cannot discern the possibility of their sudden, startling flight.

I wonder now what creatures see. When I watch birds feeding
through the red grid of my kitchen window, do they see me?
They must, because they see Midnight at the pantry door and
take off in skittish flight, cardinals first and chickadees last. But
do they see my colors? form? movement?

I am struck for the first time by the miracle of perennials—

dry, dead sticks putting forth buds or making way for new growth from the old roots. The dried remains of last year's flowers are still on their stalks while new plants spring up between their legs, seeking a share of light and air. In my borrowed garden, I clear away the old growth to make room for the new. But down the road, in Bruno's untended garden, the old stalks remain and new shoots find their way among them anyway. Maybe mine is an American impulse and Bruno, a French vintner's son, knows something I don't.

It has taken me, daughter of a farmer's daughter, forty years to discover these things, and belated as I am, I choose the slow way of learning, just observing what happens each day and guessing at what tomorrow will bring. I have no desire to go to books that might explain these things to me, how flowers grow, how trout make their way through the seasons, natural and legal.

FRIDAY, APRIL 19:

I have been listening to fitful rolls of thunder for the past half hour. The sky is dark and the air still, but just when it seems about to storm, the sun bursts through the clouds and it's a sunny spring afternoon again. Just now, the sky turned gray-green and I hear the first faint drops, slow and tentative.

The thunder brought me home from the stream where, again, I fished without catching anything. It makes little difference to me whether I get a bite. I am still learning my rod and reel. Last Friday, I took the old reel apart to learn its secrets, then I put a new reel on the rod and filled it with line, discovering every tangle trial and error can produce. It's a task that requires four hands, and I had to make do with two and a pair of knees.

In time, many hours' time, the reel was ready for casting. I attached a lure and went to the backyard to practice. As my first cast arced over the lawn, Midnight sprang out of the bushes and leapt for the lure. Its barbed hooks landed inches from his outstretched paw, and he began to stalk it like a mouse. I rushed at him before he pounced, grabbed the lure and held it high as I walked back to the house, with Midnight leaping all the while, determined to catch the glinting in the air.

After several days of casting, I have become comfortable, even intimate with my rod, but I still discover something new about it every day. Yesterday, by accident, I cast farther than I ever had before, and then realized it was the way I snapped my wrist that produced the effect. Before the cast, I had been whipping my arm slower or faster, in a longer or shorter arc, to control the distance, but now I see it is in the wrist, not the arm and shoulder, that distance is determined.

Discovering this, I realized I had known it all along; it was familiar but forgotten knowledge, something I had read or, more likely, been told by my father in childhood. Now I have learned it in a way I will not forget, on my own wrist.

Today, some instinct told me to pull the rod backward at the end of a cast, and suddenly I had solved the problem of slack that snarled my line when I started to reel it in. Discovering this, I again remembered that I had known it; the motion was one I'd seen my father make hundreds of times, but I never realized it had a purpose. I thought it was one of those poses that belong to men, like standing with hands on hips, head bowed, after exertion. I thought the rod-jerking motion intrinsic to men, not to fishing, just as I once thought the hands-on-hips posture belonged to men, not to deep breathing.

There was a time when certain actions, performed by me, made me feel both exhilarated and confused. Exhilarated because I knew I was trespassing where no girls were allowed, and it was dangerous, exciting. Confused, because it made me wonder if I was a true girl if such actions came unbeckoned to my body. Once, when I was standing, head bowed, hands on hips, after a long run in a touch football game, my college boyfriend said, "I hate to see you standing like that." I became self-conscious, and for the rest of the game tried to avoid that stance, but my body wouldn't cooperate, and then I realized it was because bodies, any bodies, want to do that when they need to catch a deep breath.

THURSDAY, APRIL 25:

Today I bought a "sportsman's tool" at Ames—a pocket-size wrench, pliers, wire cutter in one. I'm using it to cut two of the three hooks off all my lures, so that when I catch an undersized fish, I can return it to the stream undamaged.

Tuesday, an hour before sunset, I went to the part of the stream that runs directly behind the house and waded my way upstream to a stretch of fast-flowing water that has several deep, eddying pools in it. I planned to start fishing above the fast water and work my way downstream, making a few casts into each of the pools.

At the first pool, I hooked a six-inch brook trout. When I tried to release the fish, I saw it had swallowed the lure, two hooks imbedded up and one down in its throat. I tugged the line, and the trout flapped in my hand, rolling its eyes in panic. I put it back in the water, hoping against reason the fish might free itself by thrashing. A minute later, I hauled it back onto the rocks and tried to work the lure free with my hands, but it was clear the only way to remove the lure was by jerking the line so hard it would tear the fish apart.

I put it back in the water again, took it out again. Each time I returned the fish to the stream, it seemed more listless, and its flesh, a glistening greenish-black when first caught, was becoming an eerie, phosphorescent silver. I talked to the fish as if it were Midnight. "Oh, honey, I'm so sorry. It'll be all right. Just let me help." I cursed myself for going fishing without a knife to cut the line. At one point I decided to put the fish out of its misery, but the only way to kill it was by smashing it with a rock and I couldn't bring myself to do that. Finally I yanked the line between my two hands and it broke, leaving the lure imbedded in the trout's throat. I returned him to the stream alive, but I know he can't survive.

Wading back home as the sun set, feeling miserable, depressed, and guilty, I vowed never to fish again. But gradually, as the water swirling around my knees turned from gold to lavender and then to dark purple, I began to persuade myself that I could still spend my days in the stream, I could still fish if I did it in some way that guaranteed I would be able to release what I caught. So this morning I tried to remove two of the three hooks from my lures with scissors and a hammer. I tried cutting the hooks off, bending them straight, nothing worked. Finally, I called my father in Minnesota to ask him how to fish without maiming the catch, and he told me about the "sportsman's tool." He also suggested I try fly fishing with the rod he left behind on his visit last fall.

As soon as I mentioned I was having problems with three-hook lures, I could tell he understood. His voice became quiet and steady, full of inflectionless concern, as he described the tool and what it could do. He was talking to me the way I had talked to the fish. "It'll be all right, honey. Just do as I say and it'll be all right."

WEDNESDAY, MAY 1:

Today, just upstream from the pools under the bridge on Water Street Road, I saw fish flapping in the shallow riffles. It was about 1:00 P.M. and the sun was reflecting brightly off the water, so my eyes had to adjust before I could distinguish the dappled rolling of the fish from the play of sunlit water over stones. The fish were large, twelve inches or more, with black and yellow patches along their length. At first I saw only two or three, rolling over one another in water so shallow that for the brief moment one fish went over the top of another, it was half out of the water.

Then I noticed that when three, never less, started rolling, up to a dozen others would dart toward them from different directions and join the fray. I assumed they were mating.

I stood with rod in hand watching them for a half hour as they joined and separated in different configurations. They seemed undisturbed by my presence in the water within a few feet of them. I cast my one-hooked lure a few times to see if they were interested, but I reeled it in right over their backs without getting a response. I didn't really want to catch them, or even disturb them. I was, I guess, just testing their absorption in their mating dance. It was total.

Later, after fishing without success downstream, I returned to the bridge and the fish were still there, still rolling. Parked on the road above me was a pickup truck with two young men who asked me if I'd caught anything. When I shook my head, one of them said they "grew up around here and something's happened to the fishing. We used to just put a hook in the stream and the trout would bite. Now, I don't know. Something's happened." I told them about the fish mating a few feet away and they asked if they were mudsuckers. "I don't know," I said. "What do mudsuckers look like?"

"Like catfish," the talker said, "only narrower at the head and, well, I don't know how to say this, but their mouths, their lips, well, they look like black people's, only white."

As soon as he said that, I knew the fish I'd been watching all year and thinking were trout, were suckers. Not sleek, fast, noble trout, but lowly, lazy, bottom-feeding mudsuckers. It was a blow. While I was absorbing it, the young man added, "Suckers don't bite. You have to snag 'em." So that is why the "trout" who swarm under the fallen sycamore that spans the stream near the house don't even bother to flee anymore when I dangle the lure at their lips or flick it along their bodies. That undulating strip of white means mudsucker. And I thought they were very old, very wise trout who were demonstrating their contempt for me by not bothering to react to my presence.

I have a lot of refiguring to do. The fish I've been watching from the log are suckers, and yet the fish I have been catching, sometimes in that very spot, are trout, some of them of respectable size, ten and eleven inches. I had been thinking the trout I caught were small, because I was comparing them to suckers, which I thought were large trout. It's a miracle I've caught anything, because I've been basing my trout-fishing strategies on observations of mudsuckers. Suckers feed on the bottom, don't flee at sight or sound of me, and travel in packs. Trout are smaller, leaner, quicker, more active, more likely to bite, and much more likely to flee—like the fish I have in fact been catching. How could I mistake a mudsucker for a trout? Oh, the perils of the romantic imagination, seeing with the mind's eye instead of the body's. I will never make that mistake again. Perhaps I should say, I will try to be vigilant about that temptation.

SUNDAY, MAY 5:

Last night I dreamt that Mom and I were driving in an open-topped jeep on a country road at night. We were driving through a wooded area on a narrow road that went up and down hills, round curves and over bridges, a road like many of those I drive around here.

In the dream Mom was driving and I kept telling her to be careful, because she didn't seem to see that both shoulders of the road were lined with deer. She was driving fast and I was afraid we would hit one of them. I didn't think we were in danger; my concern was for the deer.

As we approached a small bridge, my attention was fixed on the shadowy forms and red eyes caught in the glare of our headlights, when all of a sudden, a black bear lunged out of the woods. Before I could scream, he leapt through the car, grabbed Mom's head in his jaws and landed with her in the stream under the bridge.

Terrified and in shock, I stopped the jeep and ran back to the bridge. The bear had the back of Mom's head in his jaws and was holding her face down in the water. I felt her terror, her utter helplessness in the face of being drowned or mauled or both. I knew that even if the bear released her for a moment, she wouldn't be able to escape because she doesn't know how to swim.

Her submerged body was motionless in the bear's grip but I could tell she was pleading with me to save her. I tried to think of ways to get the bear away from her so she could breathe, but everything I could think of seemed more dangerous than doing nothing. If I threw stones at the bear, he might get angry and clamp his jaws tighter around her head rather than release her. If I jumped into the water to reach her, he would probably kill me as well as her.

I knew that each second I delayed brought her closer to drowning. I didn't know which was worse—doing something that would probably result in my dying with her or letting her drown thinking I hadn't even tried to help. The conflict between wanting to save myself and not wanting to abandon her was overwhelming, and I awoke with the most intense feeling of terror and pity I have ever felt in my life, waking or sleeping.

Going back to sleep was unthinkable. I got up and went down to the kitchen. A feeling of hopelessness, of sickening personal failure, stayed with me for hours. I have never before had a dream in which my mother's life was in danger.

MONTEVARCHI, ITALY
THURSDAY, JUNE 6:

In the open arches of the Loggia dei Lanzi, at the far end of the main piazza in Florence, Cellini's statue of Perseus holds Medusa's severed head in his outstretched bronze arms, his left foot astride her graphically decapitated body. A pigeon sits calmly on top of her head, sharing in Perseus' triumph. At the other end of the loggia, Giambologna's Sabine struggles mightily against the rapist who has her in his grip. Two pigeons squat on her head and his, undoing all the sculptor had done to turn stone into struggle. Meanwhile, in the vast open spaces of the piazza, mechanical birds swoop and soar, doing their vendors' bidding. Pigeons are nature's revenge on art.

WEDNESDAY, JUNE 12:

The coldest winter since 1929 has left the olive trees in Tuscany barren this summer, perhaps dead. The new growth that springs from the roots of the blackened, leafless trees would normally be trimmed away, but this year the tenderest shoots are left alone, because nobody knows if the old trees will revive. (*Recrescono* is the word Dino adds to my vocabulary, hoping that I will understand him this year.) The palette of the landscape is altered drastically. Hillsides that used to shimmer with the silvery gray-green of their orchards now send gnarled, black branches up to the sky like bony fingers of supplication.

Dino, who tends the orchards at Clara's villa, says it will take twenty years for new trees to bear good fruit. "My grandchildren will all be grown first," he adds with a mixture of sorrow and the perverse pride locals everywhere take in having been chosen for a rare, natural disaster. This year the blight bestows a distinction of sorts. Next year it will be just a familiar scar.

In the larger orchards, some trees survived and some didn't, no one knows why. The fig tree by the old well, thought dead a month ago, is beginning to cover its nakedness with leaves.

SUNDAY, JUNE 16:

Some paintings, like Titian's *Assumption of the Virgin* over the main altar at the Frari in Venice or the Botticellis in the Uffizi, are hard to see. Too many holy cards and posters stand between them and me. After so much reproduction and imitation, it is almost impossible to grasp the boldness, the newness, the marvel of their invention. They have been plundered of their wild originality, tamed by flattery. This is, I guess, the hack's revenge upon genius

Statues seem less vulnerable to this particular fate. When an original stands next to a very good copy, there is no mistaking the two. The copyist may reproduce every curve and bulge of muscle, every detail of stance and expression, and yet one breathes and the other doesn't. In Della Robbia's *Choristers* in the Museo del Duomo, the legs of the youngest choristers dance; the legs of the copyist's choristers look like they might crash to the floor under the burden of the stone's weight.

It almost makes one believe in the concept of soul. And it certainly makes it easy to understand why some sculptures were thought to contain spirits, and their sculptors to be sorcerers.

TUESDAY, JUNE 18:

This morning, I met Mom and Dad at the airport in Rome and drove them straight to the villa. After fifteen hours in the air and three on the road, I expected them to be content with a lazy afternoon on the loggia, but they still feel the thrill of foreignness more keenly than jet lag. I satisfied them with a mushroom hunt, followed by a long walk through the vineyards to Moreno's house and the promise of Florence tomorrow. Last year it took nine months' coaxing to get them abroad for the first time in their lives. This year they began lobbying for a return invitation months before I was ready to issue it.

For Mom, who grew up on a farm in flattest Iowa, who escaped alone into big Midwestern cities before retreating to the safety of their suburbs, Italy is adventure beyond imagining. She feels she is "seeing the world" for the first time, and no hill is too steep, no food too exotic, no alleyway too dark to explore. I've hired Moreno to cook and clean for us, so Mom will be protected from any errant impulse to make this a busman's holiday.

Over dinner, I translated conversation as best I could between my parents and Moreno, who was astounded to learn we live a thousand miles apart. "Perchè?" he kept asking, and no answer helped him understand how parents and children could withstand such separation. Moreno, who is thirty, lives with his parents in the home where he and his father were born. When Mom asked how long his family had lived on this hill, he answered without hesitation, "Since Adam and Eve."

SUNDAY, JUNE 23:

Last night Clara suggested we join her and some friends for dinner at a *festa* in the nearby village of San Leonino. We arrived early but still had to park our car two miles below the tiny hilltop town and walk up the steep road that circles San Leonino and leads into its narrow, twisting streets, usually deserted but now crowded far beyond their capacity. Elbows tucked to sides, we inched our way into the crowd, hoping the moving wall of shoulders would sweep us in the direction of our meeting place with Clara's friends. Suddenly the melodious hum of Italians having fun gave way to an uproar of loud shouting, and the already-compact crowd parted in the middle, pressing itself flat against the stone walls of the Renaissance houses lining both sides of the street. Seconds later, a dozen donkeys charged through the two-foot-wide opening in the crowd, tossing their bareback riders into the outstretched hands of townspeople who knew what to expect. I craned my neck to locate Mom and saw her crushed against stone, pinned in place by several layers of cheering villagers, laughing so hard the tears streamed down her face.

A half hour and several donkey charges later, we made it the two hundred yards to the dining pavilion and met our companions for the evening, three Englishwomen, two Italians and an

Eritrean, the latter in Italy just long enough to heal very visible wounds before returning to battle against Ethiopian soldiers. Mom, who had never met a foreigner of any kind before these last two summers, relished every syllable of every accent. She was stung when the youngest Englishwoman upbraided her for not knowing that Eritrea was fighting for independence from Ethiopia, but she was also exhilarated to be held accountable for such information. "I can't remember when I've had more fun," she said this morning.

TUESDAY, JUNE 25:

It's taken me a week to discover that, despite appearances, both Mom and Dad have brought medical problems to Italy. I would still be in the dark if it hadn't become necessary to explain Dad's sudden compulsion for nude sunbathing and Mom's equally sudden aversion to ice cream.

Dad, I am now told, has been diagnosed as having a rare, precancerous skin condition called pseudopsoriasis. Fortunately, this skin disease is cured, not caused, by high doses of ultraviolet light, so Italy is just what the doctor ordered. Mom's problem causes more distress but less anxiety, because the doctor, after extensive blood tests and CAT scans, has assured her that she is exceptionally healthy. He thinks a late-blooming milk allergy may be responsible for the back pain and digestive problems she suffers during the night. During the day she is fine, except for the pangs of denial she suffers whenever we pass a tempting display of *gelati*—pistachio, hazelnut, double chocolate, banana, all forbidden. She deeply resents this diagnosis, at times defies it. "I grew up on a dairy farm," she says, and orders the smallest cone.

Each morning when I ask her how she slept, she says, "Oh, I wish you wouldn't ask."

WEDNESDAY, JUNE 26:

This morning, sitting on the patio shelling peas from the garden, I saw two small lizards in fierce but brief combat, their bodies locked together like wrestlers in a pit. Then they broke apart and faced off at ten inches, each absolutely still as he eyed the other. I flicked a pea in their direction, and as it hit the ground, they rushed at each other and fought even more fiercely, each apparently thinking the other had been the provocateur. My pea flicking was a very God-like act, I think.

FRIDAY, JUNE 28:

Yesterday, Mom and I drove down to Montevarchi for the Thursday morning market. (Dad stayed at the villa to sunbathe, *tutto nudo,* on the patio.) Mom was dressed in pants and the gray gabardine jacket I bought for her at the Florence market last summer. She looked completely at ease, pleased with herself, the day, the world. We were both quiet, content to enjoy the warmth of the sun on our faces. As we strolled down Via Roma toward the open stalls of the market, she turned to me with an almost conspiratorial smile on her face and said, "You know, I just love to walk with my hands in my pockets. I don't know why."

It was as if she were asking me to explain why she felt so good. The look, the stride, the glow of well-being she basked in at that moment were familiar to me. They are mine. The hands-in-the-pockets saunter, an old habit with me, is new to her. I suspect it comes more naturally to her when we are together, but it isn't as if she is consciously modeling her manner on mine. She has become younger in the last couple years, and I attribute it in part to Dad's retirement. For the first time in nearly fifty years, they are equals, no longer businessman and housewife but companions who walk through the same world.

She is beginning to take on the bearing of an independent young woman.

Her body, honed by daily morning exercises before the TV with Joanie Griggins and long walks around nearby lakes with Dad, is trim and fit. A stranger coming up behind her, seeing her with hands in her pockets, shoulders back, a spring in her step, could easily think she was a teenager. Approaching her from the front, they would see a very confident, relaxed woman of middle years. Nobody would place her in her seventies, and learning of her age, nobody would describe her as "trying to look young." She is effortlessly young, her face unlined, her eyes clear and curious.

I have been proud of her beauty for as long as I can remember. Hers is a box office beauty that changes as the times change. In the forties, when I was a very young child, she was artfully, glamorously beautiful. She had the figure and the features to do the forties right. Spike heels, bright red lipstick, eyebrows penciled on in thin arcs, long-skirted suits with fitted waists and padded shoulders. She brushed waves of silvery hair away from her face to heighten the effect of strong cheekbones and piercing blue eyes. You never noticed she was only 5 feet 2 inches.

Looking at pictures of her from that time, I know she was after a very sexy look, but I never noticed how adults responded to her. What filled me with pride was the clear infatuation of my classmates. When it was her turn to be on playground duty during our recesses and lunch hours, they clustered around her, staring, adoring, hoping to win a look or a touch. I felt superior, generous, and did not exert my claims to her at these times, preferring instead to stay at a slight distance and watch my classmates vie for the attention that was mine every day.

By the mid-fifties, her beauty had been domesticated. In pedal pushers and sandals, she no longer inspired comparisons to Marlene Dietrich. One was more likely to think of June Allyson and, later in the decade, Donna Reed. Prematurely gray hair had made her striking in her twenties and thirties. As a strawberry blonde in her forties, she blended in. But children still singled her out; they were smitten at first sight. To them, she was Hollywood, the silver screen fantasy of a Mom, her beauty as approachable as a plate full of cookies.

Now her beauty is her own. She doesn't look like a Mom or a wife or the star in anybody's movie. She looks like Bea, whoever she is.

SUNDAY, JUNE 30:

Even here I notice fish—silver fish in the jewelry shops on the Ponte Vecchio in Florence, glass fish in the shops radiating out from San Marco in Venice, stone fish carved in the holy water fonts at the cathedral in Siena.

This afternoon, driving back to Montevarchi from the pine forests of Vallombrosa, I rounded a curve and saw dozens of fishermen casting their lines into a wide stretch of the Sieve River. I pulled over to the side of the road and got out of the car to observe their methods. They used poles two or three times the lengths that Americans use, poles so long they nearly spanned the river. Testing my Italian, I asked two other onlookers what kind of fish were in these waters. "Trota e carpa," they said. And "barba." I looked puzzled by "barba," and one of the men gestured a beard onto his face. "Oh, catfish," I said, and he shook his head. "No, non gatto, barba."

We went on in this fashion for ten minutes, with them telling me where to find the biggest trout on the Sieve, and me divulging the secrets of the stream that runs through "il mio piccolo villagio a New York." It was gratifying to swap information, one local to another; the fact that our localities were a great distance apart didn't seem to make much difference.

In Mary McCarthy's *Stones of Florence,* she tells the story of a trick Brunelleschi played upon a woodworker he disliked. When the woodworker arrived late for dinner at Brunelleschi's house one night, B. treated him as if he didn't exist, as if there were indeed a woodworker of his name, who had a very specific physiognomy and personality and personal history, but who was not the man standing in B.'s doorway. The woodworker became so convinced that he was not himself that he was afraid to go home lest he find himself already there. When news of Brunelleschi's trick and its success spread throughout Florence, the woodworker was so humiliated that he left the city for good. This is the way New Yorkers drive one another to California. It is also the way some corporate chiefs soften up their employees for transfers. Sometimes it is the way I feel after staying in Italy too long. I become so convinced I'm Italian that it is hard to believe I have another home. I'm afraid to go back to Glenco Mills lest I find myself already there.

FEAR OF
THE DARK

EDINA, MINN.

WEDNESDAY, SEPTEMBER 4:

Last night, after learning Mom's tumor was malignant, I began packing for an indefinite stay in Minnesota. "I want my daughter," Mom said, planting a new phrase deep in my heart. I promised her I would be there by noon today and booked a 10:00 A.M. flight out of Newark. I packed and worried into the middle of the night, then set the alarm for 6:00 A.M., allowing enough time for the two-hour drive to the airport. When I awoke at 8:00 A.M. and realized I would miss the plane, bolts of lightning traveled through my veins. I booked a later flight, called Mom, lied and drove the Taconic Parkway at the speed of my heartbeat, ready to defy any state trooper who dared to come between me and my guilt.

On the plane, I kept thinking of something that has worried me since Mike's first call last Tuesday. I have never been able to stand the sight of Mom in pain. I respond to it bodily. If she burns her hand on the iron, I wince. If she coughs, my chest heaves. Once, when we were shopping together in downtown Evanston, Mom tripped on a crack in the sidewalk and smashed headfirst into the pavement. My whole body started tingling, and when I saw the fright in her eyes, I almost fainted. The right half of her face looked broken, caved in, and I lied when she asked me if there was a mirror in the shoe store where we waited for an ambulance. I remember the effort I made to keep looking at her, as if there was nothing wrong, as if her beauty was intact.

I have witnessed only a few, rare accidents, spaced over decades of her healthy life. I have never had to repress, or even think about, my body's impulsive identification with hers. How will I react now that the threats to her are so much more extreme? What help will I be, what comfort can I give, if I am simply the mirror of her suffering? I wonder if all daughters feel this. Do we all have to go through a second weaning?

As I stood in the crowded aisle of the plane waiting for the line of passengers to move, I was peripherally aware of a very tall woman standing behind me. I caught a glimpse of long red hair but was too lost in my own thoughts to register what was familiar. When the line began to move, I looked up, she looked down, and we stared blankly at each other for a second. "Freya?" I said. "Le Anne?" she answered. We were friends, good friends, for six months in 1968, when we were both out of place in California. As we walked down the ramp toward the arrival gate, I learned she had moved back to Minneapolis, where she was born and raised, two years ago. Before parting, we quickly exchanged phone numbers and introductions—me to her husband and twin sons, Freya to Mike and Dad.

On the drive from the airport Mike and Dad told me more about the treatment the medical center is recommending for Mom. The first step is surgery, not to remove the tumor but to expose it directly to the highest possible dose of electron-beam radiation. As soon as she recovers from surgery, she will receive daily radiation treatments, delivered externally, for five weeks. She will also need a nerve block to control pain, because even if the tumor is rendered inactive by the radiation, it will still be there as a fibrous mass exerting pressure on nerves close to her spinal column. When Mom asked if any other follow-up treatment would be necessary, the oncologist said, "No, just routine checkups every six months for the first two years." Dad says "first two years" were the sweetest words he ever heard.

THURSDAY, SEPTEMBER 5:

Yesterday, when I first walked into the house, I saw Mom's face tremble for a moment, but by the time we released each other from a hug, she was composed and smiling. She looks good: rested, calm, fit, without the pallor or weight loss one would expect of someone supposedly only weeks from death. The irony is that she is in perfectly good health except for the fact she is dying. And now, with her family gathered around her like support troops called to the front, she seems to feel the enemy is outflanked.

During the day I am tempted to think some mistake has been made. It is only during the middle of the night, when the codeine wears off and I hear Mom prowling the house until the next pill takes effect, that I feel the nearness of the threat. Last night I lay awake wondering if pain feels different when you know it can kill you. Does it hurt more when it has been called malign? Her night pacing fills me with a dread I did not feel this summer when I heard the brushing of her slippers over the cool tiles of the villa floor. We were innocent then, unaware the pain had designs on her. Now I imagine her alone in the dark, feeling stalked and defenseless. I get up, join her in the kitchen, turn on lights. There is strain on her face, but I do not know what she is thinking.

Mom has cat eyes. You can see straight through them to her brain, catch them in the act of perceiving. They seldom tell you what she is thinking or feeling, just that she is seeing, constantly, actively. They are the eyes of the observer, not the observed. Look into them and they reveal only their beauty. Some people find her eyes scary, especially in photographs, when they seem to turn the lens back on the camera. Others, like me, are reassured by them. We know we are being seen, taken in, and that makes us feel less alone.

SATURDAY, SEPTEMBER 7:

Dad and Mike and I were in the kitchen watching Martina Navratilova play Hana Mandlikova in the finals of the U.S. Open, and the third set of their match had just begun when Mom reminded us it was time to leave for five o'clock Mass. We wanted to stay for the end of the match, but balking was out of the question.

It had been an unusually hot day, and the church was clammy from air-conditioning. Lollipop yellow light streamed through modern stained-glass windows onto the Minnesota shrub garden that surrounds the altar. Before Mass began, we were asked to rehearse a "new" song composed by a parishioner to be sung at the offertory. It was "The Impossible Dream" from *Man of La Mancha* recycled as a hymn. The gospel reading for the day was about Christ's healing the deaf man. After we applauded the official debut of the song we had rehearsed, the priest offered our prayers for the sick of the parish, three of whom were mentioned by name. Mom cried quietly into her handkerchief, and I feared her tears were stimulated by the repeated references to the sick and dying.

When the priest started to deliver communion, I decided to receive. I wanted to spare Mom any pangs my staying behind might give her, and I also thought the church had probably changed enough for me to receive communion without pretense to being a good Catholic. The last time I had been divided between my disbelief and my desire to spare Mom's feelings was six years ago at my grandmother's funeral. I remember thinking that if I didn't receive communion, I would add to my mother's grief over her mother's death; but if, as a non-believer, I received communion, I would be committing a mortal sin. The fact that I was a non-believer who still believed in mortal sin didn't escape my attention, but it was not a contradiction I could resolve in the thirty seconds I had to decide whether or not to file out of that pew in Fort Dodge, Iowa. I decided to risk my soul for my mother's sake and hope that God, in whom I did not believe, would forgive me.

Many things have changed in six years, including church rules about who can receive communion. Even Dad, who has never been a Catholic, is invited to receive communion on his rare visits to Saint Patrick's. Practices about how the host is received—onto extended tongue or into cupped hands—have also changed. As a child I was taught that only the right thumb and index finger of an ordained priest could touch the host. His other, unconsecrated fingers were held stiffly apart in tea-sipping fashion during the host-handling parts of the Mass, and the touch of a layman's hands upon a consecrated wafer was defilement beyond imagining. Sometime in the last ten years, however, it seems that our hands became clean.

As I stood in the communion line today, I watched how those ahead of me received the wafer so I could show proper form when my turn came. Finally I stood alone before the priest; he looked straight into my eyes, held the host inches in front of my face, and said, "This *is* Christ's body," with an emphasis that seemed aimed directly at my disbelief. Then, still looking into my eyes, he paused for what seemed an eternity before saying "Amen" and placing the crisp wafer in my sweating palm. He had come close to withholding the host from me and I felt chastened, exposed and more than a little unsettled. I had never seen this priest before in my life. How was he able to single me out? Had he noticed I was the only communicant to place my right hand on top of my left, which forced me to deliver the host lefthanded to my mouth? Had everybody noticed?

I returned to our pew, and kneeling between Mike and Mom, knowing that the three of us were joined in our hopes if not our beliefs, I felt comforted. I was entitled to this communion and I took its consolations as my own.

A little later, when we were waiting for the last communicants to return to their pews, Mom, who had continued to cry quietly throughout Mass, turned to Mike and me and explained that her tears were tears of happiness at having us with her at Mass. After Mass, as we walked toward our car in the church parking lot, she turned to us again, eyes wide with unabashed elation, and said this was one of the happiest days of her life.

Back home, while Mike and Dad started charcoal for a back-yard barbecue, Mom asked me what I thought she should do about having her name added to the roll call of the parish sick. She was torn between wanting the prayers and not wanting public notice of her illness. I said it wasn't necessary for her to be identified to be included in the prayer, because it was a prayer for all the parish's sick, not just those listed by name. The prayer does, however, include the phrase "for all the parish's sick, especially _____, _____, and _____," and I could tell from the look on Mom's face that she wasn't convinced she would get the full benefit of the prayers if her name wasn't in the "especially" clause. We mulled this dilemma in silence for a minute; then drawing on my training in church sophistry, I suggested she ask the priest to use her maiden name in the prayer; that way, she could draw God's special attention without alerting the neighbors. She liked that solution. Relieved, we sat down with Mike and Dad for a dinner of hot dogs, hamburgers and potato chips, which, in their own way, were as effective as communion. We shared the food of normalcy, of life as usual, the meal of the innocent, everyday all-American family.

SUNDAY, SEPTEMBER 8:

Freya and I began seventeen years of catching up today. We last saw each other in the summer of 1968, when she decided that Stanford's English department was no place for a poet and I decided it was no place for a woman with a husband in Boston. She still writes poetry. I am no longer married. Those were the first updates we swapped.

The most surprising news is that Freya, who in 1968 shared my desire to escape the Midwest, now lives in the house next door to the one in which she grew up. It's a grand house on a bluff overlooking the Mississippi, built as summer quarters for a wealthy Minneapolis doctor at the turn of the century. On the same estate is the smaller house in which Freya's family generated unhappy memories. She says her husband, Tom, fell in love with the large house when she took him on a tour of her childhood haunts a couple years ago and immediately began lobbying for a move from California.

It's been a hard two years for Freya, full of ghosts and sickness. All her life, Freya had been the healthy member of her family, the undeserving one, the daughter who must give, never receive sympathy. But since she returned to the bluff, she herself has been sick, of Lyme disease, which nearly crippled her before it was diagnosed. She's better now, ready to turn the bad time into poetry.

When I told her what brought me here, she was wary, on my behalf. She warned me how the sick can tyrannize the healthy. I assured her that the tyrant in my family was cancer, not its victim.

MONDAY, SEPTEMBER 9:

This morning Mike and I went to 8:00 A.M. Mass with Mom, who received the Sacrament of Anointing—the new version of Extreme Unction. After our conversation on Saturday evening,

Mom had gone to Mass by herself the next morning and stayed afterward to ask the pastor, Father Mahon, to include her in his offertory prayers for the sick. She explained that she had a "little problem" and would be having surgery on Wednesday. Father Mahon told her that she was "in luck," that he had "something better than that" for her. Very occasionally, he explained, Saint Patrick's holds a special Mass to administer the Sacrament of Anointing, and it just so happened that such a Mass was to be held the following morning for another lady of the parish. Unlike Extreme Unction, which is administered only when one is in immediate danger of dying, the Sacrament of Anointing is given at any time one's health is in serious danger, and since Mom is scheduled for surgery, she qualifies as endangered. Like a nuptial Mass, or a requiem, it has readings appropriate for the occasion— in this case, prayers encouraging the sick in their faith, hope and acceptance of God's will.

When the three of us entered the chapel, we were ushered to seats in a front pew. In the pew to our right sat the other woman to be anointed and her husband. We were surprised to find ourselves suddenly on show, and didn't know how to respond to the curious glances we received from those already seated. The other endangered woman was a daily Mass goer, so both she and her medical condition were known to the regulars in the chapel. Most of those present probably knew Mom by sight from her years of Sunday Mass going at Saint Patrick's, but only a handful of them knew her personally and none knew of her medical problems.

By the time Mass started, there were about one hundred worshipers in the chapel. I had expected an 8:00 A.M. Mass on a rainy weekday to draw a handful of pious, probably elderly ladies of the parish, and was surprised to see an almost equal number of men and women, most of them middle-aged married couples. It looked like a group of typical Minnesotans; rain dripped off belted trench coats onto the women's pastel pants suits, and the men shifted uneasily in their soggy plaid sports jackets.

I knew from childhood catechism lessons how Extreme Unction had been administered in the past, but neither Mike nor I nor Mom had ever attended a Mass of Anointing, and had only a vague idea of what to expect. No special attention was directed to us until after the gospel reading, when Father Mahon left the altar and stood in front of the other woman's pew; his assistant, young "Father John," came and stood before us. Father John said a short prayer for Mom's physical and spiritual well-being, then raised his right hand to place a drop of oil on her forehead and on each palm. Then he placed his cupped hands on top of Mom's head, said, "May God bless you," and asked Mike and me to step around to the front of the pew and do the same. When we laid our hands on her head, Mom began crying, quietly.

We returned to the pew and stood, one on each side of her, as the rest of those present began to file slowly by. Each person stopped, placed both hands on Mom's head, blessed her and wished her well. Every one of them was a true believer in the healing power of God, and the intensity of concentration they brought to their moments of contact with Mom was overwhelming. With few exceptions, they looked straight into her eyes, expressing an unaccountable intimacy and a deep desire to pass on something healing in their touch. They went between Mom and the other woman, creating what felt like a palpable force field of energy. As they continued to file by, Mom gripped the top of the pew with both hands, looking as if she were holding on against a strong, steady wind. She clearly felt that powerful medicine was being administered, and so did I. I had never felt such intensity of good will, and if nothing more than that were at work in this chapel, it was enough to quiet my skepticism.

When everyone had returned to the pews, the Mass continued, and when it was time for communion, I had no hesitation about receiving. But again, as on Saturday, young Father John gave me a long, direct look and seemed to pause before placing the host in my hands. Why was he singling me out this way? How could he possibly intuit my poor standing as a Catholic? Minutes later, as I knelt at my mother's side watching the others receive communion, I suddenly realized what I had done wrong. When the priest raises the host and says, "This is Christ's body," the communicant is supposed to answer "Amen," signaling assent to the statement. Father John had been waiting for my "Amen," which never came, so he spoke it for me before parting with the host.

After Mass, coffee and doughnuts were served in a room adjacent to the chapel. The men and women who had displayed such exceptional force only minutes ago now seemed quite ordinary again. They did, however, show unusual tact. There was curiosity as well as concern in their eyes, but as we mingled and munched, no one used the occasion to pry or ask troubling questions. No one, that is, except me. When I thanked Father Mahon for arranging the service, I asked him what the other woman's problem was. "Inoperable brain tumor," he said. "No hope." They seemed godforsaken words for a priest to utter, but when I passed them on to Mike, he said, "Her chances are probably better than Mom's." It was not the first time I regretted having a doctor in the family. In Mike's case, a doctor who once, briefly, wanted to be a priest.

ROCHESTER, MINN.
TUESDAY, SEPTEMBER 10:

This afternoon, when Mom was admitted to the hospital, she looked so healthy and happy it was hard to believe she really needed to be here. It seemed unreal to her as well. During the drive from Edina to Rochester, she turned to me and said, "You know, I can hardly believe I'm the one who is entering the hospital." I presumed she was referring to Dad, whose health had never been as good as hers. But then she added, "It seems like it should be one of you." I looked at her in amazement. Had my sweet mother actually entertained thoughts of surviving her children? Had she perhaps even been reconciled to such thoughts?

Shortly after we settled into Mom's assigned room, a nurse came by to take her medical history. When the nurse asked her birth date, Mom suggested Mike and I leave the room. The nurse looked at her quizzically and asked if she were joking. Knowing better, Mike and I left the room. "You're as young or old as you feel," is Mom's standard answer to questions about age. She doesn't ask anyone over ten his age and doesn't want to be asked hers. By now this stance has become a matter of principle, but I suspect it had its origin in her being a year or two older than Dad in a time when women didn't marry men even a day younger than themselves. This is only speculation, however, since I really don't know my parents' exact ages. I also suspect Mom planned to discard this principle when she reached ninety. In her long-lived family, each birthday after eighty-nine is celebrated with great fanfare. The last eight of her mother's birthdays had been occasions for huge family reunions. The last and largest reunion was her funeral, held six years ago on her ninety-ninth birthday.

WEDNESDAY, SEPTEMBER 11:

When I entered Mom's room this morning, she was unrecognizable as the woman I had kissed good-bye fifteen hours earlier. She had been allowed no food or water or medication since midnight; by 1:00 A.M. the cancer pain had taken hold and, as it increased with each hour of the night, she had been made to endure six enemas. There would have been a seventh and eighth if the nurse administering them had not finally taken pity on her and asked the doctor on call if a pristine colon was absolutely necessary before pancreatic surgery. "Not really," he had said, but by that time Mom had lost what strength she might have had to endure the agony of a night without painkillers.

The woman who entered the hospital yesterday looking fit and happy entered surgery this morning looking sick and depressed. Yesterday, an onlooker could not have told which one of us was the patient. Today there is no question. Mom has been separated out. From the day she first heard her diagnosis, she has tried so hard to remain one of us. But during the night she entered a world apart. She belongs to the cancer ward now.

The orderlies arrived at 10:00 A.M. to take Mom to the operating room. As we were saying our good-byes, a nurse interrupted to say Mom would have to remove her dentures. Until this summer, I did not even know that Mom wore dentures, and, in the years she has worn them, she has made sure that no one except her dentist has ever seen her without them. From the moment she entered the hospital, her person, her vanity, her control had been under assault, and the indignity of being ordered to remove her dentures was too much for her to take. She got mad. She told the nurse that she never removed her dentures and she would not remove them now. The nurse insisted. Mom refused. She said that she wore her dentures when she slept and she would wear them during surgery. The nurse explained that it was dangerous for patients under anesthesia to wear dentures, and that there could be no exceptions to operation room policy. Mom knew she had lost. She asked Mike and Dad and me to leave the room. When they wheeled her out a few minutes later, she had a sheet drawn up to her eyes; she winked and waved good-bye.

Knowing we had a several hours' wait ahead of us, Mike, Dad and I went to the Clinic View Inn for breakfast. I don't remember what we talked about, but I know that each of us was thinking about the alternatives that would face us when we heard the doctor's report after surgery. The surgeon had told us that if they found the cancer had spread to her intestinal tract, they would remove part of her duodenum, which would make the surgery itself prolonged and dangerous. Even if there was only microscopic evidence of metastasis, they would recommend chemotherapy as well as the course of external radiation we were already braced for. Mike and I both felt that if there was any detectable spread of the cancer, we would be back where we started three weeks ago; facing a certain death sentence with no chance of reprieve. Treatment would only add its own torment to the ones cancer had in store for us. It would be up to Mike and me to counsel Mom to reject treatment, up to us to tell her there was no escape from death within months.

After breakfast, we returned to Mom's hospital room to continue our wait. I tried to read *Lake Wobegon Days;* Mike immersed himself in a Ken Follett thriller; Dad just sat and looked out the window. Every fifteen minutes, one of us would go to the nurses' station and ask if Mom had entered the recovery room yet. Finally, at 2:00 P.M., the surgeon walked into our room. Before we could ask, he assured us that the operation had gone very well. The tumor was larger than they had anticipated from the CAT scans, but it was still within the radius that the electron beam could completely cover. The surgeon had seen some leakage from the tumor during the operation, but they found no evidence of spread to other organs or structures, and the tumor had not encroached upon the bile ducts within the pancreas, so there was no danger of jaundice.

That news seemed so positive that the three of us became manic with relief. It would be a couple more hours before Mom was returned to her room, so we left the hospital and walked out into a sunny late-summer day. Mike and I followed Dad, who aimed us toward the shrub gardens and flower beds that are scattered among the buildings of the medical complex. We stopped at a fountain with a cast-bronze sculpture of a flying boy hanging onto the tail of a dolphin. I reached into my purse and brought out a handful of pennies to toss into the dolphin's tail. We spent ten minutes pitching pennies, landed two in the tail and cheered each good toss as if we had just saved Tinker Bell.

Walking the side streets looking for a place to eat, we turned a corner and saw a sign, NEWT'S PLACE: EAT, DRINK AND BE MERRY. Clearly, we were meant to eat there on this day. Nobody else was, though, and we had our hamburgers in perfect privacy. Also several Bloody Marys, which we drank in a spirit of pure elation. We wanted to bring a Newt's menu back to Mom as a souvenir, but we couldn't find one that wasn't covered with obscene graffiti. "If you don't want AIDS, sit down and shut up" was written across one. We left Newt's empty-handed but wiser about what's on the minds of Rochester's young.

We returned to the hospital about 3:30 P.M. but found Mom's room empty. At 4:00, they wheeled her into the ward. Without dentures, her face was utterly transformed, caved in and ravaged, a mask of age and pain. Her body was swaddled in tubes—IV, nasogastric, abdominal drain, catheter. She was barely conscious, mumbling a chant of "Pain, Pain, Pain," and "Freezing, Freezing, Freezing." She spoke the words as if they were capitalized, as if she were encountering pain and cold in some pure, absolute, unforgiving state. She spoke them as if there were no other words in the world.

Dad and I asked for more blankets and laid them over her, careful not to disturb the tangle of tubes that seemed to be holding her together. Dad stroked her sunken cheeks softly with the back of his fingers. I asked the nurses if she had been given any painkilling medication after the anesthetic wore off. They explained that they could not inject any morphine until her blood pressure had risen back to normal. I asked them if Mom's dentures could be put back in, because I did not want her to regain consciousness and know that we had gazed upon her toothlessness. The nurse inserted the dentures, and Mom was transformed again. With strength of cheek and jaw and brow restored to balance, the defenseless victim of pain became the woman nobly enduring pain. Encouraged by the change of face, I tried to penetrate the fog of pain long enough to convey that the surgery had been successful. Her eyes seemed to widen with elation for a second, then she collapsed again into her chant of "Pain, Pain, Pain."

I looked around the room for help and saw Mike huddled in a corner near the window, sitting in a chair with his back to Mom's bed, reading his Ken Follett thriller. Dad looked over at Mike at the same moment, and the two of us, one on each side of Mom's bed, exchanged a glance that said nothing. We both saw; neither of us could judge. Intuition told me it is hard to be a son and a doctor.

Suddenly, we were spared. Mom fell into a sleep so deep that it was not necessary to administer morphine until 7:00 P.M. Dad and I moved chairs close to the bed and kept watch. Every fifteen minutes or so, her eyes would startle open, wide and blue; she would look confused for a moment, then focus intently and say, "Le Anne" or "Newt," before her lids snapped shut again. Once, she stared wide-eyed at each of us in turn, with surprise and pleasure on her face, saying, "Le Anne. Mike. Newt. My family. I love you all."

THURSDAY, SEPTEMBER 12:

Another day of unrelieved misery. Not even morphine can control the double pain of cancer and an eighteen-inch V-shaped surgical incision that spans Mom's torso from side to side. Hospital procedures require patients to start walking on the first postoperative day, and so Mom, bent double with incisional pain, was forced to shuffle around the nurses' station, pushing ahead of her the rack on wheels that keeps her hooked up to her catheter as well as tubes in her nose and both arms. Dad and I were stationed at her elbows to make sure she didn't pitch forward into a tangle of tubes and bags.

Despite the pain, Mom did not resist the nurses' efforts to make her sit, stand, walk; though heavily sedated, she has grasped that the operation was successful and that movement will speed her recovery. Whenever the nurses ask her to do something difficult, she rouses herself from her morphine fog and mumbles, "If it will help me get better." I keep thinking how horrible it would be to endure postoperative pain if one knew surgery had been unsuccessful.

FRIDAY, SEPTEMBER 13:

This morning Mike and I arranged a meeting with an assistant to the radiologist in charge of Mom's case. Mike returns to Philadelphia tomorrow and, before he leaves, we wanted to get more information on the course of external radiation Mom will begin in three weeks. I also wanted to ask what the chief radiologist meant when he said they've had "good results" treating patients like Mom, but Mike doesn't want to know the exact numbers. "What's the point," he says. "She has no other choice."

The assistant was both more sympathetic and less reassuring than his boss, who has a greater interest in getting patients to sign on for his research project. The chief radiologist had told us the side effects of the external radiation would be minimal, but his assistant seemed to think otherwise. Since they will be irradiating her entire abdominal cavity in an effort to prevent metastasis, he said we should expect six weeks of nearly complete appetite loss, with serious weight loss, fatigue and general muscular weakness. It would be very important, he said, to build up her weight as much as possible between now and the beginning of the treatments.

When Mike and I returned to Mom's hospital room, we did not share this information. Why should Mom anticipate future miseries when there were so many present ones to contend with?

I left the hospital about 2:30 P.M. to take a long walk, but once on the sidewalks of Rochester, I found myself too weary for even the mildest exertion. I went back to the motel, fell asleep on the sofa and had a strange series of short dreams. All the dreams involved some scenario in which my eyes were closed and it was very important that I open them, but my lids were so heavy that it seemed impossible to raise them no matter how hard I tried. In one sequence, I had jumped into the fast-flowing stretch of the Taghkanic Creek just downstream from my fishing hole. I was riding the current the way I rode the Eisbach in Munich this summer; the water felt great, exhilarating, and I enjoyed being swept along with my eyes closed. But I knew I was coming near the place where a large, fallen tree spans the stream and I needed to open my eyes so I could avoid being smashed against it. I tried and tried to open my eyes, but my lids wouldn't budge. Knowing I was coming closer and closer to a fatal collision, I made one last, stupendous effort to force my lids up—and light flooded my eyes through the open slats of the motel blinds. I shut my eyes against the light and immediately fell asleep again, to dream another dream of eyes that wouldn't open. I can't remember the other dreams in detail, but there were six or seven of them, and they all ended with my struggling to open my eyes to save my life and finally succeeding, only to have my eyes filled with the glare of the late-afternoon sun in Rochester.

SUNDAY, SEPTEMBER 15:

On the first day post op, when Mom took her first walk around the circular nurses' station, she was able only to shuffle slowly in her red slipper socks, her hospital-issue Supphose sagging below the hem of her hospital-issue gown. Stooped and trailing tubes, she looked pitiful, a cartoon of broken body and spirit. As I escorted her round the ward, I felt envy and awe toward the patients who could actually lift their feet as they circled the room.

On the second day post op, when Mom could lift her feet, my envy switched to the patients who could walk without nurses hanging on each arm like two more tubes.

On the third day, when she could walk unassisted, I noticed that there were patients who were not limited to walking round the circular nurses' station, like old ponies fit only to carry small children round the fairground track. Some patients were trotting down the long stretch of corridor toward the elevators.

Today, with the last of her tubes unhooked, Mom mastered the corridor and we even went down to the sun deck on the fourth floor, which seemed a grand accomplishment. But even there I found others to envy—patients, for instance, who did not seem to think that a late-summer day's breeze was a dangerous blast of gale-force wind. It was a balmy seventy degrees, but Mom, propped up by several pillows, sat in a deck chair swaddled in blankets from slipper-socked toes to stiff upper lip. I think she would have pulled the blanket up over her head if that wouldn't have defeated the purpose of coming out to take "a little fresh air."

MONDAY, SEPTEMBER 16:

Today's trial was excruciating gas pains as Mom's intestines tried to accommodate real food after several days of intravenous feeding. This is, I am told, a classic postoperative ordeal, but in Mom's case, it is exacerbated by the pummeling her innards withstood during surgery. Since the pancreas is located behind the other organs in the abdominal cavity, the doctors had to "rearrange" all the other organs in order to do their work. They also checked for tumors in her intestines by handling and squeezing them. Now she must literally work the kinks out in order to process her first solid food since surgery.

The pain was intense—"You don't know," Mom said after nearly passing out on her way from bed to bathroom. When the nurse said that walking would help relieve the pains, Mom began marathon treks up and down the corridors and round the nursing stations in other wards. On one lap, Mom said it felt "as if little men in space suits were floating around my stomach, bumping into things." I suggested she not tell too many people about the little spacemen in her stomach or they might switch her to another ward. "Don't make me laugh," she said, clutching the little pillow she holds against her scarred midriff for comfort.

TUESDAY, SEPTEMBER 17:

The anesthesiologist visited Mom's room early this morning to say he wanted to do a trial run of the celiac block today before doing the actual block tomorrow. The procedure involves inserting two long, thin needles into Mom's back and then injecting alcohol through them to deaden the nerve that transmits pain from the tumor in her pancreas to her spinal column. In the trial run, he would inject water rather than alcohol, and since the water would have a temporary numbing effect on whatever it touched, it would help him pinpoint the exact location of the nerve before he injected alcohol, whose effect is permanent.

As he pitched the virtues of a trial run, the anesthesiologist seemed unduly nervous, as if he half expected us to reject his suggestion. Several times, he said he was sure "Mike would want it done this way." There were indeed a couple reasons to balk. A trial run meant that Mom would have to go without codeine for several hours and let her tumor-caused pain build, so that she could tell the doctor if the injected water was having an effect on it. It also meant that she would have to lie still for a half hour or more with her recently cut-up front pressed against a hard table while the anesthesiologist stuck needles in her back.

Mom had been prepared to endure that once, but she didn't like being asked to endure it twice. Still, if a trial run helped ensure the success of what was supposed to be a total, permanent solution to her tumor pain, she would do it. She would happily do just about anything.

At 2:00 P.M., when orderlies came to take her to the operating room, Mom was in good spirits despite the considerable pain that had been building all morning. This time, when the nurse asked for her dentures, Mom pointed out that she was not having general anesthesia and saw no need to remove them. She got her way and left the room almost buoyant.

She returned an hour later looking as if she had aged ten years. Her face was ashen and her skin, usually smooth, was marked with a tracery of fine lines. "It was the needles," she said. The needles, stuck repeatedly into her back through inches of muscle, without any anesthetic, were "hell," she said. "Enough pain for a lifetime." The doctor had ordered two male nurses to hold her down while he inserted the needles, not because she was being difficult, but because it is not humanly possible to stay still while muscles are being punctured.

The expression on Mom's face suggested that she could have told us more but preferred not to. It was time to start forgetting, time to block the memory of today's pain so she would have the energy to face tomorrow's. Dad stroked her creased cheeks with the back of his fingers and she fell into a deep sleep. I watched as her skin regained its color and smoothness and tried to remember if I had ever heard her use the word "hell" before. I recalled her saying "damn" once, when I was about ten years old. She had been vacuuming the stairs that led to the basement, and as she reached the bottom step, the Electrolux slid down the stairs from the top and landed on her big toe. "Damn," she shouted and I was shocked. I went with her to the emergency room of Saint Francis Hospital; when the doctor pronounced her big toe broken, I forgave her for shattering my illusions with her shout.

Last night the anesthesiologist came into Mom's room about eight o'clock with a sheepish smile on his boyish face. "You probably don't like me very much anymore," he said to Mom. "Well, I could have done without the pain," she answered, giving him back the girlish smile he was fishing for. I resent the way these handsome young doctors sidestep pain with smooth talk and flirtation, but if Mom was buying it, I wasn't going to interfere. I kept my mouth shut and counted on a few well-timed glares to get my message across.

He had come to get Mom's signed release for the nerve block procedure, a ritual that involves explaining possible side effects and their likelihood. He said that she would barely feel the needles this time, because they would feed her Valium intravenously during the procedure; she would remain conscious but feel no pain. When Mom asked him about side effects, he said that he had to inform her that there was a very remote possibility of lower body paralysis, but that she shouldn't let that concern her. Mom looked as if she had been slapped in the face.

In all our previous consultations about the nerve block—with the anesthesiologist, the oncologist, the surgeon, the radiologist—nobody had ever even hinted at serious side effects. I asked the anesthesiologist what the odds of paralysis were, and he said, "Oh, not more than one in a thousand, more like one in ten thousand." Mom was silent, but I could see she was as disturbed as I was by his cavalier attitude toward statistics. "I do this procedure several times a week," he added, "and I've never had a case of paralysis." Since this doctor looked as if he couldn't have been out of medical school for more than a few weeks, this was less reassuring than he intended it to be.

We all knew that the only alternative to a nerve block was ever-increasing dosages of addictive painkillers, each of which has its own unpleasant side effects. Remembering that the radiologist had said it was sometimes necessary to repeat the nerve block after six months or so, I asked if Mom would have any need for painkilling medication after the nerve block. "Absolutely not," he said with a big smile. "She won't even need an aspirin. This will provide one hundred percent relief of pain for the rest of her life." I wondered if he offered lifetime warranties to pancreatic patients on the assumption that they wouldn't be around for more than six months.

I looked at Mom to see if she had been persuaded and saw that she was not going to be talked out of her fear of paralysis. However many months or years she had left, she wanted to spend them on her feet. "Do I have to make up my mind right now?" she asked. "No," he said. "I've already reserved the operating room for tomorrow morning, and you can tell me whether you want to go ahead when I come by to see you at eight A.M." The doctor seemed surprised by Mom's sudden willfulness, but, to his credit, he left the room without applying any further pressure on her.

A few minutes later, however, the chief resident strode into the room while we were discussing Mom's choices and said, "I hear you don't want to go ahead with the nerve block." Without waiting for Mom to respond, he told her she was making "a very bad mistake." On previous visits, this doctor had displayed the flirtatious charm that seems to be the official medical center manner, but now he was abrupt and overbearing. He talked to Mom as if she were a naughty child refusing her medicine. "What are you afraid of?" he bullied. "The risk of paralysis is only one in one hundred, not more than one in fifty." Mom looked him straight in the eye, paused long enough to make him feel uncomfortable under her gaze, then said, "I'm going to take my time to make up my mind."

Left to ourselves, we mulled odds that had ranged from one in fifty to one in ten thousand over the past hour. Mom wondered why she couldn't just continue to use codeine to control her pain, as she had for the past couple months. Dad reminded her that she had to take codeine every four hours now, even during the night, and that the frequency would increase as her body got used to the dosage. Mom wondered why she should have the procedure now, why couldn't she wait a few months to see if it was necessary?

Dad and I wanted her to go ahead with the nerve block, because we wanted an immediate solution to the pain that held her and us hostage. If she could go home free of pain, maybe we could believe she was free of cancer, and maybe our belief would turn out to be true. We didn't press our case though. It was her body, her risk. Only she knew why the threat of paralysis frightened her more than any of the other risks she had already faced.

The next morning, when Dad and I entered her room, Mom told us she had spent the night praying and decided to trust in God. She didn't think He would let her be paralyzed. But when the doctor arrived, already dressed in his scrubs, to say he was ready if she was, a sudden pallor betrayed her doubts about both God and man.

After Mom had been taken from the room, I told Dad that I was going out for a walk. In fact, I had made an appointment to see the chief radiologist, but I didn't want Dad to know. I intended to ask him questions Dad and Mom and even Mike had chosen not to ask, and I didn't want them to know I had the answers. As I walked the path between the hospital and the medical building, I looked over my shoulder to make sure Dad couldn't see me from the window in Mom's room. I felt like a teenager sneaking off to forbidden places.

Sitting in the doctor's waiting room, I wondered why I was the only one who wanted a clearer sense of Mom's odds. In part, I was the only one who needed to know what to expect. If Mom had only months to live, I wanted to spend them with her, and I needed to make arrangements to leave my New York life vacant. Dad's life did not need to be rearranged, and Mike was not in a position to rearrange his no matter how much he might want to. They could afford to remain innocent; I couldn't. I had to plan for Mom's death, and I had to do it in stealth. But even if there were no practical reason for me to know more, I suspect I would still have made this appointment. I wanted to know the best and worst possibilities ahead of us.

When the doctor summoned me into his office, I blamed my need to know on geography, and asked him to tell me how many patients he had treated with this protocol and how many were still living. He said that he had treated about one hundred patients with pancreatic cancer over the past two years; 50 percent had survived a year after treatment and 20 percent were still alive at the end of the second year. There were no third-year statistics yet, but it was possible those who had survived two years were cured. I asked him what kind of life the surviving patients enjoyed, and he said they were leading "normal, healthy lives." In six months, he said, he would have a clearer indication of how Mom had responded to treatment.

The doctor, apparently used to family members who expect better odds, dispensed this information very impersonally, his monotone cool, formal, slightly defensive. He seemed surprised that I was overjoyed with his numbers. A 20 percent chance of two-year survival might seem dismal in most circumstances, but for pancreatic patients, it seemed miraculous. A 20 percent chance of survival left room for genuine hope.

I returned to Mom's room a few minutes before she did. She was still groggy from the Valium IV, but as the orderlies wheeled her past Dad and me, she gave us a big smile, lifted her legs out from under the sheet and kicked them in the air to show us they still worked. "It didn't hurt at all this time," she said as nurses helped her from the stretcher to the bed. "How does your back feel?" we asked. "Fine," she said. "I don't have any pain." All three of us were giddy with relief. Mom could leave the hospital tomorrow free of the pain she'd been enduring for months, and with a reasonable chance of surviving several more years in good health. There is still the external radiation treatment to endure but that is a month off and not painful in the excruciating way that surgery is.

We were all beaming when the anesthesiologist entered the room, looking nervous. He asked Mom how her legs felt, if there was any numbness or tingling. She told him they felt fine and did a few unsolicited kicks for him. He looked relieved, gave Mom a patronizing tweak on the toe and asked Dad and me to step outside for a moment.

The procedure had not gone as well as expected, he said. He usually injects 50 cc's of alcohol through each of two needles positioned at both ends of the celiac nerve, but when he began to inject alcohol through the second needle today, Mom roused herself from her Valium haze and mentioned that her left foot felt hot. He immediately stopped the procedure. Because he had not administered the full dose of alcohol to the nerve he didn't know how completely it would eliminate Mom's tumor pain. "Maybe seventy percent," he said. "She might want us to repeat the procedure in a few weeks." Although he didn't say so, it was clear that he had stopped injecting alcohol when Mom complained of a hot foot because that was a sign the alcohol was affecting the nerves that control the legs. Mom had been on the verge of becoming that one patient in ten thousand (or was it one in fifty) that he had told her not to worry about.

By 1:00 P.M., Mom was complaining of a terrible, burning pain in her lower back. It was not her tumor pain, she was sure. "That's gone," she said. "This is lower in my back." I went to the pay phone in the visitors' lounge and called Mike in Philadelphia. When I described Mom's state, he said the pain was probably caused by the nerve block. He explained that alcohol destroys anything it touches, not just the nerve that is targeted, and that some of the alcohol must have trickled down onto the muscles of Mom's lower back. Her pain was probably being caused by destroyed muscle tissue, and it would take several days to heal. I called the anesthesiologist and he agreed with Mike's assessment, adding that the nerve block often causes intestinal turmoil for a couple weeks as well. Why, I asked, hadn't they warned us about this last night? How is Mom supposed to build up her weight and strength before beginning her radiation treatment if she is weakened by pain and intestinal distress?

By mid-afternoon Mom's pain was so intense she needed an injection of morphine. Instead of the relief from pain and medication that we had expected from the nerve block, we got pain and medication redoubled. We had so much wanted their promised relief—"She won't even need an aspirin," the anesthesiologist had said—that this setback was deeply demoralizing. Mom succumbed to depression for the first time since this crisis began, and I plunged with her.

When visiting hours ended at 8:30 P.M., Dad said he was too tired to eat out and suggested we make sandwiches at the motel. I feigned a large appetite in order to purchase some privacy, and spent a glum couple hours alone in a bad Italian restaurant across from the hospital. After dinner I decided to go back to the hospital and check on Mom. Two other patients in the ward had major surgery today, and I suspected their needs would take precedence over hers.

It was 10:30 P.M. when I entered the hospital but nobody questioned my movements, and I reached Mom's room unnoticed. She was awake, in severe pain, her morphine injection a half hour overdue, her call light ignored. Kim, her favorite nurse's aide, came into the room every ten minutes to offer sympathy, but he is not authorized to administer painkillers; only nurses can inject morphine and they were busy tending a disoriented patient who kept trying to pull out his IVs.

Another half hour passed before a nurse was free to answer Mom's call light, but my presence seemed to reassure her, keep the panic at bay. I couldn't lessen the pain, but I could spare her the fright and despair patients feel when their suffering is ignored. She said I had looked like an angel to her when I ducked my head in the door tonight, and her saying so immediately lifted my depression. Waiting together for her morphine, we were strangely happy.

THURSDAY, SEPTEMBER 19:

We left the hospital this morning with a few days' supply of codeine and a round of cheery good-byes from the nurses. The farewells seemed inadequate, perhaps inevitably so. From the moment Mom was admitted to the hospital, these nurses became the most important people in the world. She depended on them initially for comfort, and ultimately for survival; in the first post-operative days, when her body literally could not function without them, we demanded that their concern for her be as profound as her dependence upon them. We expected compassion as our due and we got it. Not until we were leaving did I realize how much we had asked of the nurses, and how much they had given. And yet, at parting, there was no time to acknowledge that extreme experience had been shared. There were, as always, new patients, new urgencies, new families demanding to be treated as the most important people in the world. And so we exchanged those inadequate, cheery good-byes. They pretended that Mom is all better now, which she isn't, and we pretended that theirs was simply a job well done, which it wasn't. My respect for good nurses is boundless.

Doctors are another matter. No doctor even came by to discuss what special care Mom might need at home, and no prescriptions had been authorized. We would have left without even an aspirin if I hadn't insisted upon something for the pain that still burns in Mom's back.

Before leaving the hospital, Mom took codeine to help her through the two-hour drive home. As she sat in a wheelchair on the pavement outside the hospital entrance, Dad lowered the front passenger seat of his Renault into a reclining position, and we placed pillows against the seat to support Mom's distressed lower back. We used an overnight case as a footstool, hoping raised legs would put less strain on her still-healing incision. The move from wheelchair to car caused a few loud groans, but once Mom was settled, with a pillow clutched against her abdomen and blankets up to her ears, she was comfortable enough to take notice of the rain clouds that stretched from Rochester to Minneapolis.

SATURDAY, SEPTEMBER 21:

Drugs are becoming more and more of an issue. Mom's need for painkillers is greater than ever. The celiac block, which was supposed to eliminate the need for them, has created pain so intense it requires more medication than the tumor did. The anesthesiologist said the acute pain in her lower back would last only two or three days, but it is now four days since the procedure and the pain shows no sign of subsiding, which makes me doubt whether the block was effective. If the pain is entirely caused by alcohol-damaged muscles, it should eventually go away, but if this pain is also directly caused by the tumor, Mom may never get off narcotics. This uncertainty causes its own depression.

Today, Dad showed strain and impatience with Mom for the first time. The battleground was pills. He's trying to deny Mom's need for them, and that fills her eyes with fear and repressed anger. When she asks for a pill, and he says, "Oh, I don't think you need one yet," she doesn't contradict him, but I see her eyes moisten and focus on some distant place beyond Dad and me; her chin starts to crumble and then she sets it, making her jaw jut forward a little. She is silent but I know she is crying and yelling in that place where her eyes are focused.

She is too weak to get up and get her own pills, and so Dad is the dispenser, with power to give or withhold. His seeming lack of sympathy for her suffering infuriates me, even though I know his behavior is rooted in a fear of addiction. My impulse, barely checked, is to sneak her codeine whenever she wants it and his is to withhold it even when she clearly needs it. Pill time has become a family sickness, with me playing mediator between her requests and his refusals.

Today, for the first time, I also sensed Dad's concern about his own health. A lesion appeared on his right forearm, the first since the sun solved his skin problems in Italy this summer. As he sat at the kitchen table sorting through medical bills this afternoon, I saw him open a drawer and take out a pamphlet he had stashed there on skin cancer.

The day, which started disastrously, got better as the hours passed and Mom's condition improved. By evening, her need for codeine reduced itself by half, and her ability to do things for herself doubled. She even tried to wash dishes after dinner, with a pillow pressed between herself and the sink, but after a plate or two, I insisted she stop, promising her many future opportunities to dip her hands in dishwater.

I wonder how much of her improvement was the result of feeling she had to get better, or else.

Mike didn't call today, and his silence feels like defection. We three cannot be left alone in this. I am supposed to fly to Toronto on Tuesday to interview Margaret Atwood for *Vogue,* and I'm afraid to leave Mom alone with Dad unless we've worked out some understanding about how Mom's pain should be handled. When I made the arrangements to do the interview, the doctors had assured me that Mom's recovery from surgery would be nearly complete by this time. I had thought I would be able to go straight from Toronto to New York and pick up the pieces of my life there, but that seems impossible now.

Mom's pain persevered today and so did Dad's pressure to cut down on codeine. Mom cried when he refused to get her a pill this morning, because, by his reckoning, not enough time had elapsed since her last one. I fumed, entertaining dark thoughts about the control Dad is exerting over Mom and, indirectly, over me. What right does he have to assume power over her pain? Why must we pretend father knows best, when father is fixated on drugs as the source of all evil? Cancer and pain are the evils of this situation, and if we need the lesser evil of drugs to fight them, so be it. It seems foolish to worry about the long-term effects of addiction when we are in a short-term fight for her life. She needs relief from pain so she can eat, sleep, build up her strength before starting the next round of treatment in two weeks. She has gone from 120 pounds to 104 since she entered the hospital and we have to put that weight back on her before radiation starts taking it off again.

Mom is divided between her own needs and her habit of pleasing Dad. After their fight, she confessed to me that she is worried about the strain she is causing him. She worries about his heart, his blood pressure, and then gets angry at herself for not being able to control her pain without medication. To restore calm for a few hours, I suggested we try to get Dad to go fishing this afternoon. About 2:00 P.M. he set off into a chilly, gray afternoon with fly rod and hip boots in hand.

As soon as he left, I called Mike in Philadelphia and told him what was happening. He agrees that Dad's concern over pills is misplaced and that it is crucial to keep Mom out of pain so she can regain her strength. I asked him to call back this evening and play doctor, without letting Dad know that I had put him up to it. For a moment after getting off the phone, I resented having to influence Dad through Mike, as if father and son were the only ones capable of making decisions in this family. But in fact, I know this is not a matter of male privilege. As son, Mike has no more influence on Dad than I do as daughter; it's only as doctor that he has leverage.

With Dad out of the house and her pain temporarily under control, Mom relaxed. She thought she felt strong enough to go outside, so we bundled her into sweatpants and a hooded sweatshirt for a stroll to the corner and back. It was the first time she had walked outside since entering the hospital, and she held my right arm in a grip so tight that I quickly lost circulation below the elbow. Our progress down the street was very slow, and while her left hand clutched me, her right hand was tucked casually into her sweatshirt pocket, a one-sided picture of repose for the benefit of any neighbors who might be lurking behind drawn curtains.

Exhausted and elated by our eighty-yard round-trip, Mom returned to her perch on the living-room sofa with the air of a woman ready to sit down and relax after a long day's work. Rather than ask if she wanted a pill or some food or a drink of water, I simply sat down across from her and we began to talk. The conversation turned to her sisters in Fort Dodge and I found an opening to ask about Aileen. I broached the subject matter-of-factly, as if I expected to receive news of Aileen as routinely as I receive news of my other aunts. My instincts must have been sound, because Mom responded easily, without hesitation, as if she'd forgotten we have spoken of Aileen only twice in our lives.

Until this afternoon, I wasn't even sure that Aileen was still alive. I learned that Aileen is living in the Marion Home in Fort Dodge, that she was moved there from the mental institution shortly after Grandma died. Mom visits her whenever she goes to Fort Dodge, and Aileen always asks about "Mike and Le Anne." She knows all the basics of our lives, she even has pictures of us in her room at the nursing home.

The image of Aileen surrounded by pictures of nieces and nephews she has never been allowed to see made me unspeakably sad, but I tried to conceal my reaction, because I didn't want Mom to stop talking. It was the other sisters in Fort

Dodge—Alice, Veronica, Anna Marie and Katherine—who arranged for Aileen to be taken out of the mental institution after Grandma's death. Mom said they were all surprised to discover that the only entry on her medical records, after all these decades in the institution, was "Series of strokes. Age 14."

At fifteen, when I first learned of Aileen's existence, I was told she was retarded. Later, when I learned from a cousin that Aileen reads and writes, I again asked Mom why her sister was institutionalized. At that time, which was shortly after Grandma's funeral, Mom said that Aileen had never been "quite right" after an automobile accident when she was about thirteen, and that as she got older, she became "difficult to control." This afternoon I asked Mom what exactly had been odd about Aileen's behavior as a teenager. The only thing she could recall was that Aileen, who is older than Mom, would sneak out of the house in the middle of the night and walk the mile from the farm into town, usually showing up at one or another relative's house in the morning.

I asked Mom if Aileen had ever wanted to leave the institution, and she said, "Well, I suppose so. But I don't really know. It's all so long ago. I don't remember."

I took that as a cue that Mom was getting tired and stopped asking questions, but she went on without prompting. "Aileen was beautiful," Mom said, "more beautiful than the rest of us." She was the third of the seven sisters, after Bertha and Alice. "There were six years between Bertha and Alice," Mom added, "because in between there was a tubal pregnancy. Then came Aileen and the rest of us girls and the three boys, one every two years."

Mom said Aileen was very lucid when she last visited her, but when Sister Innocentia (née Bertha) visited the Marion Home recently, Aileen did not recognize her. The other sisters were surprised by this, and when they made inquiries, they discovered that the nursing home staff had been drugging Aileen into incoherence. The sisters demanded that Aileen be taken off drugs and they also asked if she could be assigned a new roommate.

Mom says Aileen shares a room with a "poor woman with Alzheimer's"; the roommate sometimes "acts crazy" but Aileen's behavior is "normal."

Our talk was interrupted by the sound of a car entering the garage. A few seconds later Dad came in the back door empty-handed, without even a nibble to speak of, but clearly in better spirits than when he left. He was pleased, overjoyed really, to hear that Mom and I had taken a walk. When Mike called an hour later, Dad was willing to be guided by his advice.

MONDAY, SEPTEMBER 23:

I must make my peace with this house. I feel like a guest here, entitled to the privacy of my assigned room but with no established rights in the open spaces. The only piece of furniture from the house I grew up in is the narrow bed on which I sleep at night, and I dearly wish they had left that behind in Evanston. It is thirty inches wide, fit for the five-year-old I was when they purchased two undersized beds so Mike and I could share a small room until they built an addition. Now I lie in it, unable to toss and turn as I listen every night for sounds of distress.

The bedroom feels like a guest room in a home unused to guests, furnished with items too functional to discard but too featureless to put on display in rooms that are lived in. Even if I made the room mine, it would still be too small and dim to linger in during the day. There is barely room enough to walk around the two narrow beds, and sunlight, when there is any, filters in through two windows set at shoulder level, presumably as protection against peeping neighbors.

I need a corner to call my own, but it's not clear where I am going to find it. There are no nooks in this house, no doors to close behind me except in the bedrooms and bathroom. The rooms flow into one another, living room and dining room and hall connected by inlets of wall-to-wall carpet and paths worn by Dad's restless pacing. There are television sets in the kitchen and den and basement, so that he can catch whatever's flickering as he prowls the house in search of diversion, a dish to wash, a fly to tie, a broken appliance to fix. He used to paint and sculpt in the basement for hours at a time while Mom read in the living room, but now he seems unable to bestow his attention on anything for more than a few minutes. Mom stays fixed on the living-room sofa, gazing out the picture window at freshly mowed lawns and gray skies, but Dad's path crosses mine several times an hour, no matter where I retreat.

The truth is, I have always resented this house. I wanted my parents to stay in Evanston, so I could return to the people and places I left behind. I counted on them to keep my room, my friends. Or move to a warm climate and offer beaches as compensation for a lost home. It never occurred to me that Dad might accept a transfer to frosty Minnesota at an age when he should be thinking about heading south. I assumed that danger was long past.

The dreaded transfer to the home office hung over us all through my childhood; I remember protesting, sincerely, that "my entire life would be destroyed" if Dad's bosses at the *Minneapolis Star & Tribune* insisted on his leaving Chicago, as they threatened every other year during the 1950s. I know Mom felt her life had indeed been destroyed when they moved here after thirty years in Evanston, but given Dad's fears of forced retirement, she didn't raise objections to a surprise promotion at age sixty-one.

In Evanston, Mom had friends on the block, Ruth and Em and Von, women she laughed with the way she laughs with her sisters. The neighbors here are just neighbors, people who draw your curtains in the evening when you are on vacation. Evanston had two sides of a track, a lakefront of old mansions to the east, a growing sprawl of ranch houses to the west, a ghetto, a downtown that went through cycles of uplift and decay. Here, towns are graduated like income taxes, with a different suburb for each

66

$10,000 gap in bracket. Edina is $60,000 to $70,000, a three-bedroom, two-car-garage community, without sidewalks to stroll or alleys to explore. No one ever plays in the street. Custom permits lawn mowing and snow blowing in the front yard, but all other signs of life are kept out of sight, behind closed curtains or in backyards bordered by fences.

They've been here twelve years now, and Mom has adjusted, but I still pull into the wrong driveway sometimes. The streets named for meadows and prairies that no longer exist all look alike to me, and I have no markers, no memories, to tell me this home is mine.

TUESDAY, SEPTEMBER 24:

After my 2:00 P.M. flight to Toronto was rained out, I spent the rest of the afternoon in the airport rather than return home. Three weeks of family inseparability has left me so starved for solitude that I was content to wander from gate to gate thinking my own thoughts. Weather delays were followed by equipment problems and it was close to midnight when I arrived at Margaret Atwood's home in Toronto. She had to get up early to see her daughter off to school the next morning, but we stayed up and talked for an hour. I told her about my mother and she told me about medical crises she has been through with her father and Graeme's father. "It's our cohort's time," she said. "All my friends are going through it. All we ever seem to talk about is our parents' health."

The room I slept in was lined with bookshelves. After our conversation, I was less surprised than I might have been to find several rows of medical books. I got into bed with *The Cancer Handbook* and turned to the section on the side effects of radiation treatment. I studied probability charts for hair loss, nausea, skin burns, severe fatigue, depression, loss of appetite, and took comfort in a footnote that said it was very rare for any one patient to suffer all the possible side effects of radiation. I fell asleep about 2:30 A.M. and dreamt that my body was being irradiated. The dream, which lasted all night, had very little detail; I was lying in bed, my body surrounded by a red glow, which it was both receiving and emitting; there was no pain, just a disturbing awareness that the red glow could kill.

WEDNESDAY, SEPTEMBER 25:

After our interview this morning, I took a cab to the Windsor Arms hotel and checked in. Margaret had offered me a place in her home today and tomorrow, but I didn't feel comfortable accepting her hospitality. I have never stayed in the home of anyone I've written about. Besides, I was looking forward to the privacy of a hotel room. I can't even remember the last time I had a day to myself.

The hotel is a short walk from the University of Toronto, and after lunch I set out to find Saint Michael's, the Catholic college within the university. It was the only Catholic college that I applied to when I was in high school, and though I've never seen it, I've always thought of it as my path not taken. If I hadn't been accepted at Rice, I would have gone to Saint Michael's. I would never have met and married and divorced Peter, I probably would not have gone to Harvard, perhaps not even to New York. I would not have had the friends and lovers and jobs that I have had. So much of my life has been a matter of accident that I wonder what would have followed from a change of circumstance as basic as four years in Toronto instead of Houston. Maybe I'd have grown up to be the good Catholic wife and mother that I was supposed to be.

It was a clear, sunny day and as I walked through the campus, I tried to imagine myself one of the students who were lounging in the college courtyards. In many ways, I would have been more at home surrounded by the Victorian Gothic of Saint Michael's than I was with the neo-Mediterranean pastiche of Rice. But then, I didn't go away to school to feel at home.

The chapel, doors open, had to be entered. Its cold stone would have made the real difference. In the hush of the empty chapel, I half expected to hear the swish of long skirts dragging against the marble floor. But, of course, nuns, even if there were any lurking in the recesses of this Jesuit chapel, don't dress like that anymore. I sat in a pew toward the rear of the church and waited to see what would stir in me. I soon found myself enjoying the cool air, the light falling gently from high windows, the quiet. It was simply peaceful here. It didn't feel haunted.

I began to pray, asking that my mother be restored to health or at least to ease. I even asked forgiveness for the anger I had harbored toward the church all these years, though I quickly added that I had very good reasons for my anger and I didn't want anyone listening to my thoughts to think that I had changed my mind on any of those issues that had made me turn from the church. But I allowed that maybe the church knew something I didn't about sickness and death, maybe it was better at comforting the dying than guiding the living.

On my way out of the chapel, I stopped to browse through the rack of pamphlets at the rear of the church. I picked up one titled, "Mamma, Why Did You Kill Us?" and began to read. It is the allegedly factual account of a last confession given by a woman who has been visited by all the unborn fetuses she had aborted. I put fifty cents in the donations box and took the pamphlet with me so that I could rekindle my anger in the place of my choice.

THURSDAY, SEPTEMBER 26:

This morning I went to see the "Treasures of Budapest" exhibit at the Royal Museum. It is an exhibit of artifacts confiscated from the homes and synagogues of Budapest's Jewish community by the Nazis. Hitler had planned to build a museum to house this collection—the last remnants, he hoped, of an extinct race whose diabolical nature would be manifest in its artifacts.

I went through the exhibit very slowly, paying close attention to the variations each craftsman had brought to the same ritual objects. What held my attention longest were the utensils used in Jewish funeral rites, the special combs and nail clippers to groom the head and hands of the dead. I had been ignorant of Jewish funeral traditions and was very moved by the respect and care this community gave its corpses. What madness to think these objects could be made to testify against their makers.

I wonder whether this would have been my focus if I'd seen the exhibit when it was in New York this summer. I doubt it. I suspect I was drawn to these details because I have entered that "more onerous citizenship." The phrase is Susan Sontag's, from the first paragraph of *Illness as Metaphor*, which I began to read in my hotel room last night.

"Illness is the night-side of life, a more onerous citizenship. Everyone who is born holds dual citizenship, in the kingdom of the well and in the kingdom of the sick. Although we all prefer to use only the good passport, sooner or later each of us is obliged, at least for a spell, to identify ourselves as citizens of that other place."

I have never been a citizen of that other place, but I am being given a key to the city, and I fear I will have to struggle every day against the temptation to throw it away or stuff it in a locked drawer. In the bookstore yesterday, I browsed through every volume that had "cancer" in its title, but I couldn't bring myself to open any of the books on death and dying. I think I avoid them as if they were death itself, as if their purchase committed me to a course I must follow to an inescapable end. We are not the Jews of Budapest. We are postwar. Illness does not lead to death; it leads to medicine.

I returned to the same situation I left. There has been no improvement in Mom's back pain, and she complains of a weird sensation in her stomach, the feeling that it is falling out of her whenever she stands up. That sensation, rather than incisional pain, is why she holds a pillow tightly against her abdomen when she walks.

Over Mom's objections—she didn't want "to bother the doctor"—I called the anesthesiologist to ask why she was still in pain ten days after the nerve block. The doctor who first promised immediate total relief, then retreated to "maybe two or three days' discomfort," now says a nerve block sometimes causes two to three weeks of pain. And, oh yes, that sensation in her stomach, it's from the nerve block. No, it won't go away. She'll have to learn to live with it. But don't worry, it doesn't hurt anything.

I have decided to stay another week.

SATURDAY, SEPTEMBER 28:

I am surprised by the ferocity of this attachment. I have often wondered what remained of our connectedness as a family. Had our bonds been so attenuated by time and distance that we were linked by nothing stronger than AT&T? There was affection, of course, and memory, but did our love have a present tense or was it stranded in the past imperfect? After such wondering, I am brought up short, reined in with one strong pull. It seems I was deceived by the length of the tether; the knot holds fast.

I must have known this, but in a family as reticent as ours, the knowing is always clouded, a matter of instinct and inference. Often the route of communication is dream. These past weeks have made me remember two extraordinary but nearly forgotten experiences I had in August 1974, when I was twenty-nine and new to New York, alone and starting over. I call them dreams, but at the time they felt like waking memories, flashbacks stirred by awakening to a sudden blast of bright morning light that made the close confines of my loft bed shimmer and dance. Eyes open, twenty-nine years after the fact, I dreamed my birth.

Sleek and wet, I popped out of darkness into dazzling light, and was held aloft by something firm and warm. I looked down in amazement at the other, enormous part of myself, the part from which I came and to which I was still attached. Then I saw a hand with scissors cut the long, thick cord connecting the two parts of my flesh and my whole body suddenly filled with air and just as suddenly emptied itself in a long red scream of fear and protest. Before I could suck in more white air and turn it red, I was lowered through the air and placed on top of the large, round, warm flesh from which I had been severed. A ripple of calm spread slowly through my clenched body and exited as a sigh.

In the second dream, which came later in the same week, I was an infant, sitting bowlegged on a rug in the middle of a room surrounded by seated adults. The adults were a chorus of voices crisscrossing the air high over my head and a set of trousered knees cupped round the front edges of upholstered chairs. I wanted to be raised onto one of those knees, I wanted my ears to be in the flight path of the sounds, but I also wanted to go exploring, see what was hidden in the darkness of the open doorway that beckoned on the far side of the room. The awareness was wordless, but my infant self knew it was on the verge of a momentous decision, one whose consequences were clear and irrevocable. I could rise to my feet and walk, revealing to the adults a capacity they did not suspect was within my power. The room, and the room beyond this one, and the one beyond that, a possibly endless progression of rooms and doorways, would be mine to explore if I just stood up and walked. But if I rose by my own power, those knees would never be effortlessly and innocently mine again. I could not hope to be swooped up, willy-nilly, by whatever adult felt an impulse to lavish affection. I would have to choose a knee, make my desires known, ask for affection. In the dream I know what I will do, what I have to do. Braced for loss, I prepare to stand and walk.

I have no memory of hearing my parents describe that day, but often, in my young years, they would boast of how I had walked at nine months, my small body pitched forward in a kind of continuous, pigeon-toed free fall. It is one of the stories of my fabled "independence." A similar boast is made about my brother. They tell how on the first day of kindergarten, Mike told my mother that if she escorted him the five blocks to school as she planned, she would "ruin his life forever." Respecting his pride, she let five-year-old Mike set off for school alone, but then she followed him, sneaking through alleys on a parallel course to his long march up Main Street and down busy Ridge Avenue, catching glimpses of her firstborn at corners and in the breaks between buildings.

The day Mike left Chicago for his first year at Harvard, I stood next to my mother as she smiled and waved good-bye to the handsome young man who looked back one last time before disappearing round the curve of a gangway. Back home, she closed the bedroom door behind her and emerged several hours later, her lips sealed, her eyes red and swollen. I knew the silence was for me, her tacit blessing. I too would be allowed to leave. I too would receive a wave and a smile from my mother, who is proud to have been born on the Fourth of July. We have reaped much from our independence and we have paid a great price. It is the family allegiance, our link and our separation, our pride and our pain.

AVAILABLE

LIGHT

GLENCO MILLS, N.Y.
THURSDAY, OCTOBER 10:

I just returned from the fish hole, where I sat for hours on my double-trunked log peering into clear water. I saw a large fish emerge head first from under the carpet of fallen leaves that covers the stream bed. He looked like he was giving birth to himself, wiggling his way out of the earth full grown. I also saw a molting crayfish scuttle across the bottom and take cover under a maple leaf.

Two small fish, about four inches long, seemed to be playing with each another. They are, I suppose, too young to mate but their movements reminded me of the lizards I watched mating on the patio in Italy this summer. One fish would swim up to the side of another, and when he was exactly parallel to the other fish, sideswipe him. The sideswipe would knock them apart, and both fish quickly circled back for another collision. It looked very like the soccer drill in which two players stand side by side, jump into the air and butt shoulders. The butting would be repeated four or five times in quick succession, until one of the fish gave up and darted away. A couple minutes later, they would repeat the cycle.

At other times the two fish seemed to sniff each others' tails, like dogs do, or stroke one another with a slow swish of delicate tail, like cats. A larger fish flipped on its side and seemed to scratch itself against the leaves on the bottom of the stream. It was almost as if the presence of leaves in their world made the fish behave like land creatures for a day. Every other time I spied on them from my perch on the fallen sycamore, they swam without touching each other.

TUESDAY, OCTOBER 15:

Mom had her first radiation treatment today. She said it was "scary." She must lie absolutely still on a hard, narrow slab, which is then raised several feet in the air. She is not scared of falling. What frightens her is the sound of technicians literally running for cover as she is being lofted toward the source of radiation. She will take this ride five days a week for the next five weeks.

WEDNESDAY, OCTOBER 16:

Mom and Dad spent their forty-eighth wedding anniversary at the Clinic View Inn watching the sun play on the checkerboard of light and dark gray marble that forms the facade of Rochester's main industry. Mom dined intravenously, her first portion of take-out chemo pumping into her veins from a contraption strapped to her waist. Dad fixed himself a grilled cheese sandwich.

I placed a bid on a house last week, and I haven't had a good night's sleep since. Before I left for Italy last spring, I promised myself I would begin house hunting as soon as I returned, but that plan, like many others, changed the day I learned of Mom's cancer. I figured that my whereabouts for the next several months were too uncertain for me to undertake the momentous aggravations of house buying.

But last week a realtor called to say he had something in my price range, and I let myself be talked into "going for a look-see." Before the afternoon was over, I was in his office signing "a binder," which committed me to paying 1 percent of the purchase price if my bid was accepted, which it promptly was. Lawyers are drawing up contracts now, and I have seldom been so ambivalent.

The house is adequate and affordable, a no-frills, two-story, white clapboard house on three acres near Kinderhook. It looks like a child drew it. Draw a rectangle, draw four squares inside it for windows, draw a rectangle bottom center for a door, put a triangle on top for the roof. Don't forget the chimney and, above, a sun with spokes around it.

The interior has a few surprises. Like a kitchen in the second-floor hallway, and a beauty parlor downstairs where the kitchen should be. If you are over 5 feet 8 inches you either duck your head or crack it when you go up or down the stairs, because the stairwell was cut through the first-floor ceiling in a strange way. Neither the present owners nor I are over 5'8", but my neighbor Lenny discovered this feature the hard way when he inspected the house for me yesterday.

Lenny knows houses, how their innards work, and he assures me this one is sound. No rotting wood, no cracks in the foundation, good furnace, new water heater, well-maintained septic system, plentiful insulation. It's ship-shape, just like the owner says. Needs some roof work, but otherwise I could just move in and start setting hair. Lenny said I could get out of it whatever I put in, meaning the money I put into purchase and renovation will probably be a good investment.

When I drove past the house yesterday, I saw my prospective next-door neighbor. An old lady, swathed from neck to toe in several layers of ragged clothes, stood in her front yard poking a pitchfork into a large pile of burning leaves. She came in and out of sight through billows of gray smoke, looking so much like a fairy-tale witch that I had to laugh. I choose to think of her as an asset, a bit of local color in otherwise nondescript surroundings. I also choose to think of the large, boggy area behind the house as a pond site. I can create the charm that is missing, put shutters on the windows, add a sun room and a front porch. There's no trout stream to explore, but I can stock a pond and watch its ecology change from hour to hour.

I know I am acting in panic, but I don't know what else to do. Real-estate prices in the county have doubled in the past year and are still rising. I'm afraid if I don't buy now I will be priced out of this area. And buying now means buying hastily, because each time the phone rings, I think it may be a call that summons me to Minnesota, for one month or two months or six. I don't have time to search the county for a house with a face and character I could love.

I'm thinking of the house I bid on as a poker chip, my stake in local real estate, so that if prices keep rising, so will the value of this house, and when circumstances are right, I'll be able to sell and resettle. I did not want to buy a house in this spirit, but I don't see any other way to stake a claim in this county.

My friends' counsel is of two kinds—"Don't buy it if you don't love it" or "It's impossible to make a bad investment in real estate." I toss and turn each night between these two poles of advice, and feel a wrenching disappointment. I don't want the cold comfort of a good investment. I want a home.

For years I have promised myself that I would search out Aileen, travel alone and unannounced to Iowa, find whatever institution she called home and learn what she had to say of her life. I had no fantasy of rescue, just a desire to let her know I claim her as my aunt, as she claims me as a niece. I wanted to break the silence. And now it is too late. I learned this morning that a stroke has left Aileen paralyzed, speechless. As paralyzed, as speechless as I have been, will now always be, to her.

I remember a woman sitting at a picnic table brushing my hair. It's a hot summer day in Iowa and I am three years old, dressed in a red-check sunsuit that earns my mother a scolding from a stern-looking nun who is also at the picnic table. My nun-aunt thinks my bare arms and legs are "indecent." The lady brushing my hair doesn't seem to mind. She just smiles and looks out over the biggest, greenest expanse of lawn I have ever seen. The nun I will see once or twice a year, usually at the train station in Chicago, when she is en route to a new teaching assignment. I never see the other woman or the big green lawn again. I never even think about her again until the summer I am fifteen, when I'm in Fort Dodge, swapping gossip with my cousins.

One cousin, an altar boy, says a woman came up to him last week after he served Mass at the mental institution outside of town and said she was his aunt. Denny told her she was mistaken but the lady was very certain. She even knew the names of Denny's five brothers and sisters. Denny's story makes another cousin remember the time she went with Grandma to a meeting of Gold Star mothers. Each Gold Star mother was asked to stand up, and say her name and the number of her children. When Grandma rose, she said she had ten children, which surprised Betty, who knew the correct number was nine, counting Leo, who was dead. At the time, Betty thought Grandma was just exaggerating, but now we are convinced a terrible secret has been kept from us.

I wait until we are back home in Evanston to confront my mother. She is vacuuming and I am sitting on the living-room sofa, brooding, as I have been for two weeks. When she asks me to raise my feet so she can vacuum under them, I pounce. Why didn't you tell me you have another sister? I shout the question, and glare, accusing my mother of fault, of grievous fault, for the first time in our lives. Her face pales and she loses her grip on the vacuum attachment, which crashes to the floor. The sight of my clenched jaw and steely eyes makes her cry, but I don't flinch. I am ready to reject whatever explanation she may have to give.

She tells me that Aileen is retarded and has lived in a state institution since she was eighteen. Grandma sees her every week, and her brothers and sisters all visit her whenever they can, but the family decided never to mention her to the next generation, because we might be frightened. "Frightened of what?" I demand with the righteousness of a teenage do-gooder who spends her Saturday mornings teaching Catholic doctrine to retarded children. "It was different back then," my mother says. "People didn't understand what they do today. There was the thought that these things might be hereditary, and we didn't want any of you kids to worry about it."

The explanation is not good enough. From that day, I never think the same of my elders. My parents, my grandmother, all my aunts and uncles, their cousins, everyone in Fort Dodge who ever knew Aileen, at least one hundred people, most of them relatives, had entered into a cruel conspiracy to deny Aileen's existence to my generation. I was stunned by their wrongheadedness, their unanimity, the utter staunchness of their silence. Not a single slip of the tongue in all these years, except for Grandma's Gold Star mother's boast.

I never forgot Aileen again, but I never saw her, and I never mentioned her name to any member of my extended family until October 1979, when we were all gathered in Fort Dodge for

Grandma's funeral. The evening after the funeral, I was getting reacquainted with several of my female cousins, when one of their husbands looked up from the newspaper he was reading and said, "Who is Aileen? This obituary says Grandma Meyer had ten children, and is survived by nine, including a daughter Aileen?" We cousins looked at one another, trying to fathom in a glance who knew what. The husband looked at all of us as if he had just found himself transported back in time to a Salem witch trial.

The silence broke, and the pent-up words, released at last, began to rush and tumble in a frenzy of recrimination. Each of us, it seems, had stumbled upon the secret of Aileen at some time in our adolescence; each of us had confronted our mothers in anger and disbelief; and each of us, in turn, had kept the secret, sharing our mothers' and grandmother's guilt. None of us knew why.

My oldest cousin had some answers, though. She says Aileen is not retarded, she reads and writes. She was just a bit slow and very beautiful, the kind of girl farmhands take advantage of. Suddenly I understand, or think I do. The mental institution was a form of birth control, the only kind allowed a beautiful Catholic girl who didn't understand the sinfulness of farmhands. There are priests to blame, no doubt.

Maybe that's why my mother seems to feel so little guilt about Aileen, so much guilt about birth control. My nun-aunt used to accuse her of the practice, belittle the size of her brood and exhort her "to get in the line of duty." Those visits at the train station often left my mother in tears. And tears of pure torment were rare. I caused them only that once, when I shouted my question over the roar of the vacuum.

Since the time of Grandma's funeral, I have felt in league with my hidden aunt. I was always told that I was named for Leo, the uncle who died the year before I was born. I choose to believe Aileen was also encoded in my name, waiting to be deciphered.

Driving back from a weekend with friends in Montgomery County, I decided to make a stop in Hoosick Falls. Like most of the mill towns in upstate New York, Hoosick Falls is visibly depressed. The grand Victorian mansions erected for the glory of mill owners are now white elephants, the respectable black-shuttered Georgians beg for renovation and the modest white frame houses of former mill workers would be happy just to be occupied. What civic pride is left expresses itself on the shiny bronze plaque that announces Hoosick Falls as the hometown of Grandma Moses.

There were no signs indicating where I could pay my respects, so I pulled up before a house that had a tag sale sign posted on a power line pole near the curb. Several card tables were set up on the driveway, bearing such items as used radio batteries, broken camera parts and a red plastic basket of the kind that comes with Chicken-in-a-Basket dinners. No item was priced over twenty-five cents.

It was about 4:00 P.M. and the man presiding over the sale was beginning to pack up his possessions in cardboard boxes. When I asked him if he had a good day, he shook his head. "Nope," he said, "seems folks would rather look at leaves," and then he shook his head again as if to say, "It takes all kinds." I asked for directions to Grandma Moses' grave and was directed up Main Street and then right at the top of the hill toward Maple Grove Cemetery.

Maple Grove is a large cemetery and, again, there were no signs to help visitors, so I asked a woman walking her dog among the tombstones where I could find Grandma Moses. The woman was dressed in dark slacks, a plain khaki trench coat and a pink linen jockey cap exactly like one that blew off my head and into the Seine on my first awestruck trip to Paris twenty years ago. She pointed me toward the right grave and then kept on talking.

She told me she had lived in Hoosick Falls for ten years, ever since she retired. She lived in Brooklyn and Elizabeth, N.J., before that, but decided to move here, where her parents had been born, after she retired. Her father went to the Catholic high school, her mother to the public school. Both were dead and her friends were dying too. It wasn't the same anymore, anyway, since she retired. "You don't stay in touch," she said. "Oh, there's calls and letters, but it's not the same, and everyone's dying. I never would have moved here if I knew I was going to live ten years. I thought I was only going to live five."

She said she was seventy-two, and she looked fine to me, but as we talked, she cast her eyes enviously at the graves around us. She seemed to think good health was a dirty trick God was playing on her. When she suggested I come with her to hear "a beautiful five-o'clock Mass" sung by the nuns and monks at Cambridge, N.Y., I declined, saying I wanted to reach my home in New York City before it got dark. I didn't want her to know I lived within easy reach.

I excused myself and drove the cemetery road up the hill to its crest, where Grandma Moses had been honored with the best view in Maple Grove. Looking west, I took in the sight of the Berkshires in full fall plumage, all gold and red and orange and glistening in the not-quite-setting sun.

TUESDAY, OCTOBER 29:

I met this morning with my lawyer in Hudson, who had just received the signed contract on the Kinderhook house from the seller's lawyer. I asked if I had to sign it immediately, and he said I could think it over for a few days before committing the 10 percent of purchase price that is required upon signing. Since I still have all the same reservations, I decided to sleep, or not sleep, on it for two more days.

Over lunch I browsed through a new issue of *The Columbia County Home Buyer,* and on the last page saw a picture of a house, within my price range, that looked too good to be true. I called the realtor, who said she could not show the house today, but she told me where it was located and I went by this afternoon.

It's just ten minutes east of Glenco Mills, in the village of Ancram. "Village" is the official designation for Ancram, but it's more like a hamlet, about thirty houses clustered in a deep valley along a bend of the Roe/Jan Creek. The heart of the village has one blinking light, a post office, a town hall, a volunteer fire department, a general store, a Lutheran church, a tavern, a wine shop, a gourmet food store and, mirabile dictu, The Ancram Opera House. The village is not shabby like some of the small towns around here, but neither does it have the spruced-up look of recent renovation. It just looks like a place that's been lived in and died in for a long time.

The house for sale has neighbors on each side, but behind it is an unbroken vista of wooded hillsides and farmland. Across the road in front is a town park and cemetery, behind which runs the Roe/Jan, one of the best trout streams in the state. Looking east over the park, one sees the foothills of the Berkshires rising blue in the distance.

The exterior of the house is far more imposing and handsome than anything I thought I could afford. It's a two-story, white clapboard, green-shuttered folk Victorian with a main section and a smaller, attached, side wing set back about six feet. Both parts of the house have front porches running their entire length, with ornate posts supporting their wainscoted ceilings. The house is locked and unoccupied, so I peeked in the windows for a glimpse of the interior, but curtains blocked my view of everything but wide-board pine floors.

My heart started racing the moment I rounded the curve that brought the house into view and it hasn't stopped racing since. I've made an appointment to have the realtor show me the interior tomorrow, and I'm already wrestling with guilt at the prospect of withdrawing my bid on the Kinderhook house. I hate the idea of disappointing the owners, who think the sale is beyond doubt, but not as much as I hate the idea of living there.

WEDNESDAY, OCTOBER 30:

I met the realtor at 2:00 P.M. and was ushered inside a house that has not been tampered with since its birth. The floors are six-inch-wide pine, the walls lath and plaster; each wing of the house has its original carved oak door, and the original molding still frames all the windows. The realtor showed me a picture of the first owners standing in front of the house in 1880. Every detail of the exterior is the same.

Most old houses in this area have to be restored to this state, their wood floors discovered under generations of linoleum, their plaster walls freed from layers of paneling, the coherence of the original layout deciphered from clues hidden under lowered ceilings.

I suspect the condition of the house is due more to frugality than to a deliberate code of strict preservation. The first floor of the smaller wing, which houses the kitchen and dining room, is in good condition, but there are bad cracks in the plaster throughout the main section. The upstairs looks like it has been abandoned for years, which is probably the case. The realtor says a ninety-year-old widow lived in the house until this summer, when she decided it had become too difficult to maintain. She probably stopped climbing the stairs to the four upper bedrooms when there was no need to change sheets anymore.

The house needs more work than I wanted to undertake, but it's a house that deserves a new life. And land that deserves tending. The lot is a pie-shaped acre, narrow at the front and then gradually broadening as it goes up a steep grass incline behind the house before leveling off for another two hundred feet. In the level part a few tall maples and elms rise above an impenetrable jungle of brambles, berry bushes, wild honey-suckle and sumac, all draped with miles of tangled grapevine. Just beyond the back property line the land dips down a bank to a little creek and then rises high to a wooded hillside flanked by a broad expanse of meadow.

I told the realtor I was ready to make a bid. She looked at me like I was crazy, not for wanting the house, but for acting so suddenly. I explained my reasons for urgency and told her about the binder I had placed on the other house. She assured me the other binder was no obstacle as long as I hadn't signed the contract, but she suggested I make my bid contingent on a contractor's assessment of what work needed to be done. I offered the same amount of money I bid for the Kinderhook house, and the realtor thought it would very likely be accepted. She also recommended a contractor and said she could arrange for me to meet with him soon.

THURSDAY, OCTOBER 31:

The realtor called this morning to say my bid had been accepted by the owner's daughter, who would be representing her mother in all our transactions. I immediately called Edina to share the news, but Mom was too depressed to respond. When I described the house, she mustered an occasional "that's nice," until I mentioned the cemetery across the road. "Oh," she said, "I wouldn't buy the house then." I told her it was an old cemetery on a hill, with sixty-foot pines towering over monuments to the town's Civil War dead, a picturesque parcel of local history surrounded by playing fields and a trout stream, but she was having none of it. A cemetery was a cemetery, and she wouldn't want to live near one. I dropped the subject.

It has been difficult to communicate with Mom since she began radiation treatments. She often doesn't feel like coming to the phone, and when she does, her speech is monosyllabic and affectless. She says she "hates" radiation. The treatments, which are directed at her entire abdominal cavity, have sapped her energy and destroyed her appetite. She isn't nauseated; she just has no desire to eat, and as much as she dislikes looking "scrawny," she says even the smell of food is "a turnoff." When I ask her if she is depressed, she says, "No, not really. I know it's just something I have to get through."

Dad sounds stalwart, exhausted but inured to the daily four-hour drives to Rochester and back. He too is just doing what needs to be done "until Mom gets better." Neither of them ever seems to doubt the ultimate success of this treatment.

FRIDAY, NOVEMBER 1:

I made another tour of the Ancram house today, this time with a contractor at my side. Bob took me down to the basement and showed me the wooden posts that support the main section of the house. Like everything else, the posts are over one hundred years old and they have rotted at the bottom where they meet the damp dirt floor. This is what caused the house to settle, tilting the rooms toward the center and cracking the plaster. The settling has not yet affected the exterior of the house, which he says is in excellent condition, but it will start to show damage soon if the problem is not corrected.

Bob says he would jack the house up four or five inches and replace the old support posts with new ones sunk into a concrete base. The jacking will cause the lath and plaster in the main section to crack so badly that it will need to be removed, both upstairs and down. Since the framing of the house would then be exposed, he might as well insulate and rewire the house before putting up new walls and ceilings. The molding around all the doors and windows will have to be removed, but Bob assures me he can do this without damaging the wood and then he can put it back up over the new walls. None of this will affect the smaller wing of the house, which has no basement under it and so has not settled. All that wing requires is some extra bracing under the dining-room floor.

Bob is a very soft-spoken man and he made the needed work sound manageable, even routine, but my heart sank at the prospect of undertaking such a feat of renovation. Certain that the house had just escaped me, I asked him what it would cost to do all he recommended. "Well, I need to work up an estimate to be sure," he said, "but I guess it would be somewhere around seven thousand dollars." I couldn't believe my ears. Some paint jobs cost that much. He was offering to take this house apart and put it back together again for less money than it would cost me to build a kitchen in the Kinderhook house. I wanted to sign him on to begin work immediately, but he reminded me that I didn't own the house.

SATURDAY, NOVEMBER 2:

I asked Lenny to inspect the Ancram house for me this afternoon and let me know if he agrees with the contractor's assessment of the work that needs to be done. During the week, Lenny works for the state, restoring historic mansions that have come under government protection; on his days off, he saves old houses from the wrath of unsuspecting weekenders who thought they were buying a hassle-free haven from the stresses of city life. I've know Lenny only a few months, since marital problems forced him out of his home and into a rented room across the road from me in Glenco Mills, but I trust him unreservedly.

Lenny is a romantic about houses, and he fell hard for this one. In fact, he was jealous at first sight; only decency and our budding friendship prevented him from giving me bad advice. As he poked an ice pick into the lowest clapboards looking for dry rot, he admitted a temptation to tell me the house was structurally beyond repair so that I would back off and he could come forward with the winning bid. He was so smitten that he encouraged me to buy the house even when he misheard me and thought the contractor had given an estimate of $70,000 instead of $7,000 for his work.

He stuck his graying curls through the trapdoor into the attic and swiveled his neck in admiration of the rafters. He ran his fingers over the lathing in an unfinished upstairs room and smiled to himself. Behind the house, he lifted the cover off the hand-dug well and whistled his appreciation of its perfectly laid stone walls. I watched as a little shower of grass clippings and dirt fell into the open well and said, "Is that the water I will drink?" He said yes, it was spring water and implied it was a rare privilege to drink from such a well. "This looks just like the well my grandfather had on his farm," he added. "There's not many of these left."

"What about the bugs?" I asked, my eyes fixed on the life forms scudding across the surface of the water. "Well," he said, "you could get a cover with a tighter seal, but the bugs are mostly on the surface of the water anyway, and you draw from the bottom, where there's a filter. I don't know whether you would want to do this, but my grandfather used to put a fish in the well every spring to eat insects." The important thing, he said, was that this property was situated in a way that protected the well against runoff from nearby farmland, which would otherwise pose the risk of contamination by toxic pesticides. I could see for myself that no pesticides had reached this well. I resolved to drink bottled water and raised another question.

"Is that enough water for the whole house?" I asked. Lenny said the fact that the water rose to within a few feet of ground level meant that the spring feeding it must be bountiful. I acted reassured, but I didn't really share his enthusiasm for vintage water supply. The old well seems fine for coin-tossing, but it's hard to imagine drinking and bathing and washing dishes in its water. Maybe I am just being citified and squeamish. I am used to taking water from faucets and not asking questions about how it got there. Who knows what contaminants I've been ingesting all my life? And how bad can this water be if the lady who has been drinking it is ninety years old?

I asked Lenny how long his grandfather lived. "Eighty-two years," he said, and then pointed across the road. "He's buried there."

SUNDAY, NOVEMBER 3:

I called the realtor last night to ask if she had received a signed copy of the binder from the sellers. "No," she said. "The sellers want to meet you first. There's no problem, they're still prepared to accept the bid. It's just that it's their family home and they'd feel better about it if they met you." She said the sellers were free to meet me at the house any time on Sunday, and I asked her to make an appointment for 11:00 A.M.

Paranoia set in as soon as I got off the phone. What if they don't like me? What if they don't want to sell their "family home" to a single woman, an outsider from the city, without a husband or children or a dog or even an occupation you can put your finger on? Within an hour, I had painted myself into the slimmest margin of respectability, a quarter inch from full pariah status. I imagined the sellers painted by Grant Wood, or worse, Norman Rockwell. I can't remember when I last suffered such a bout of insecurity. Probably not since I had to wear an eye patch to the seventh-grade Girl Scout dance.

When I arrived at the house, there were already two cars in the driveway. I walked up the porch steps and was greeted at the door by the realtor. Clara, the owner's daughter, was standing in the dining room. I took one look at her handsome, open, foursquare face and knew there would be no problem. Nobody would mistake us for sisters, but we might well be taken for second cousins. Her manner was so much like mine that she made me think of what I might be like if my parents had not left small-town Iowa for New York and Chicago. We are one generation off. Clara, who was born and raised in Ancram, lives a half mile down the road; her children are the ones who will lead lives like mine. She talked proudly about her oldest daughter, who is studying design at the Pratt Institute in Manhattan, and of a younger daughter who hopes to be a doctor.

We talked as buyer and seller, but also as prospective neighbors, and we shared a certain sadness about mothers, hers ninety and ailing, mine seventy-five and trying not to die. That's why she is anxious to sell and why I am anxious to buy. She wanted to meet me because she wanted to be able to tell her mother that her house would be loved and cared for.

Clara signed the binder, and we agreed to urge the lawyers to have contracts ready by November 15, so we could aim for a January closing.

TUESDAY, NOVEMBER 6:

Now that my life is under control again, I feel out of place. Most of my energy is spent worrying about Mom, but when I asked her and Dad today if they would like me to come for a visit, they suggested I wait until Mom finishes her radiation treatments. I thought I could relieve Dad of the tiresome daily drives to Rochester and perhaps boost Mom's spirits, but he says he doesn't mind "the routine," and Mom said, "I'd rather wait until I can enjoy you." This is the first time they have discouraged a visit since I left home for college.

We agreed that I would fly out on November 22, the day of Mom's last scheduled treatment, so that I would be there to cook when her appetite starts to return.

THURSDAY, NOVEMBER 14:

Mom was supposed to begin a five-day course of chemotherapy today to supplement the last week of radiation treatments, but the doctors say her white blood cell count is too low (below 3200) to risk it. I called Mike to ask what this meant, and he said, "They're playing a game of brinksmanship with Mom. They are trying to give her as much radiation as they can without killing her, and it's a fine line. With a white cell count like that, she is open to all sorts of opportunistic infections. A cold could kill her."

SATURDAY, NOVEMBER 16:

I drove to Ancram today in a light snow and met some of my new neighbors. I share a curve in the road with The Grog Shop and Jodie's Gourmet, establishments owned by Lizette von Gal and her daughter Jodie, housed side by side in a former grange hall. Lizette lives in an apartment above the stores and Jodie lives with her two boys, Zack and Merc, in a small house on the same property. I think they will be friends, but it is hard for me to meet new people now. Nothing seems important but Mom, and it doesn't seem right to burden strangers with my cares.

MANHATTAN
FRIDAY, NOVEMBER 22:

I came into the city on Tuesday to spend a few days seeing friends before flying to Minneapolis today. On Tuesday night, I went with Simone to hear The Women of the Calabash play their amazing percussion on everything that bangs and rattles; on Wednesday I went to the Bronx Zoo with Candace and saw all that soars and slithers through their brand-new tropical rain forest; on Thursday I had lunch with Frederika, who is getting ready to leave the *Times* for Italy and a life with Vittorio. And then I caught a cold. I called Mom and Dad this morning, and they agree we can't risk bringing any viruses into the house. Milena says I can stay in her apartment until I'm germ-free.

EDINA, MINN.

MONDAY, DECEMBER 2:

I bled on my father's long red underwear. I was wearing them while we shoveled snow together, digging out from behind the three-foot wall a snow plow left at the end of our driveway this morning. The exertion brought on my period, and when I saw the red on red, I laughed out loud. Unbeknownst to him, Dad will now wear the camouflage suit of an honorary woman. I bestow the honor on him freely. In the past few months, he has become a caregiver, adept at meeting needs before they are spoken. He cooks, he washes dishes, he cleans house, he does laundry, and he does it well, without complaint or illusions of moral grandeur.

I am reduced to the role of a helper, *sous-chef,* runner of extraneous errands, second shovel. It has snowed steadily since Thanksgiving, twenty-four inches in five days. Many times I've thought of James Joyce's Dubliners in "The Dead," but the association is not entirely bleak, because it seems life is slowly returning to this house rather than seeping out of it.

When I arrived last Tuesday, Mom looked better than I expected from her descriptions of herself over the phone. At 104 pounds, she is very thin but not emaciated. Her face looks fine, unlined and in good color. Her muscles have been terribly weakened, though, especially in her thighs and upper arms. She barely has the strength to walk from her perch on the living-room sofa to the kitchen and back.

The bathroom scale has become a scale of judgment. Each added pound boosts her spirit, just as each lost pound battered it. Her appetite is beginning to return, and she has gained two pounds since I arrived. She weighed 120 before her operation in September, and although she had tried to lose five of those pounds for years, she now wants every one of them back.

Dad and I ply her with food all day long. It seems one of us is always cooking from morning to night, just to supply her with 1,200 calories of food she can tolerate. Radiation destroyed her desire for sweets, but she can be tempted by small portions of tart and tangy dishes—meat or pasta with sauces full of sour cream and butter, pretzels and dips, deviled eggs. The problem is that for every pound we add to her, we add two or three to Dad and me. Besides which, megadoses of cholesterol and snow shoveling are not the best regimen for Dad's angina-prone heart.

TUESDAY, DECEMBER 3:

I discovered that Dad keeps a journal remarkably like mine. His entries are just notations, but they testify to the same experience. His notes for last spring read:

4/4 Bufflehead Duck, Normandale Lake
4/15 Great Horned Owl
5/9 Black Crowned Night Heron
5/22 Red-necked Grebe

In September, there are mentions of a cormorant (double crested) and pure white squirrel seen in the backyard on September second and again on the eighth. Then comes:

9/11 Surgery
9/14 Tubes out except incision and IV
10/15 1st radiation
10/18 Removes chemo pump
11/21 Last radiation/white blood cell count below 3200

I remember that white squirrel. Dad mentioned it to me on the phone and then I saw it myself on September 8. We all felt it as a portent. What else can you make of a well-timed sighting of a snow-white squirrel? But what did it portend, this furry, backyard Moby Dick?

When the doctors warned us about appetite loss as a side effect of radiation, they said radiation affected the "hunger center" in the brain in ways that are not fully understood. I think this "hunger center" must control more than one's appetite for food, because radiation seems to kill all appetites, to destroy desire itself. Now that Mom's appetite for food is returning, so is her desire for other forms of sustenance—for conversation, reading, news, stimulus of all sorts.

This afternoon Mom opened a book for the first time since September. It was a volume of Freya's poetry that I had checked out from the local library. She read it cover to cover in an hour, with pleasure, then realized her arm ached from holding it up. After dinner she read some of Freya's father's poetry, also borrowed from the local library, but found it less compelling, too weighty for weak arms.

The reading put her in a conversational mood. She talked for the first time about her Grandma Meyer, her father's mother, describing her as dour, charmless, unsmiling, with a severe middle part in hair she pulled back tightly against her skull to make a tidy knot of a bun. It made Mom's head hurt to look at her. She baked gingersnap cookies and put fresh ones in Mom's lunch pail on the way to school every day, but that seems to have been her only virtue. "She wasn't mean," Mom said, "but she didn't make me feel good."

Her eldest daughter, Annie, was also dour, a spinster who lived in her mother's house but undertook all the housework for her four brothers' families whenever one of their wives had a baby, which was often. We agreed that might make one dour, especially if one had sisters-in-law like my grandmother, who laid claim to Annie's services ten times.

These memories were provoked when I mentioned that my friend Douglas was just now returning from Germany. During the three rainy, cold July weeks I traveled with him from Hamburg to Munich this summer, I wrote defamatory postcards to my parents, assailing German food, climate and character, and urging them to greater gratitude toward every forebear who had the good sense to emigrate. It was these postcards that brought my dreary great-grandmother Meyer to her granddaughter's mind.

Like most stereotypes, though, this one doesn't bear much scrutiny. Mom thinks of her Grandmother Meyer as German, but I know from the local parish register that she was born in France, and her husband, Edward, was born in Switzerland. Perhaps both came from families that left Germany during the 1830s, but that is only speculation. Whatever their origins, borders still separate them. Edward and Clarissa, though husband and wife, were Lutheran and Catholic, and so rest in peace in separate cemeteries, on opposite sides of Clare, Iowa.

For years Mom feared the same fate for herself and Dad, but the Catholic church now allows believers to be buried next to their unbelieving spouses. Dad and Mom have plots in a Catholic cemetery in Fort Dodge, and once Mom asked me if I would like to join them there. Actually what Mom asked me, as we were leaving the cemetery after her mother's funeral six years ago, was "Do you think you will ever get married again?" It was the first time she ever asked that question, and the timing seemed bizarre. Then she added, "Because if you don't get married again you can be buried here." The church apparently does not allow divorced daughters to be interred with married-for-life parents. The final interesting twist of logic is that the church does not consider a person divorced until he or she is remarried, no matter how long one has been legally sundered.

Mom's other grandmother, her Irish Grandmother Hood, is

remembered fondly tonight, as a woman full of hugs and smiles, a New York City–born mother of ten, and a winner in Iowa's religious wars. She was the proud Catholic mistress of a grand house that had once been a Methodist church, and unlike Great-grandmother Meyer, she is buried in Clare next to her Canadian-born husband, John.

MONDAY, DECEMBER 9:

Tonight we remembered Mrs. Dunham, who lived in the apartment above ours at 1010 Main Street in Evanston, with a parakeet and a framed picture of her son, Donald, in uniform. We moved from that address when I was six, but I remember an apartment full of overstuffed chintz furniture, an old lady with yellow hair who smelled of talcum powder and a caged bird who said, "My son Donald, my son Donald." Mom says Mrs. Dunham was "a crock," whom Dr. Richards kept overdrugged, and that she was very proud of her son, Donald, whom she had won in a custody battle. Many years later, when I first read *Great Expectations*, Miss Havisham reminded me of someone, but I didn't know who.

We also remembered Mrs. Long, who used to knit me wool hats that Mom loved and I hated. I particularly remember a powder-blue hat with ear flaps and a pom-pom on top that looked foolish and made my face itch. And Marjorie Robinson, a skinny girl several years older than me who wore raggedy dresses and smelled funny. She was too old for the park sandbox, but she often played there with me for hours, creating cities out of sand and populating them with twig people about whom she told elaborate stories of intrigue and violence.

I was scared of Marjorie and mesmerized by her, and I had a vague sense that Mom was pleased when I played with her. "Yes," she says tonight, "because none of the other children would, and it wasn't her fault she was strange. Marjorie's mother was weird too; she always had so much to say she spit and garbled her words. But what she said was interesting."

We matched memories of 1010 Main Street while nibbling thick squares of fudge. Mom's sweet tooth is beginning to return, so this afternoon Dad made a batch from Mom's recipe while she coached him from the sidelines. He beat the fudge 'til his arm ached, but she kept saying, "I don't think it's hard enough yet. Just a few minutes more."

Mom's appetite for television, though never ravenous, is also returning. When I came home tonight after a dinner out with Freya, Mom and Dad were curled up on the sofa in the den watching *Alice in Wonderland.*

As I was falling asleep, I remembered how, as a very young child, I experienced most people and places as radiating an aura of either darkness or light. It was a like a halo around people's bodies that I thought I actually saw. Usually, I associated the darkness with menace and stayed at a distance, but sometimes it attracted me, like a scary fun-house ride I knew couldn't really hurt me. Marjorie and Mrs. Dunham were like that.

TUESDAY, DECEMBER 10:

One day last week, when Dad and I took advantage of just-cleared roads to go to the grocery store, a neighbor watched our departure and, knowing Mom was alone, called to complain about the way Dad was keeping her "a prisoner." We arrived home just as Mom was getting off the phone, and the angry tears in her eyes made an explanation necessary. Dad didn't say anything after Mom described her conversation, but he stared out the kitchen window toward the neighbor's house with a more venomous look than I have ever seen on his face.

In fact, there is some truth to the neighbor's charge. Dad does keep everyone but the family at bay, including not only the neighbors but the church people who offer to bring Mom communion every Sunday. Mom is complicit, but I'm not sure whether she cloisters herself out of free will, out of a radiation-induced obliteration of desire, or out of fear of displeasing Dad, upon whom she is utterly dependent.

Dad has reason for behaving as he does. When neighbors do visit, Mom is too proud to let them know how weak she is. She puts on makeup and clothes that camouflage her thinness, abandons her usual reclining position on the sofa to sit up straight in a living-room chair and gives a good imitation of the Bea they have always known. Visitors, receiving so many false clues, respond with hours of garrulous conversation that leave Mom exhausted and ill. Then Dad gets mad at the neighbors for their lack of consideration, and the neighbors, innocent of everything but their own good intentions, think he is acting irrationally when he discourages further visits.

Dad is the heavy, because no one sees the strong will lurking under Mom's pleasing surface. She is beginning to show it more overtly to Dad, though. When he gets impatient with her ceaseless needs, she calls him on it; there's a quick clash of tempers and then both subside into peacekeeping. The flashes of temper startle me, because neither of them ever raised their voices in my earshot, ever, ever. I'm startled but reassured. Without a little anger in the house, we would all implode.

Mom told me tonight how I got my name. I knew I was meant to be Anne, until a late decision was made to commemorate my uncle Leo in my name. But I didn't know the particulars. It was decided, it seems, on a stormy summer night two weeks before my birth, when Grandma Meyer, my mother's sly Irish mother, was visiting from Iowa. Leo had been killed in the war a year earlier, and she wanted her son remembered, but she kept her designs on my name secret until the night of the storm. Then, fearing the lightning and thunder might bring on an early labor, she made her move. "What is it you want to call the baby if it's a girl?" she asked, knowing perfectly well what their answer would be. When they said, "Anne," she kept her poker face and said, "Is that *all* you're going to name her?" "Well, yes," they said, but she had them on the defensive. She set them up for a compromise by suggesting a few certain rejects, like Katherine Anne, Elizabeth Anne, Mary Anne. Then she hit them with Le Anne, and it was unanimous, instantly.

Tonight I also learned that when Mom was pregnant with me, she wanted a girl very much, but she was trying hard to guard against disappointment if it happened to be a boy. When the nurse came to her room after my birth to tell her she had a girl, Mom said, "That's all right. I don't mind a boy." The nurse tried again. "No, Mrs. Schreiber," she said, "it's a girl, you have a daughter." Mom insisted, "That's fine, I like boys." This exchange was repeated a dozen times over several hours before Mom grasped she had gotten what she wanted.

WEDNESDAY, DECEMBER 11:

Most parents bore their children from infancy with unsolicited retellings of stories about how it was in their day. Not mine. For reasons I've never fathomed, I must eke out every shred of information about life before my existence. If I relied on what they offer freely, I would think the world emerged from nothingness into postwar suburbia. It's not that they have anything much to hide; they just seem to think that reality coincides with the brand-new world their generation built after the war. Life before ranch houses, bi-levels and pop-up toasters is irrelevant to current conditions.

I can at least imagine something of Dad's childhood; I've seen pictures of his grandfather's blacksmith and saddlery shop, advertisements for the Schreiber buggies they made before the business turned into the town's first Dodge dealership; I've seen Indianola, Iowa, nicknamed "the holy city," and the ornate Victorian house Dad grew up in there, and Simpson College, where he formed a band and played his cornet in the street, defying blue laws which forbade dancing as well as cardplaying and drinking. I've looked through his college yearbooks, in which he is cast as the campus rake, escort of prom queens and driver "of the Dodge with a good pickup."

But there are no remnants of Mom's farm life to be seen. Her parents' farmhouse burnt to the ground one Christmas Eve in the twenties, making photographs of that time as rare as Mom's memories. By the time I was born, her father had died and Grandma Meyer had long since moved to Fort Dodge. Clare, Iowa, their farm town, has barely existed since the Depression, when local businesses shared the fate of the community's foreclosed farms. What little information I have about Clare—about the bank robbery of 1922 and the night the Ku Klux Klan burnt a cross in front of the Catholic church—comes from a parish history published in 1979. That's when I learned my great-grandparents were not all Germans, thank God, but Swiss and French and Irish.

Fortunately, I've been able to use this visit to expand my limited stock of lore. Mom is feeling well enough to converse at length, but not well enough to add much new experience to her life, so I can lure her out of the present into reminiscence. I'm happy for the smallest detail, like the news tonight that there were stained-glass windows in the outhouse on my grandfather's farm. Or that for many years my grandmother made "a hobby" of writing letters to radio ministers.

"What did she write them about?" I asked. "Well, I don't know," Mom answered. "I guess if she liked what they said, she told them so, and if she didn't like what they said, she'd give 'em what for. She had a correspondence going with dozens of them all over the country." I would love to know if she wrote to Father Coughlin, and what she said, but I guess I'll never know. I'll just have to hope she gave him what for.

———

I now know why my mother, whom I never saw run or jump or make any extravagant movement, always delighted in my own physical recklessness, why she never scolded me for all those skinned knees and scraped elbows and bumps on my head.

One day when my mother was five years old, she was trying to jump across the gap between rugs in the dining room and parlor. She missed, slid on the freshly waxed floor and slammed abdomen first into the front end of a narrow wooden chair arm. The doctor diagnosed a hernia, but rather than operate on a young child, he advised that she limit her physical activity until the age of eighteen, at which time he would operate. At five, Mom hated the thought of a future without running and jumping and climbing trees and playing basketball, then as now every Iowa schoolgirl's dream of glory, but her mother was vigilant about minding the doctor's orders. Mom later realized this doctor had blighted her childhood unnecessarily, and she vowed her own children would never know such constraint.

THURSDAY, DECEMBER 12:

Before I left for the airport this afternoon, Mom did a final weigh-in for my benefit. She tipped the scales at 112, eight pounds heavier than when I arrived. I've added five pounds and Dad six, so family tonnage is up a total of nineteen pounds, and we haven't even begun Christmas bingeing yet. Nancy will take responsibility for the next five. Mom and Dad plan to fly to Philadelphia for Christmas, and I will join them there at Mike and Nancy's.

MANHATTAN
WEDNESDAY, DECEMBER 25:

I spent the afternoon with Candace serving turkey and fixings at a day center for homeless women on West Nineteenth Street. When Dad called last week to say Mom didn't feel strong enough yet to make a trip east, I became too depressed to spend the holiday in any traditional gathering. Candace was feeling the same way for her own reasons, so we decided to make a virtue of our distress and do good deeds.

As it turned out, it was the homeless women who cheered us up, by their capacity to take pleasure in a good meal and a warm room. Each woman received an impressive cache of gifts, donated by corporate benefactors, but that pleased them less than the meal, which couldn't be stolen from them. Most of them planned to wear their new stocking caps and sweaters and gloves out of the center, but they offered gifts of cosmetics and perfume to the volunteers.

With the exception of one woman, who we presumed was a volunteer until the center's director asked her to stop serving food, none of the homeless women seemed mentally ill, as they are often said to be. Just unlucky, and so indistinguishable from the volunteers that, once we took off our yellow aprons, Santa Claus couldn't tell which among us was meant to receive the corporate largess he was distributing.

GLENCO MILLS, N.Y.
SATURDAY, JANUARY 11, 1986:

It has been so cold this week that the stream is frozen from bank to bank at the fish hole. Today, with Milena as my lifeguard, I walked out on the log that spans the stream and pounded the ice between its two trunks with a heavy length of sycamore branch. The banging of branch against stream produced a low thud, which I presumed to mean thick, solid ice. Gingerly at first, I put the weight of one leg on the ice, keeping the other on the log. The ice held. Moving closer to the bank, I stepped off the log, planting both feet on the ice between the two trunks, which I planned to use as arm holds in case of emergency. The ice held.

With greater confidence, I stepped over the log and walked

downstream on the ice to where Milena stood on the stony bank. The ice thinned and disappeared at the riffle, where the fast-flowing water keeps it from forming. Just beyond the riffle, however, was a large floe of ice, about twenty feet long by fifteen feet wide. Water surrounded the floe except at two points, where it was connected to the bank and to the solidly frozen part of the stream by channels of ice about three feet wide. I decided to try to break through the two patches that held the floe in place, hoping to set the huge slab free to float downstream.

I attacked the patch nearest the bank first, hacking away at its sides with my staff of sycamore. After much slamming, I had whittled the patch down so that only a one-foot width of ice connected the floe to the bank, but that one foot was too thick to break by the same method. A straight up-and-down pounding, post-hole style, seemed to work, but that entailed my standing so close to the ice I was breaking that I might very well have ended up floating downstream myself. Since I was close to the safety of the bank, I decided to risk it, and after ten more minutes of hard labor, I had freed that side of the floe.

Tasting victory, I sized up the other point where the floe was attached to a solid mass of bank-to-bank ice. The connecting patch was midstream, and the surrounding ice looked thin, making my task easier but trickier. Unwilling to risk a plunge into fast-rushing water at midstream, I decided upon a rock-heaving approach to the problem.

Until now, my efforts had gone unnoticed by Milena, who was exploring the bank upstream. I called her over to admire my progress and, despite some resistance, succeeded in enlisting her help in boulder-gathering. The largest stones were upstream about one hundred yards, so we flailed our way through shoulder-high dead weeds, slipping on snow-covered rocks, to pick up the biggest boulders we could see bulging under the snow. Armed with two boulders each, we trudged back to the floe.

Afraid to venture too far out onto the ice with the added weight of the boulders, we stood about six feet from the patch we wanted to shatter, and raising the boulders over our heads, heaved them, one at a time, onto the narrowest point of the strip connecting the floe to the mass of bank-to-bank ice. Our aim was good and we chipped off some of the patch, but it still held after we had expended our first round of ammunition. Milena was thoroughly engaged in the project now and we returned upstream for more boulders.

As I walked back toward the floe, panting under the weight of stone, my arms still sore and tingling from the reverberation of wood slammed against ice, watching Milena struggle to keep her footing on the slippery rocks ahead while prickly weeds scratched her face and caught in her hair, I started laughing riotously. This was the kind of labor they forced convicts to do, and we, of our own free will, were spending a gorgeous Saturday afternoon moving boulders from one spot to another to throw them at a block of ice. Why? Because without a piece of land to tend, we play at improving nature, environmental engineers at large, liberators of ice floes and protectors of fallen logs. This enticing county is all roped off from me, fenced and posted against my trespassing. Only the stream is everybody's, and therefore mine. Until I have an acre of my own, so be it.

Still laughing, I carried my load of stones to the floe's edge and paused a minute to refine my strategy. It occurred to me that the narrowest strip of the ice patch was not necessarily the weakest, because the patch did not lie flat upon the stream. It sloped down from the ice floe to the unbroken span of bank-to-bank ice, like a bridge over water. The most steeply angled part of the bridge, though the widest, might be the easiest to break. Acting on this hunch, I picked up the largest boulder with both hands, raised it with effort above my head, held it aloft for a second while I focused my eyes on the exact spot I wanted to hit and then, blowing the air out of my lungs, heaved it. The boulder landed precisely on target, the bridge of ice shattered and the floe was free at last.

Free but motionless. It did not go rushing downstream, bobbing wildly and careening round bends, smashing against bridge pylons, tree limbs trailing in its wake. It did none of the things I imagined it would. The floe was as rooted to its spot on the stream as the fallen sycamore is to the bank which once held it straight and tall. Its roots, I suppose, are the boulders of the stream bed, apron strings to ice crystals.

MONDAY, JANUARY 13:

Mom says she is beginning to feel like herself again. She has gained only two pounds since my visit in December, but her appetite is returning to normal and she feels strong enough to begin exercising. I am trying to persuade Dad to let me take them to a warm climate for a couple weeks so Mom can take long walks with sun on her face rather than blustery winds whistling up her spine. He is giving me the usual "we'll see" response. I suspect him of moralistic resistance to escaping the rigors of a Midwestern winter, but if I pitch sunshine as medicine rather than pleasure, perhaps he can be tempted.

MONDAY, JANUARY 20:

Last week, there was a stretch of five days when the coldest temperatures of the winter were recorded. The mercury seldom rose above zero even in the middle of sunny days. Then, last Thursday, the weather abruptly changed and we've had six days of unseasonably warm temperatures, between forty-five and sixty degrees.

I had been in the city when the weather turned warm, so today I decided to inspect the fish hole and see what changes the thaw has wrought. The ice floe is gone, which I expected, but so is the sycamore log, my cradle over water. The massive root system that kept its double trunk attached to the far bank must have been torn loose by the force of ice blocks rushing downstream during the thaw, accumulating behind the fallen sycamore until their weight was great enough to wrench it from the earth. Now it rests lengthwise in the middle of the stream about twenty yards below its former position. Instead of spanning the deepest part of the fish hole, it is stranded on the stony streambed in shallow water, where the ice floe was rooted ten days ago.

The accumulation of ice behind the trunk before it gave way must have been tremendous, because the rocky low bank on the near side of the stream is covered with piles of foot-thick slabs of ice. Many of the squarish slabs are twelve to fifteen feet wide, resting on one another at precarious angles like the big blocks of limestone on the shores of Lake Michigan. The densest piles of ice are on the bank forty feet upstream from where the trunk was rooted, so the sycamore must have held fast against free-floating slabs of ice backed up that deep, with the rushing water of the swollen stream trying to push its cargo past the barrier. I wish I had been there the moment the trunk gave way and the pent-up ice went shooting through the broken gate.

That might have been compensation for the loss. Now that the sycamore no longer spans the stream, I realize what a rarity it was. The swollen stream cast a few other bridges over its waters this week, but none compares to the one that's gone. The newly fallen trees are too small or too rough-barked or too steeply angled or too bristly with branches for comfort. How often, I wonder, does a large, double-trunked tree, perfectly formed for seats and footrests along its entire smooth-barked length, fall across a trout stream, offering itself to passersby like me? Once in ten years? Twenty? I won't know until I find another one. Right now, it feels like a death in the family.

TUESDAY, JANUARY 21:

I am swinging on a pendulum again, this time between fury and despair. When I called Edina last night to raise the sunshine issue again, Mom complained of back pain for the first time in months. The pain is severe enough to ruin both her sleep and her appetite, and she is beginning to lose the weight she worked so hard to regain. "I'm so tired of having clothes hang off my bony backside," she said, as if that were the bottom line of pain.

I got off the phone feeling sick. Why, why must the pain return now, just when she was beginning to recover from the radiation treatment and could perhaps look forward to the period of normal health she was promised? It's possible the "cure-all" nerve block is wearing off, but my fear, of course, is that the return of pain means the return of cancer. Mike thinks the tumor must be growing, but he doesn't see any point in calling Mom's doctors for an opinion. "Why look for bad news when there is nothing we can do about it?" he said last night when I asked him to call.

I can make the calls myself, but doctors are quicker to return calls to doctors than to daughters.

THURSDAY, JANUARY 23:

The radiotherapist finally called today, forty-eight hours after I left the first of several messages, but he didn't remember Mom and he didn't have her file at hand, so he said he would have to call me back later. That was eight hours ago.

FRIDAY, JANUARY 24:

The radiotherapist called this morning with a refreshed memory. He says the latest CAT scan, taken a month ago, shows that Mom's tumor has reduced its size by half, so it couldn't possibly be causing her pain. I was too elated by this news to express my amazement that he hadn't bothered to convey it to Mom.

I called her immediately, but she was less impressed by the information than I was, because she still has the pain. I also called Mike, who sounded curiously defensive. Was it because I took the initiative in calling the medical center? Because his own diagnosis was wrong? Because he is skeptical of the radiotherapist's assessment? None of the above?

SATURDAY, JANUARY 25:

The weekend before last, when the weather was so cold, I was struck by the complete absence of critter life. Even in the big expanses of woods at Olana and behind the Ancram house, there were no tracks of any animals but deer. Then yesterday afternoon, when the temperature was in the fifties, I drove past a woodchuck, apparently seduced out of hibernation by the false promise of a January thaw, lying dead in the middle of Water Street Road. Unlike the dead animals one sees on the road in springtime, this woodchuck was round and furry, so intact he looked like he was taking a nap. I guess motorists just didn't have the heart to flatten him. Like me, they veered around him, giving respect to the first untamed piece of fur they had seen in months. Or maybe he was just too freshly dead to be flattened yet.

TUESDAY, JANUARY 28:

I turned on the television this morning a few minutes before the twelve-o'clock news was to begin and saw a Y-shaped plume of white smoke filling a sky-blue screen. All afternoon and evening I watched that Y form and dissolve. I have seldom felt as isolated as I did today, without friends or colleagues or neighbors or even men-in-the-street to help me grasp the reality of that sky-written epitaph. The television became my friend, my fellow mourner.

I called Milena and Candace and Mom, but there was nothing to articulate over the phone except the usual inadequate words of shock. I wanted to look at other faces, bodies, hands, to help me understand that seven brave people had lost theirs. I accept their loss as an extraordinary loss, somehow different from the deaths others suffer every day, but I don't know why. I summoned up a memory of Sally Ride, whom I have met, and I tried to imagine how I would feel if she had been aboard Challenger this morning, but the very fact of acquaintance made me imagine her loss as fundamentally like that of anyone I have known.

Somehow distance, lack of acquaintance, is important today. We are all trying to make the remote personal, to keep faith with seven strangers by reclaiming them from the alienating abstractions of death, technology and celebrity. It takes an immense effort.

THURSDAY, JANUARY 30:

A half dozen of us—principals, lawyers and loan officers—met at the bank this morning for the closing on the Ancram house. After two hours of writing checks, I wanted to mark the occasion with something besides my signature, but there was nobody to join me in celebration. My friends all work in the city during the week, and Clara, the seller, was so visibly downhearted I didn't want to put her through the ordeal of pretending to be otherwise. She told me her mother broke her leg in a fall three days ago; she didn't need to explain that, at ninety, her mother's chances of walking again are very slim.

I drove straight from the bank to Ancram, hoping something there would dispel the chill of this dreary day. The house offered me its worst aspect. There was no dance of sunlight to draw attention from the chipped and peeling paint of the clapboards.

The leafless trees could not hide the black power lines slung like jail bars across the heavy gray sky. A week of warm weather has left only a few scattered patches of dirty snow in a landscape of matted yellow grass and mud. As I walked through the drizzle toward the porch, the ground squished with each step and sucked at the soles of my boots.

The house, heated just enough to keep pipes from bursting, was cold and damp. I left a trail of muddy footprints as I walked through the rooms, eyeing the cracks in the plaster and the tilt of the interior door frames, no longer parallel to either walls or ceiling. The house will never look worse than this, I thought, and still I have no regrets. The sun will shine again, leaves will return to the trees, the yellow grass will green, and I will turn back the clock, make this old house young. Suddenly I was glad no one was with me. The dreariness of the weather made the house seem so forlorn today that any friend would have reacted with forced optimism, and the falsity would have made it that much harder for me to find true cheer.

FRIDAY, JANUARY 31:

I met today with Bob, who will begin work on the house next week. It was a bright, clear afternoon, but remembering yesterday, I made some decisions that will fill the house with all available light. I asked Bob to remove the wall that divides the front half of the main section into a parlor and bedroom, so we can create one big room that receives light from north, south and east.

The back half of the main section has another bedroom, which I will probably use as a study, and if we double the window there and leave the door open, it will allow afternoon light from the west to stream into the front room as well. Bob says we can use the molding from the door we remove between the two front rooms to frame the double window in back so it will match the others in the house. Lenny will probably disapprove of my rearrangements, but I discovered today, after only twenty-four hours as a home owner, that I am not a purist, not at the expense of space and light.

Taking a last look as I backed down the driveway this afternoon, I realized why this house feels so familiar. It is my fantasy of a house like the one my mother grew up in, the house that left no trace of itself, the house I have to invent whenever I imagine my mother's childhood. Most of the houses in this area are too New England, too colonial or Georgian, to have been planted in an Iowa cornfield, but this one, with its tall tin-roofed rectangles and its Victorian front porches, would be at home there as well as here.

It's likely the two houses were built within the same decade. My grandparents married in 1900, twenty years after the first owners posed for their portrait in front of this house. I know my grandfather and his three brothers were large landowners, each with a farmhouse at the four corners of an intersection bearing their father's name. My grandmother told me that was one of the reasons she married Albert E. Meyer, ten years her senior, instead of a brash suitor named Lefty O'Hearn, about whom she still speculated more than seventy years later. So Albert E. must have been in possession of that house by 1900, when he won nineteen-year-old Kate Hood for his bride.

I imagine his house very like mine but larger, large enough for ten children, with an enormous kitchen, where his wife, the former schoolteacher, cooked for the farmhands as well as her ever-growing family. She told me once, the same day she talked about Lefty O'Hearn, that she used a fifty-pound bag of flour every week for her baking. Those bags of flour may be what started her thinking about what her life might have been like if she hadn't married a farmer.

I know the memory of all that baking still haunts my mother. Nothing tastes sweeter to her than sliced white bread, store bought; she still remembers her glorious first bite, how it tasted "like angel food cake." It's the taste of freedom to her, the manna of cities and suburbs.

And I, the daughter made strong by Wonder Bread, I am moving into the kind of house and town my mother was determined to escape; she links such places to confinement, to the chore-ridden existence of a farmer's wife with ten children and fifty-pound bags of flour on her hands. She didn't marry until she was twenty-six, because she wanted to make sure she found a man who would take her away from farms and small towns, as Dad did. Within two years of their wedding, they drove east through the Holland Tunnel into Manhattan, where Dad helped launch a risky new venture called *Look* magazine.

It's taken me these forty years to get out of there, out of Chicago and Houston and San Francisco and Boston, out of journalism and New York City and into Ancram. Mom probably thinks I'm crazy.

SUNDAY, FEBRUARY 2 :

Several times recently I have taken long walks through woods thinly covered with snow in search of deer. I found tracks on the hill behind the house in Ancram and in Taconic State Park, but they were not fresh enough to lead me to quarry. This afternoon I drove to Olana and parked my car at the top of the estate, behind the mansion Frederic E. Church built as his majestic perch high above the Hudson. I began walking down the fire lane into the woods, then veered off the path into a clearing where I had seen deer last year. I didn't know for sure what fresh tracks looked like, but the ones I found there were so distinct I was convinced they had just been made. The prints, crisper than any I've ever seen, looked like a cross section of an apple or a small set of lungs, two lobes almost touching.

I stood very still and scanned the woods. Three deer were hiding behind a thicket twenty yards north of me. They bounded away and I walked to the thicket. The snow was pocked with tracks in all directions, but I could tell which ones I wanted to follow. A soft, powdery snow filled the front and sides of the print as if the hoof had not rested there long enough to leave a clear mark. Droppings also helped me choose among the prints. The freshest, I guessed, were the pellets strung singly through the prints like beads, as if the deer had kept running while dropping them.

I followed their trail for about forty-five minutes, until they led me into a very large thicket of wild honeysuckle bushes. To judge by the carpet of droppings, this was headquarters for an entire herd. I crouched low to make headway through the thicket, but even on all fours, I felt my face whipped by icy branches as I crept over ground so littered with fresh droppings that the smell nearly overpowered me. The stench finally forced me to withdraw and I backed out of the thicket into a suddenly darkening day. I had given no thought to the time, and now realized I had about a half hour of light left to find my way back to the fire lane.

I was not confident enough in my interior compass to attempt a direct route, so I was forced to backtrack through my own meandering footprints. I arrived panting at the fire lane just as the sun set, and imagined the deer following me at their leisure, analyzing the signs of panic in my tracks.

MONDAY, FEBRUARY 3:

Bob began work today. He jacked the house up one inch, but I wasn't there to hear the groaning. He says he will boost it a little at a time so the rafters and studs will have time to adjust. I did hear the whine and screech of molding being pried from its mooring and see the windows framed by a naked arch of lathing.

WEDNESDAY, FEBRUARY 5:

What a difference two days make! Two days and a crowbar. The upstairs is gutted, its walls and ceilings bared to the skeleton, its floor a gritty gray beach of plaster dust littered with mounds of splintered lathing. Bob says he will tie the lathing into neat bundles of kindling, but it seems I will have no use for them, because the center chimney has to be removed. Bob had me stick my head into the attic to see it listing like the Tower of Pisa between the floor and the roof line. He thinks the house will be happier without it anyway, that the weight of all that red brick is what made the house droop in the center. I know he is right, but I'm sorry to lose the possibility of a potbelly stove at the warm center of cold winter nights.

WEDNESDAY, FEBRUARY 12:

I slept late this morning after a night of tossing and turning on my gimpy left shoulder. I smashed deltoid first at high speed into the ice at Olana on Monday trying to skate circles around Candace. We were playing tag like indestructible twelve-year-olds, so I probably deserve every pang and twinge. My body finds it hard to remember it's forty without an occasional reminder. The fact is, I don't fall like I used to. More to the point, I don't get up like I used to.

I planned to remain sedentary today, mending in place at the kitchen table while I tried to paint what I see out the window. But at 10:15 A.M. my next-door neighbor Frank knocked on the kitchen door, offered me a package of his homemade pork sausage and asked if I would like to go on a wild-turkey hunt with him. My paints were already arrayed on the table, but since I don't get many such invitations, I decided to accept.

For reasons unclear to me, Frank asked that I meet him in

fifteen minutes at the crossroads in Churchtown, where he would be waiting in his pickup. We rendezvoused and I followed him to his lodge, the workshop of a recently deceased taxidermist whose widow has donated the studio and three hundred acres of woodland for the use of her late husband's hunting buddies. After a tour of the lodge, Frank led me into the woods. It was a warm, clear, sunny day, near forty degrees, but the snow was still knee deep on the untrodden trails.

We walked silently for hours, up and down hills, along ridges, covering more than five miles, with me always following six paces behind in Frank's snow-breaking footsteps. As I trudged in his wake, my eyes glancing right and left off his broad back, it suddenly occurred to me that Frank was probably close to my age. I have assumed he was much older, not because he looks it, but because it is hard to comprehend we belong to the same generation.

We never saw a wild turkey, so there was no need for Frank to draw his long-barreled pistol. We spotted several deer, or I should say, Frank directed my attention to deer several times, demonstrating by a sudden wave of his arm how much more alert I must learn to be. Fortunately, deer are out of season, so I did not have to witness the skills that have kept venison steaks in my freezer these past two winters.

After a couple hours we stopped to roast hot dogs and drink purple, fizzy wine, passing the bottle back and forth between us. Back at the taxidermy shop by midafternoon, we watched as a doe and her baby buck high-stepped through snow at the tree line to forage for the apples we threw into the field behind the lodge. We were silent, as we had been all day, content to exchange no more than a half dozen words over as many hours.

We walked to our cars and I thanked Frank for showing me his hunting grounds. Just as I was about to drive off, he tapped on my window and I lowered it enough to hear him say, "Don't tell anyone what happened in there today." I looked puzzled, and he added, "My wife might hear about it." He glanced right and left with a shifty look in his eye, then tried to kiss me goodbye through the window, but it was rolled up too high and his lips landed on cold glass.

FRIDAY, FEBRUARY 14:

Order is beginning to emerge from the rubble. Bob rigged a chute from an upstairs window to his pickup truck and hauled away several loads of lath and plaster today. Now that the upstairs walls are reduced to studs, I see how easy it is to move them around. We decided to push one wall of the smallest bedroom back a foot to create space for a separate door to the second bedroom, which otherwise has to be entered through the third bedroom. The two larger bedrooms will be more private and the smallest bedroom will become a walk-in closet. Then I can remove the closet in the upstairs foyer, put a second window where the closet was and fill the entire upstairs with light, as I have done downstairs. I've eliminated two bedrooms so far, but I've still got four left, and that's more than I ever wish to fill. I've already learned that extra bedrooms are a liability in a country house within striking distance of nature-starved Manhattanites.

SUNDAY, FEBRUARY 16:

Mike called tonight in a panic over Mom's back pain, which continues to worsen. He is convinced the treatment has failed, that the tumor is growing and Mom has only a few months to live. He and Nancy want to take the children to Edina for a visit so they can see their grandmother while she is still capable of responding to them, but Mom, innocent of his verdict on her life, keeps saying she would rather wait until she feels better before "entertaining the kids."

I phoned Mom tonight, hoping the call might provide reassurance that she is better than Mike fears. Dad answered, and we talked about *New York Times* stock (he's sorry he sold his) and water drainage (he is sending me an eight-foot plastic tube that can be attached to a downspout to funnel water away from the Ancram house). Nothing in his voice suggested gloom in the household.

When Mom came to the phone, she sounded more animated than I had heard her in months. Yesterday she and Dad drove to Rochester for her monthly round of tests. When Mom complained of back pain, the oncologist in charge of her case said, "Mrs. Schreiber, there is nothing more we can do for you. You are cured. You are no longer a cancer patient."

If Mom is reporting his words accurately, I am shocked at their irresponsibility. Even if the tumor is quiescent now, the patient is far from cured. I suspect he used those lines, or something very like them, to wash his hands of the messy problem of pain. The placebo effect was strong. Mom proudly reported that she had gone for a mile walk around Lake Cornelia yesterday for the first time since last summer, and today she went to a ladies' luncheon to celebrate a neighbor's birthday.

I asked if she was planning a visit to Fort Dodge, trying to sound as if I meant "Now that you are feeling so much better, wouldn't you enjoy taking a trip and seeing your sisters?" What I was really thinking was "Don't you want to see your sisters while there is still time?"

"Oh," she said, "did I tell you Aileen died? She was buried today." There was an odd lilt in her voice, a crackling of guilt for not having notified me of Aileen's death earlier and for not having attended the funeral in Fort Dodge. She excused herself by adding that her sister Veronica "was ill with the flu and couldn't make the funeral either . . . and she lives there." There was no hint in her voice that she shared a common fate with her sister Aileen.

After getting off the phone with Mom, I called Mike. "Those bastards" was his comment when he learned that Mom had been told she was "cured."

TUESDAY, FEBRUARY 25:

I am in such a foul state of mind that I was ready to let the neighborhood stray freeze to death last night. I was on the phone to Nancy when Kissa began scratching his nails against the metal of the kitchen storm door. His screeching filled one ear while the other heard Nancy wish a pulmonary embolism on Mom. "It would be quick, painless, and it could happen any time," she said, seeming to expect me to share her enthusiasm at the prospect. The ever-present possibility of sudden death is why it is so important that I help persuade Mom to let the kids visit soon.

I know Nancy well enough to know she didn't mean her words the way they sounded to my doubly tormented ears. But in my heart I accused her of trying to orchestrate my mother's death to her convenience—a trauma-reducing visit between her children and their grandmother, followed by a tidy sudden death and the immediate release of her husband to his normal concerns.

Nancy must share Mike's belief that Mom's cancer has returned and she simply wishes her an easy death. What confuses me is their lack of grounds. How can Mike be so sure of his prognosis in face of the radiotherapist's insistence that her tumor is inactive? Does he know something I don't? I never know when he is reacting as a doctor, with medical understanding beyond mine, or when he is reacting as a son, with responses as mercurial and unreliable as any of ours. Should I trust his judgment, share his panic, or take reassurance from Mom and Dad, who remain calm, full of hope, no matter what the day's setbacks and uncertainties?

My thoughts were so jumbled when I got off the phone that the sound of Kissa's clawing made me feel a skein of bloody lines was being etched on my brain. I slammed my booted foot into the storm door and saw a black ball streak across the glistening white surface of moonlit frozen snow. About midnight I checked the outdoor thermometer, and seeing it was ten below zero, felt a surge of pity for poor homeless Kissa. I bundled up and walked down the road toward the house of the weekender who lets Kissa fend for himself five days of the week. I thought I heard something crying in the distance, but the loud crunch and squeak of my footsteps on the snow-packed road made sounds hard to discern. A full moon was high in the sky, and as I neared Kissa's weekend house, calling his name, I caught clear sight of him fleeing from my approach. He'd rather freeze than spend the night with me, and I can't say I blame him.

WEDNESDAY, FEBRUARY 26:

This morning I saw a fat black cat limping through the backyard toward the bushes at the edge of the creek. For a moment I thought spry, skinny Kissa had been transformed by a night's freezing, perhaps died and been reborn with more bulk on him to withstand the cruelties of man and nature. But at noon he leapt onto the back porch, his appearance and manners unchanged. I gave him food and shelter but apparently not enough attention. As I sat at the kitchen table trying to finish an assignment that's due tomorrow, he prowled over my papers and tried to eat the books I'm supposed to review.

WEDNESDAY, MARCH 5:

Bob has finished insulating and rewiring the entire main section of the house, and will begin putting up Sheetrock tomorrow. He says it will take him two to three weeks to have walls ready for me to paint. I'm tempted to hop a plane for Puerto Rico and spend a week lying on the beach before beginning the two months of hard labor it will take to get the house ready for moving in on June 1.

If I take a trip next week, I can be back by March 17, when Mom is scheduled for another CAT scan. Mike is recommending a bone scan as well, in case Mom's back pain has been caused by radiation damage to her spine. He fears very bad results from this series of tests, and if he is right, I will leave immediately for Edina.

It seems I am always planning two futures, two next weeks, two next months, and waiting for doctors to tell me which one will come to pass. I don't think Mike understands how his fluctuations of mood and diagnosis affect me. Whenever the son in him loses hope, the doctor in him gives Mom one or two months to live, and the daughter in me begins dismantling her life.

My city apartment is for sale, my rental in Glenco Mills expires June 1, the Ancram house is unlivable without two months of work I have to do myself. I'm spending money without making it, because I'm afraid to accept assignments on deadlines I might not be able to meet. Whenever Mike says Mom is dying, I am guilt stricken for being here rather than there. I have none of the usual excuses—no job, no children that demand my daily attention. How do I explain that I must make a home for myself, perhaps a home for Dad as well, a home to return to, survive in? I can't explain my urgency to Mom, who still believes she is immortal. I can only hope I have these months to make a home I can leave for hers, a home I can offer to him.

PUERTO RICO

WEDNESDAY, MARCH 11:

We and every other tourist on the island just returned from the Phosphorescence Bay Cruise, which is the only activity ever scheduled on Vieques, except, of course, for the war games played by the United States Army on the northern half of the island. I wanted escape so badly I would have come here alone, but Candace decided to join me at the last minute and I am happy for her company.

We walk or ride bikes every day to one or another of the beach coves that ring the island. At night we do the same thing, with tonight's cruise providing the only variation. We leapt into the warm waters of the starlit Caribbean (the cruise is canceled if the moon shines too brightly) and watched sprays of silvery sparks shoot off our limbs with every splashing stroke. If silence had reigned, we might have passed for a school of shimmering gods and goddesses, but our boatload swam to an accompaniment of earthy, beer-sodden whoops.

Usually we have our choice of cove to ourselves. I spend hours with my masked face in the water, watching a small assortment of fish swim in and out of coral formations. I think about nothing except keeping water out of my nose and sea urchins out of my flesh.

THURSDAY, MARCH 13:

Tonight I took a midnight walk alone along the sweeping curve of Sun Bay. It has a long, broad, generous arc of beach with mountains rising at both tips and a deep grove of tall palms bordering the white sand for its entire half-mile length. The bay is so beautiful that I thought, as I always do under the spell of a glorious landscape, "I hope Mom will see this sometime." It's actually less a thought than a reflex. Sometimes the impulse leads to a plan of action, as it did when I lured my parents to Italy. More often it remains an idle wish. Tonight, the feeling of impossibility that rose with the wish was devastating. It was as if a heavy mist of guilt and sadness had rolled in with the waves and filled the bay. How can my eyes take pleasure in beauty that hers will never see?

MANHATTAN

MONDAY, MARCH 17:

I have been dreading this day for weeks. Since returning from
Puerto Rico on Saturday, I have been staying in Milena's apartment because I want to be poised to catch a flight to Minneapolis
if the results of Mom's tests are bad. I forgot that it takes a few
days for them to process and interpret the tests, so here I am,
stuck in the city, easy prey for my city tenant, who informs me
the bathroom ceiling is about to cave in from damage done by
water leaking from the apartment above mine. My tenant and
upstairs neighbors are, of course, too busy to tend to the problem, and since I'm in the city for a few days, they say, why don't
I just find a plumber and a plasterer, supervise their work and
we'll split the bill. Country living has made a chump of me. City
dwellers seem to know my time is no longer money and so they
are quick to spend it.

WEDNESDAY, MARCH 19:

Reprieve. The CAT scan showed no increase in the size of Mom's
tumor. The bone scan showed no damage to her spine. The
blood tests revealed no problem whatsoever. Mike is amazed, I
am ecstatic, Mom and Dad are disappointed. They never entertained the possibility that Mom's life was in danger, so they
experienced no relief from these results. They wanted an explanation and solution for her pain and they got none. The
oncologist says there is "no reason" for her "discomfort," and
when pressed, he suggested they arrange a visit to the medical
center's pain clinic. The earliest appointment they could make
was for a month from now.

When I talked to Mike tonight, we decided that he and Nancy
will visit Mom and Dad at Easter, with or without the kids,

and I will make a visit a couple weeks later, after I've begun work on the house and finished my last remaining assignment.

GLENCO MILLS, N.Y.
MONDAY, MARCH 24:

I was not born to strip wood. It has taken me forty pads of Grade 000 steel wool, three gallons of Zip-strip and twenty small corner blocks with raised and recessed concentric circles carved in them to learn this. I have also learned that March is not the month for stripping. You can either open your windows and court frostbite or keep them closed and risk fume-borne brain damage. Also, the rubber glove that can hold its own against a mixture of methylene chloride, toluol, acetone and methanol has not yet found its way to my varnish-stained hands. This knowledge leaves me with twenty-nine pieces of unstripped molding from six windows and four doorways, not to mention the doors themselves, all of which must be reckoned with before they are returned to the walls from whence they came.

I found a man in Hudson who says he will "dip" the whole batch for me for a modest price. Lenny says I'll be sorry, that I'm contemplating a serious crime against wood, but I'm already sorry and I'd rather the wood be curdled than me.

THURSDAY, MARCH 27:

Mike and Nancy are in Edina, without the kids. Their telephone voices are hearty and cheerful until Mom wanders out of earshot, and then they confess in whispers how appalled they are at Mom's fragility. Nancy says she is cooking night and day to add the 110th pound to Mom, and Mike is trying to get her to take more exercise. Yesterday he made the mistake of coaxing her into a trip to the supermarket. He felt like a bodyguard protecting her against threats from all sides. Every cart-pushing customer seemed a reckless driver armed with a deadly weapon.

Today was the warmest March day on record, an incredible eighty-six degrees. I drove to Bash Bish Falls and climbed the steep rocky face of the cliff from the base of the falls to the top, hoping to find signs of an early spring. There were no leaves or buds to be seen, but when I broke off the tip end of a twig to sail it down the rapids, the stump end wept profusely. The sap tasted sweet, like sugared rainwater, and I felt like a butcher.

MARCH 30, EASTER SUNDAY:

Tonight I was at home watching *The Right Stuff* on the VCR when I was startled by a loud pounding on my back door. Nobody pays visits at ten o'clock on a dark country night, so I was a bit scared when I went to the door. I pulled back the curtains and saw Frank, bare chested, his flabby midriff streaked with blood. He told me he had something to show me, something "I had to see," so I followed him across my yard and into the smokehouse at the back of his property. A skinned deer carcass hung from ceiling hooks. On the floor, in a pool of blood next to the doe's hide, were three fetuses—two does and a buck. They were perfectly shaped miniature deer, about a foot long, a hairless glistening mauve.

Frank picked them up one by one to show me their genitals and the buck's incipient horns. He said triplets were rare and he knew I wouldn't want to miss seeing them. "It's a shame," he said, explaining that a state trooper had found the doe dead in the road and brought her to Frank for dressing.

As Frank stood in the pool of blood, streaked red from his labor, a fetus in each hand, exuding a strange glow of pride and excitement, I did not know how to react. Part of me recoiled at what seemed to be the most perverse form of sexual flirtation I had ever experienced. Part of me saw a man who was simply trying to share a sight that awed him, and I was flattered that he trusted me to understand his exhilaration. It was clear he thought the fetuses were beautiful, and they were.

"Too bad I can't preserve them in Naugahyde [sic] or something," he said. Then he asked me if I would like the doe's liver. I said, "No," but not wanting to seem ungrateful, I added that I loved the venison steaks he gave me earlier in the year. He said he would try to bring me some steaks from the doe, but he had to give the hind to the trooper.

MONDAY, MARCH 31:

This morning about 7:30 A.M., I was awakened by a ruckus of scratching in the stovepipe that goes through my bedroom. I was too tired to do anything about it, so I just rolled over and hoped the creature would free itself or take a nap. It obliged me with quiet for an hour, but then resumed a fitful scratching that was driving Kissa wild. I had to do something, but I didn't know what kind of creature it was or what it would do once it was out of the stovepipe and at large in the house.

I banged on the stovepipe at the elbow joint where it enters the chimney. There was no response from the creature, so I figured it was no longer in that section of the pipe, although it definitely had been there earlier. The only other nonvertical part of the pipe was the damper above the woodstove. I went downstairs, flipped the damper open, and out popped a starling, who started hopping frantically in the cold ashes. The stove screen kept him trapped and safe from Kissa, who lunged and clawed to no avail.

I placed a large rock against the screen, congratulated myself for keeping such things handy and locked a very disappointed Kissa in the bedroom. Then I devised my strategy for releasing the bird. Plastic insulation was still stretched tightly over the windows, so I couldn't open them for exits. I hoped the lace curtains would be enough to discourage the bird from trying those escape routes, and tried to prearrange a flight out the front door by opening it and closing the doors to all the other rooms. If he flew up the staircase, I would have to rethink matters.

Before removing the screen I armed myself with a broom to stun the bird if he tried to attack me or to guide him on his way if that was necessary. But as soon as I lifted the screen, he flew straight into the nearest window, crashing through the transparent insulation and trapping himself between it and the window pane. He kept flapping his wings against the glass, apparently thinking if he could see daylight, then freedom must lie in that direction. I decided to try opening the window, but first I had to tear off more of the insulation. This freed him for flight again and he darted into the breakfast room through a door I thought I had closed. He crashed through the insulation over the window there, tangling his wings in lace. It was now clear I would have to catch him in my hands and take him outside.

I got a kitchen towel to protect my hands from pecking and clawing, then approached the window. He didn't dart away at first, but when I grabbed him, I did it too tentatively and he escaped my grip. This happened several times. Finally I grasped him firmly in both towel-covered hands and he became absolutely still. There was no pecking, no scratching, not even a twist of head or roll of eyeball. I carried him onto the porch and opened my hands, and he streaked across the road and out of sight.

A few minutes later I heard scratching from inside the basement door and thought, now what? I opened the door and Midnight burst out. He must have been trapped there since last night when I went down to check on the furnace. He raced into the kitchen, and I followed, but before I got there to open the back door for him, he had clawed through the insulation on both windows. I decided to call it spring and spent the rest of the morning pulling shredded strips of plastic from their moorings.

Yesterday, I decided to try out my new hip boots in preparation for the opening of trout season today. The boots are heavy and you strap them on with canvas knee braces inside the boot as well as by straps extending from the top of the boot to belt loops. This keeps them securely on my legs, but it also means I'll have two fifty-pound weights strapped to my body if they should fill with water.

With boots on, I lumbered through the yard and down the path to the stream behind the house. Last spring the path led to a rocky strip of beach from which you could enter the stream in ankle-deep water. But now the stream is so swollen with melted snow that the beach is an island separated from the bank by several feet of fast-flowing water. I stepped in, and although the water only reached mid-calf, I had a hard time keeping my balance. Even in the ankle-deep water on the other side of the island, it was hard to keep my footing. Whenever I raised a boot off the streambed, the rushing water carried it a foot downstream. It felt like moon walking, except that I knew gravity would reassert itself if I slipped.

Walking upstream was impossible, and the only way to make safe progress downstream was to slide my foot along the rocky bottom until it found the next firm footing. In knee-deep water, the force of the stream pounding against my legs was so great that I had to struggle to remain standing. One slight slip would have sent me on a long, bumpy, boot-bound ride downstream to safer, shallower waters or to fatally deep ones.

That prospect didn't appeal, so I slogged my way back to the bank wondering why trout-fishing deaths were not a seasonal epidemic. It had taken all my strength and attention to stay upright, and I wasn't fishing. How would it be with a fishing rod in hand, and my concentration focused on the hunt?

——————

On the local television news tonight, they said dangerously high water had kept a lot of fishermen out of the streams. Personally, I needn't have worried. There were no fish to distract me from boot management today. I started at the fish hole, using one of Dad's homemade nymphs on my fly rod, but without the sycamore trunk spanning the stream and slowing the water, the fish hole is less of a pool. It's become a stretch of water too fast-flowing and turbulent for fish to laze about in. After several dozen casts produced only a fingerling, I moved downstream to the bridge, where I had no better luck. Since there is no insect life on the stream yet for my flies to imitate, I didn't really expect any smart fish to strike, but I had hoped for an ignorant stocked trout or two.

FRIDAY, APRIL 4:

The molding returned from the dipper today looking like a pack of teething puppies had gnawed the varnish off. It doesn't look like wood anymore; it looks like a flattened furry animal. Bob assures me a good rubbing with steel wool will remove the fuzziness, but that still leaves the problem of holes. It seems a good deal of the wood was not wood, but wood putty, plugging up 120 years of nail and screw holes, which are now revealed for all the world to see. To judge from the degree of pitting, everything in the house must have been fastened to the door and window molding at one time or another. Perhaps Ancram was prey to strong winds or high floods or thieves in the night.

Now that the molding is stripped, nobody will tell me what kind of wood this is. The dipper ventured a "maybe cypress" but he didn't want to stand behind it. Whatever it is, it makes a very bold statement indeed; the grain looks like zebra stripe or, to a more domestic mind, marble cake. Once I've smoothed its fur and filled its holes, I'll either have to paint it or go with a Wild Kingdom look in the living room.

I have been painting eight hours a day, every day, all week. I hired Bob's stepson Joe to do the ceilings and help me apply two coats of primer to the walls of the renovated main section of the house. When we finished on Tuesday about four o'clock, Joe stepped back, looked around, saw bright sunlight bouncing off the clean white walls of the large airy room we've created and proclaimed it beautiful. "Are you sure you don't want to leave it white?" he asked, and I'll admit I was tempted.

But I was bent on color. I have lived forty years between off-white walls. It's time for a change of palette, I thought, time to be bold, Victorian, at least in this one large room of my making. I pored through color charts for weeks. Paint chips danced in my dreams, waltzed and rocked and bebopped to lyrics by Benjamin Moore and Pratt & Lambert. Would it be Kurdistan V, Cherish III, Beetroot, Botticelli or Frappe? I did not succumb to the siren song of exotic names. I chose a nameless hue, known only as RV092W. When I showed the chosen chip to Candace on the flight to Puerto Rico (I carried it everywhere), she said, "Aren't you afraid it might be a little too pink?" What does she know, I thought to myself, city apartment dweller that she is, beneficiary of biennial landlord specials.

In my mind's eye, I saw a subtle dusty rose whose muted glow changed as the light changed from morning to night. I bought eight $20 gallons. Wednesday morning I watched in disbelief as the first white wall I touched turned Pepto-Bismol pink with each swipe of the roller. I called the paint store in panic and was told not to worry, it would darken if I applied a second coat and let it dry overnight. I found it hard to believe that more would be better, but I tried to banish my doubts. This morning I drove to Ancram and entered a room that had profited not at all from a night's rest.

I packed my two large vats of paint in the car and drove straight to the decorating center in Hudson. The proprietor was not sympathetic. "That's the color you asked for, lady," he said, "RV092W." It was "a custom color," he explained, and so could not be exchanged. He would, however, add pigments to the batch at no extra charge. I described the dusty rose I was after, its muted Victorian glow, and watched hopefully as he plopped small globs of brown and yellow and blue into my buckets of medicinal pink.

Back in Ancram, I rolled in good faith. This paint was darker, duskier, it would be just fine. I gave two coats to all four walls. Twice, I hand painted ninety feet of clean edge between the walls and the white ceiling. My fingers cramped, and after several hours of alternately standing on tiptoe to reach the upper parts of the wall and hunkering down on bent knees to do the lower parts, my calves swelled to twice their normal size. I finished about five o'clock and sat exhausted on the lid of my empty five-gallon bucket to admire the fruit of my labor.

Suddenly, a blast of late-afternoon sun burst through the clouds that had covered Ancram all day. Light streamed horizontally through the windows and hit the walls with the full impact of its pent-up ferocity. The walls seemed to pulse. I felt I was sitting in the engorged maw of a meat-eating beast. A red-meat-eating beast. I have never seen anything so throbbingly pink.

By six o'clock the light had died and my walls lowered their skirts, so to speak, becoming proper Victorians once again. Maybe the peep show happens only one hour a day, I thought. I could live with that. Or get lead-lined curtains to block the light. I can't turn back now. I have five more rooms to paint, and all that molding to spackle, and floors to lay.

MONDAY, APRIL 14:

After painting woodwork today, I fished the Roe/Jan near the Ancram house for the first time. The Roe/Jan, formally known as Roeliff Jansens Kill, is broader and deeper than Taghkanic Creek, and also more active. A little boy sitting on the bank dangling worms and catching fish told me there were trout, bass, shiners and catfish in the stream. I had to take his word for it, because, in my hip boots, fly fishing and covering a lot more territory, I got nothing but wet. Hip boots are definitely not high enough for this stream; chin boots would serve me better.

Maybe I should stick to spackling. It seems I'm a natural. Those poor chewed-up pieces of molding look good as new, and after three coats of paint, no one can tell how little wood is left on them. Candace and Milena, who witnessed the before and after, call me "Spackle Plenty."

FRIDAY, APRIL 18:

Following Zack and Merc's advice, I tried fishing in the pools at the base of the dam behind the Kimberly-Clark Mill today. It didn't seem a very romantic spot to fish, but I figured if it's good enough for trout, it's good enough for me. I walked across the employee parking lot with fly rod in hand and clambered down the steep bank on a path worn through poison ivy to an outcropping of rock about fifteen feet wide and thirty feet long. The roar of the Roe/Jan plunging over the dam drowned out the hum of the mill's generators, but the frothing spray of the waterfall also made it difficult to cast into the side pools that were my targets. I nearly hooked myself several times when the force of the spray whiplashed the line back in my face. Finally I discovered that a low side-arm cast brought the fly to rest on the pool instead of me. Even there the water swirled so fast that the fly was instantly sucked into a vortex and then spit up into the air yards away in imitation of no creature in its right mind. My only hope was that the trout in these pools were too dizzy to be discriminating.

Pulling the line in to make my fifth cast, I found a stunned eleven-inch brown trout in my possession. The tug of the currents against my line was so great I hadn't even known he was taking a ride on my hook. It wasn't brilliant gamesmanship on my part, but still it was a respectable-size fish and I decided to keep him around for a while, in case I caught another and had enough to offer the friend I'd invited for dinner. Instead of threading him onto a stringer, I cleverly put him in one of the water-filled crevices on the outcropping of rock from which I was casting. Nature's minnow bucket, I thought, from which I could return him unharmed to the stream or take him home.

A few minutes later I hooked another trout, this time knowingly, and I let it play the line in sportsmanlike fashion. When I landed him, I gently carried his ten inches to the crevice where I had left the first fish, thinking my evening's menu was settled. But the first fish was gone. I shrugged and returned the second fish to the stream, figuring the odds against my catching a third fish in the same spot were impossibly high.

I resumed casting just to pass the time and began to wonder how that first fish managed to escape from the crevice. I set my rod down and returned to look for clues. On hands and knees I peered into the still water and saw a suspicious bulge in the silt at the bottom of the crevice. I reached into the water with my right hand and a cloud of mud exploded around my fingers. When the mud settled I saw my trout shuttling back and forth across the three-foot length of the crevice. Every time I grabbed, he dove straight to the bottom and stirred up a mud storm that left me in zero visibility. The water was only a foot deep, but that trout knew how to work every cubic inch of it.

I was so intent on our battle of wills that I failed to notice an audience had gathered. A dozen mill workers on coffee break had taken positions on a catwalk spanning the Roe/Jan about twenty-five yards downstream from me. The noise of the falls prevented me from hearing what they said as they gestured in my direction, but I could imagine the gist of it, and I knew I didn't even have the protection of anonymity, because one of the men on the catwalk was Clara's husband, who no doubt informed the others I was the lady who bought his mother-in-law's house.

I waved and smiled, hoping they might arrive at a reasonable explanation for my behavior, then returned to my task, which was, in fact, to save the fish. Personally, I couldn't have cared less if he lived out the rest of his life in that crevice, but I feared it would be a short, unhappy life unless I rigged up an aerator and brought him food every day. The problem was the trout still thought of me as his enemy and I knew there was no way of talking him out of it.

Bare-handed lunging clearly didn't work. I considered tying on my tastiest fly and flicking it daintily into the crevice, but it was too late in the game for that. I looked about me for a solution and spotted a plastic carton, the kind that might once have contained a half-pound of coleslaw, littering the bank. I fetched it, rinsed it in the stream and hovered above the crevice awaiting my moment.

When the trout paused to rest at the narrow end of the crevice, I plunged and scooped up his tail. He wriggled free, but before he could slap bottom, I scooped again and caught him head first in the carton. Grabbing his tail with my free hand, I carried him, half-in/half-out of the carton, to the pool, where, in my haste to free him before he flapped out of my grip into another crevice, I slipped on the wet rocks and slid into the water with him. An adrenaline rush of fear shot through me before my feet hit a ledge of rock and I found myself standing waist deep in the coldest water that ever lapped my thighs.

I climbed back onto the outcropping and thanked the powers that be at Kimberly-Clark for the brevity of their coffee breaks. On the short drive home, I passed Zack and Merc, who asked me if I had tried the pools by the mill yet. I said yes, I had just caught two twelve-inch brown trout there, and thanked them for the tip. They asked why I was shivering, but since they could see me only from the chest up, I left them wondering.

WEDNESDAY, APRIL 23:

I awoke this morning to find the ground covered with snow. I sensed it before I saw it; as soon as I opened my eyes and raised my head, I could tell there was no color beyond the windows. There must have been a strong north wind during the night, because the kitchen porch was four inches deep in drifted snow. My hip boots were covered and a crust had formed on the reels of my fishing rods. The tulips were bowed halfway to the ground by the white streaks on their heads.

The birds seemed disoriented by the disappearance of spring. On the drive from Glenco Mills to Ancram, I had to slow down several times to avoid hitting birds who were clustered on the blacktop. They were startled into motion by the sound of the car, but they flew toward the windshield instead of away from it. One robin darted across the path of the car when I was only yards away; when I braked, it accelerated in mid-flight as if it had a rocket booster in its tail feathers. How do birds speed up like that, without any perceptible quickening of wing motion?

Coming down the hall stairs this morning, I noticed a bird sitting in a nest built on top of the front-door ledge. The bird is so small I thought it might have been hatched there, but when I stood on a chair to see the nest better, the bird flew away and I saw two tiny blue eggs. Dad says it must be a wren.

When I get back from Edina, I'm going to search through my paint charts for wren's-egg blue. After the fiasco of pulsing pink walls, I've decided to take my clues from nature. The only colors I'll use upstairs are ones I can see from my windows. The straw

yellow of meadows about to turn green, the unnameable blue
of the new growth on the spruce tree, and lots of snow white.

EDINA, MINN.
FRIDAY, APRIL 25:

I hate Mom's doctors. When I arrived in Edina this morning, I
found her thinner, frailer and in greater pain than at any time
since her operation. Last week she went to the pain clinic expecting to discover an array of alternatives to drugs for the back
pain her oncologist says is not caused by cancer; what she was
offered was another nerve block, and she was so desperate for
relief that she let them perform the procedure the next morning.

Now she is at home, taking mind-fogging doses of codeine to
blunt the same intense burning pain the first nerve block caused.
Her weight is down to 105 again, she has very little appetite and
barely enough strength to walk from one room to the next. She
is surprised by her misfortune and sure, as always, that she'll
"feel better tomorrow." She doesn't remember that it took six
weeks to recover from the side effects of this "cure-all," and
nobody at the medical center reminded her.

I understand why most of the doctors cannot spend any more
time or emotion on their patients than they do. They are specialists trained to intervene at moments of crisis, to cut, to radiate, to alter chemistry, then move on to the next patient. But
why is there no place in this elaborate medical system for sustained care of the human being who continues to feel the effects
of the doctors' knives and beams and chemicals? Why must
medicine feel so much like a hit-and-run accident?

MONDAY, APRIL 28:

Mom awoke exhausted and disheartened by a bad night, her
sleep interrupted by back pain despite Darvoset, Tylenol and a
heating pad. About 11:30 A.M. I was cooking some Cream of

Wheat, which she said she would force herself to eat, when the phone rang. Dad answered, and as soon as he said, "Hi, Veronica," Mom became very alert. "Why is she calling at this hour?" Mom asked, knowing her sisters usually wait for evening long-distance rates. Dad's voice became somber and Mom, guessing the news, said, "Allie's died." She rose from her chair in the living room and walked with tears streaking her face to the kitchen. "And I can't even go to the funeral," she said, crying hard as she reached for the phone.

She calmed herself as she talked with Veronica, and by the end of their conversation, she had undergone a very visible change. She had looked pallid and drained all morning, but as soon as she got off the phone, she walked almost briskly to the kitchen table and indicated her readiness to eat. I had taken the pot of cereal off the stove when I heard the news, figuring Mom would lose what little appetite she had, but now she asked if I would mind frying her some bacon to have with the cereal.

While I met her requests, she sat at the table with a higher head and squarer shoulders than I have seen in months. "Allie was always so frail," Mom said, as if contrasting herself to her older sister, who was in fact sturdy enough to bear and raise eight children. "Veronica says Allie lost her will to live and nearly starved herself to death." I knew Allie had become depressed and refused rehabilitation after breaking her hip last year, but I didn't know until today that she suffered from lupus for nearly thirty years.

Within an hour, Mom had changed from her pajamas into a snappy black-and-white sweatshirt and a pair of pants. She put on makeup, fixed her hair and asked me to heat up some leftover pasta for her lunch. She ate two servings and a bowl of apple sauce. Later in the afternoon she called the beauty parlor and made an appointment to have her hair done tomorrow.

A better day. Mom slept fairly well and we all woke to sunny skies. When Freya and the twins came by to visit at lunchtime, the boys presented Mom with homemade paper monsters. Mom reciprocated with leftover jelly beans, and all concerned seemed pleased with the transaction. Once the boys settled in for an episode of "He-Man," Freya and Mom talked at some length about acupuncture, which Freya uses to reduce pain in the knee that was operated on last spring. Mom was more receptive than I expected and gladly accepted Freya's offer to call her acupuncturist at the pain clinic and explain Mom's case. But when Freya added that she knew of a Japanese oncologist who does research at the University of Minnesota and practices one day a week at the clinic, Mom proudly told Freya she didn't need to see an oncologist, she wasn't a cancer patient anymore.

After Freya left, it became clear that a half-hour's animated conversation had depleted Mom and she really didn't have the strength to keep her appointment at the hairdresser's, but she thought Dad would be disappointed if she didn't make herself "look good for a change." So she changed clothes, applied fresh makeup and made a very brave attempt to act like just another lady in the beauty parlor, which was not easy. The hairdresser kept us waiting for fifteen minutes, which Mom would have spent sitting in quiet torment on a backless bench if I hadn't walked around a corner and found chairs with better support. (There were comfortable chairs visible to her from the bench, but she wouldn't move to them because they were in the men's section of the salon.)

I had intended to stay at her side, but Mom so seldom goes out of the house that she had forgotten to bring her purse and I didn't have enough cash on me to cover the bill. After making sure she was comfortably seated, with a small pillow pressed firmly against her back but hidden from sight by the pink plastic cape draped over her body, I drove home to fetch her purse. When I returned, she was sitting on the backless bench, hunched and forlorn. "My back is killing me," she whispered as she painstakingly filled in the blanks of a check. Watching over her stooped shoulders, I was appalled by the physical and mental toll this simple act seemed to exact of her.

I didn't realize how constricted she has become, and neither, I think, did she. On the drive home she seemed chastened. As long as she is housebound, she is protected from her limitations. But the most timid excursion into the outer world exposes her. A trip to the beauty parlor is a herculean feat, check writing a minor triumph. Mike warned me the supermarket was a death trap, but I didn't grasp the literalness of his warning.

Yesterday I noticed for the first time that Mom is struggling with a kind of mental disorientation as well. Her sense of time—both time of day and historical time—seems particularly confused. Last night, for instance, she asked if she had seen my new house the last time they visited me in New York, which is a logical and temporal impossibility, since that visit was in November 1984, when I still lived in the city and worked for the *Times*. A few minutes later, she asked Dad if the steaks we were eating for dinner were part of the batch her brother Al had given them. "How could they be?" Dad snapped. "That was four years ago!" Dad is impatient with her lapses. He refuses to let her slip away from us.

It's not clear whether her occasional muddled thinking comes from distraction by pain, a forced isolation from everyday routines or drugs. Given all three factors, we should probably be happy she is as alert as she is most of the time. She reads the newspaper cover to cover every day, and usually asks us to turn up the volume on the television news so she can hear it in the living room. Tonight, however, she asked us to turn the volume down. Most of the news yesterday and today was devoted to the nuclear accident at Chernobyl, with elaborate coverage of the potential side effects from exposure to radiation. She doesn't want to hear it.

WEDNESDAY, APRIL 30:

As soon as I learned that Mom had spent another sleepless, pain-ridden night, I decided to call Freya's acupuncturist. She immediately confessed her reluctance to handle a case as complicated as Mom's but promised to convey the information I gave her to her colleague Dr. Ye, whom she described as "a leading Japanese oncologist" who practiced "Eastern medicine" on Wednesdays only.

About 2:30 P.M. Dr. Ye (pronounced "Yay") called, and in very broken English explained that acupuncture would be of little use to a patient with pancreatic cancer, because the tumor causes pain at the root of the nerves, pain "too deep" to be relieved by acupuncture. He asked if we had tried "a tense machine," and thinking we had encountered a language problem, I asked him to repeat the question several times. Finally I understood that there is a device called a TENS machine, which stands for transcutaneous electrical nerve stimulator, and that he thinks it might help Mom's back pain. He said he had one at the clinic and he offered to try both it and acupuncture on her this afternoon.

Mom was interested but reluctant to undertake an outing when she felt so "terrible." I forced the issue by saying I could take her to the clinic today but I would be back in New York by next Wednesday, which would be her next opportunity to see Dr. Ye. I pressed hard, certain that this byway of medicine would never be explored after I left Edina. She conceded, and within an hour I was following directions to The Healing Point, located above the pet store in the small shopping center across from the Red Owl.

I escorted Mom across a parking lot, up a flight of stairs and into the waiting room with nothing more than a desperate hope we might find something to make the walk down less torturous than the walk up. Dr. Ye greeted us at the door, and one glance told me he had been misrepresented. No "leading Japanese oncologist" would let such baggy, threadbare pants droop beneath his white doctor's coat or drape his stethoscope around the open collar of a transparently thin, short-sleeved shirt. I asked and learned that Dr. Ye is visiting from mainland China, where he says oncologists routinely combine acupuncture, herbal medicine and other traditional Eastern practices with surgery, chemotherapy and radiation. Since the two approaches to healing are kept separate here, he steals one afternoon a week from his research at the university to see patients at The Healing Point.

"I try to make the patient more comfortable," he said in a manner of speaking so modest as to be barely audible. Despite a limited vocabulary, Dr. Ye managed to communicate his impressive intelligence and his familiarity with the problems of pancreatic patients. He nodded his approval as he read the letter we had brought describing the treatment Mom received at the medical center. He was knowledgeable about nerve blocks and their side effects, but some of the details of the experimental radiation treatment were new to him and he expressed admiration for the medical center's daring. I had the distinct feeling that high doses of intra-operative radiation would soon be used to treat Chinese cancer patients.

After asking more questions about Mom's medical history and present symptoms, Dr. Ye led us into his office and helped Mom onto the table. He asked her to lie on her left side facing the wall while he pressed a finger against various points on her back, asking "Is it tender?" with each poke. Whenever he pressed against a spot just to the right of her spine at mid-back, she would say, "There!" There was surprise in her voice, because the tender spot was nowhere near the site of her pain, which is much lower in her back. Dr. Ye directed our attention to the wall, where he had hung an anatomical chart with acupuncture pressure points marked on it. Mom's tender spot corresponded to the pressure point associated with the pancreas.

He brought out a TENS machine, a hand-held device that looks like a TV remote control switch with four little suction pads attached to its wires. He applied a gel to the pads and stuck them on Mom's back, two on each side of the spine at mid-back. Then he set some dials on the TENS machine and turned on the power, sending electrical pulses straight to the targeted nerves. Next he took two needles and stuck them in Mom's right ear. When Mom looked puzzled, he pointed to another chart, which showed pressure points in the ear and their correspondence to body parts far removed from that organ. His work completed, Dr. Ye left the room, saying he'd be back in twenty minutes.

I followed and strained his English with my questions. No, the needles were not for pain control but for medicinal effect on the pancreas. Yes, TENS machines are based on the theory of acupuncture, but they are widely used by Western doctors. Their purchase or rental is covered by most health insurance companies, even though the same companies will not reimburse for acupuncture. Yes, he genuinely believed the TENS machine would help Mom. He had treated many pancreatic patients in China and he knew how great their pain was. He said he also had good results using herbs to treat the digestive problems of pancreatic patients in China; he would make a trip over the weekend to a Chinese market in St. Paul, where he thought he might find them.

After fifteen minutes of questioning Dr. Ye, who remained resolutely patient and kind, I went to check on Mom. She said she felt no pain where she had before, but her entire left side was numb from staying in one position for so long. When I tried to help move her onto her back while holding the four wired pads in place, the needles fell out of her ear and disappeared.

We were both laughing when Dr. Ye walked in and found me searching the floor. "No problem," he assured us, the needles had been in long enough. He asked Mom to come back and see him next Wednesday and he promised to find some herbs to help her regain her weight and energy. By the time we left, he had given us seventy minutes of undivided attention, for which he charged $35.

It is now seven hours later and Mom still feels no back pain. Dad is ecstatic at the prospect of fewer drugs, and of a clear-headed wife. Mom is hopeful, and a bit concerned that Mike will think her "a crock" for straying from the straight and narrow of A.M.A.–approved doctoring. At one point this evening, Mom said that when she was alone in Dr. Ye's office, she started wondering, "How did I get here, lying on my side with two hot needles in my ear and four cold suction cups on my back? Did I let my daughter do this to me? Then I thought, well, I guess everything in your life affects everything else in your life." I accused her of sounding like a Confucian after only one session with Dr. Ye.

"No," she said, "it's all that Faulkner you made me read. You're the pebble I dropped in the pond, and Freya's the ripple that led to needles in my ear. Or maybe it was the deer tick who bit Freya and ruined her knee." Dad suggested we blame it on California, where I met Freya, or on the Vietnam War, which is what sent me there in anticipation of my fiancé's Navy assignment. I confessed that in 1967 I had left my choice of graduate school to a Ouija board, which swung its pendulum west toward Stanford and San Francisco's summer of love.

Soon we were all giddy on the ripples of free association. It was midnight before we agreed to fix all responsibility on the palm-reading gypsy who foretold Mom's marriage to Dad. We went to bed praising "Dr. Yay" and his magic machine for the first lighthearted evening we have spent together in a long time.

Tonight, on the local news, there was a feature about a woman who had been smashed up in an automobile accident eight years ago and still suffers severe pain. (This is part of a public service series which is supposed to inform Minnesotans that you can get badly hurt in car accidents, even if, as in this case, the accident happens in Illinois and you only later move to Minnesota.) Anyway, as this woman is being interviewed about how unpleasant automobile accidents can be, her husband is attaching the black pads of a TENS machine to his wife's neck. The machine is never mentioned in the report but I recognized it at once; I guess they allow only so much public service in any one report.

Why is TENS kept such a secret? Why didn't the doctors at the pain clinic try it before giving Mom a second nerve block? Must we travel to China to find the kind of compassion we found in Dr. Ye today?

THURSDAY, MAY 1:

Mom awoke without pain after a good night's sleep, and I expected to see at least flashes of last night's good humor. Instead she was morose and withdrawn all morning. Finally, about noon, she reminded me that this was the day of Allie's funeral. "I wish I could be there," she said. "It's so hard for me to believe someone is dead without seeing the funeral."

Mom wants to spend the day imagining she is in Fort Dodge with her relatives, saying the rosary together at Laufersweiler's funeral home, attending the requiem Mass at Sacred Heart, driving in the cortege to Corpus Christi Cemetery and then back to Allie's home for food and remembrance. "Maybe I'll believe it then," she said.

Part of her sadness today is sheer disappointment at missing a family gathering. Weddings and funerals are the only occasions that draw her dispersed nieces and nephews, my forty first cousins, together again. It's been over a year since she last visited Fort Dodge and she doesn't know when she'll be strong enough to make the five-hour drive again. She keeps telling herself "next month," but the months are beginning to string themselves into decades like the beads on the rosary her fingers are telling right now.

About six this evening Mom started waiting for the phone to ring. She was sure one of her sisters would call with news of the funeral—who had been there, who had not, how Allie looked in her casket and what Father McElroy said in his homily. By eight, she was near tears at the thought of being forgotten. "I should have gone," she said. "We could have put pillows in the back seat of the car and I could have stretched out." Dad reminded her that getting there was only the start of a long, demanding day of standing, kneeling, walking and visiting.

"But what if they don't understand why I'm not there?" she said. In fact, her sisters had very little basis for understanding her absence, since Mom always presents herself over the phone as a woman on the verge of total recovery. I couldn't imagine Mom's sisters being punitive, no matter what they understood of her situation, but by nine I began to share her doubts.

At 9:30 the phone rang. It was Anna Marie, Mom's youngest sister, but she had very little news of the funeral. This morning, Mom's only surviving brother, Al, collapsed when he was dressing for the funeral. Al's wife, Phyllis, who is not good in a crisis, found him unconscious in the bedroom and immediately called Anna Marie for help. Anna Marie summoned Katherine and Veronica, and the three sisters arranged for Al to be taken by ambulance to the university hospital in Iowa City, where Al has been treated for several forms of cancer in the past few years.

Anna Marie went in the ambulance with Al, who had regained consciousness; Phyllis, who does not drive herself, was too distraught to depart with the ambulance, so Veronica drove her later in Al's Buick, and Katherine followed in a third car so Anna

Marie and Veronica would have a way to get home. The drive from Fort Dodge to Iowa City takes ninety minutes, so the sisters had to choose between attending Allie's funeral or staying with Al at what they feared might be his deathbed.

When they left the hospital this evening, Al was in stable condition. The doctors think he suffered a stroke, but they are not certain. It seems that when he fell, he struck the part of his head where skull had been removed during brain surgery, and that may have caused his loss of consciousness. Mom expects Al to be better by next week, but since she is putting her interpretation on third-hand information, I doubt that anything is certain.

When Mom relayed the grim details of the day to me, I couldn't help but wonder how Grandma Meyer would have told the tale. She specialized in a brand of Midwestern black humor marked by extreme concision and unabashed relish for disaster. Her quintessential story was of her parents' wedding day and went like this: "When my parents got married, they were so poor, the only possessions they had to their name were his horse and her wedding dress. On their wedding night she washed the dress and hung it out to dry, and while they slept, the horse got loose, ate the dress, fell in a hole and died."

Every time she told the story, and she told it well into her nineties, she would be overwhelmed by its hilarity. Her laughter set her rocker into such furious motion that the tears literally flew off her face and her waist-long hair escaped its pins, unfurling itself in long white banners. Her audience of daughters would catch the laughter and become useless, leaving me on guard in case she rocked right out of the chair. The wedding night story was often followed by the story of how she once killed a rattlesnake and draped it over the barn door handles to scare her husband when he returned at dusk from the fields. I don't remember the punch line, or even if there was one, just the peals of laughter the memory unfailingly provoked.

She laughed unabashedly, guiltlessly, because there was an

unspoken happy ending to all her stories. Her horseless parents somehow made the trip from Owen's Sound, Canada, to Clare, Iowa, and became the prosperous farmers who raised her. The snake didn't bite. Until last year, her children all thought they would inherit her long, laughing life. There had not been a death among them or their spouses or their children since 1944, when my Uncle Leo was killed during the war. Now Roy and Aileen and Allie are gone, and Mom and Al are full of desperate hope.

SATURDAY, MAY 3:

Mom and Dad and I went to a Mexican restaurant for lunch today, an excursion that would have been inconceivable before our visit to Dr. Ye. I thought Dad was pushing it when he ordered margaritas for all of us, but Mom rose to the occasion and I censored my call for prohibition. Better that she be tipsy on tequila than codeine.

The heady normality of the occasion made Dad garrulous, and he asked if I needed any art for my new house. This prompted me to ask him why he had done so little painting since his retirement three years ago. He has always been an after-hours painter with an uncanny knack for anticipating major changes in the art world, in which he took no part. In the fifties he was an abstract expressionist, swirling thick gobs of oil paint in dark vortices that made me think of caves and distant galaxies. About the time Andy Warhol painted his Campbell's soup cans, Dad was in the basement painting a brown National Tea grocery bag with a strip of S & H Green Stamps flowing over its minutely serrated edge. He made sculptures of found art long before there was a term for what he made out of the old streetcar springs and rusty bolts and printing machine parts he scavenged on the way home from the office. Fossil hunting and gardening vied for his attention, but painting drew it most consistently.

When he retired, I sent him a portable easel as a present, one that collapsed itself into a box the size of the attaché case he never carried to the office, because evenings were reserved for pleasure, not business. I imagined him getting into his car and driving until he saw something that made him want to stop. But the open easel sits unused in the basement, without even an empty canvas resting against its braces. I asked "how come?" and got more of an answer than I expected.

"For years," he said, "I've wondered what I could do if I painted eight hours a day, really worked at it. Maybe I could be good. I used to win prizes in college, did you know that? Nothing special, but still. And when I won the company shows at the *Star and Tribune,* the guy from the Walker Art Museum who did the judging told me he'd like to see more of my stuff. I never wanted to sell my work, but I thought maybe I could be good if I gave it the time. Now I have the time and I can't seem to bring myself to do it. Maybe I'm afraid I'll find out I'm not very good. Or maybe I'll find out I really am good and regret all the years I haven't spent doing it seriously."

Whew, I thought, sometimes it's frightening to discover how alike we are. Those words, repackaged, could have come out of my mouth anytime in the past two years, since I forced myself to find out what I would do if time were my own.

I told him I would love to have something of his for the house, maybe something based on the materials of the house, like clapboards, maybe a minimalist painting based on clapboards. "Hey, that gives me an idea," he said, and he started buzzing with the formal possibilities of clapboards and shutters and sections of molding.

MONDAY, MAY 5:

Mom always rallies the day before I leave. Yesterday, the effect of the TENS machine started to wear off and I could see the lines of strain returning to her face, but today she professes to feel fine. I suspect she is trying to assure me it's all right to go home. Ever since I've been old enough to compare her to other mothers, I have marveled at my good fortune in being born to a woman without a guilt-inducing bone in her body. This doesn't spare me guilt, but it spares me the redoubled pangs of being angry at the object of my guilt.

Tonight, because it was my last evening, we stayed together after dinner longer than usual. Mom sat in one of the curve-backed chairs, her feet tucked under her, teenage fashion, as we swapped gossip about the marital woes of friends, neighbors, cousins and the occasional celebrity. Dad joined us after washing the dishes, and something I said about a couple I know who met each other on jury duty, which is the civic-minded equivalent of choosing your mate out of the phone book, set them off on the story of their first meeting. I knew the general outlines of their courtship, but there were new details tonight.

Dad tells the first part. In 1937, he was an ad salesman for the newspaper in Perry, Iowa, and Mom, unbeknownst to him, was the new buyer for the women's department of the Montgomery Ward store. One day not too long after Mom moved to town, Dad's boss suggested he pass through the women's department when he made his weekly call at Ward's. The boss wouldn't tell him why he should make the detour, but he was very insistent about it. Dad thought the request peculiar, but he took the advice and knew why it had been given as soon as he laid his eyes on Mom.

He asked for a date that very night, Mom says, and she accepted. Glen Miller's orchestra was playing in a nearby town, and no man ever did a better impersonation of Fred Astaire than my father. (I know, because I have spent the first forty-some years of my life looking for one.) The next morning, Mom told her roommate she thought she had met the man she was going to marry. She was twenty-six (this fact is never mentioned), and though often courted, she was not given to such premonitions.

The town conspired to make the match. If Mom was having

coffee at the luncheonette on Main Street and Dad entered, the waitress would escort him past empty booths and seat him where she thought he belonged. Dad's boss kept finding excuses to send him to Ward's, and Mom's boss suddenly had a ready supply of free movie tickets. Neither of them had been in town long, so the matchmakers were not acting on privileged information. They were prompted by the visuals. That's my conclusion.

He looked like a man who was not going to stay in Perry, Iowa, and she looked like a woman who was ready to leave. I have seen the pictures. They do not look like their parents' children; she is not the farmer's daughter and he is not the blacksmith's son. They look like the movies. They look like Bogart and Dietrich, not the Bogart and Dietrich of any particular role, but the stars themselves, the ones who walked into premieres under crossed beams of light. My father is very slim, and the curve of his right arm into his pants pocket matches the arc of my mother's penciled eyebrow. His fedora is cocked to cast a shadow over the right side of his young face, and their open camel hair coats fall in straight lines toward slender ankles. They look straight into the camera with self-knowing smiles. They are very pleased with their invention; the clothes were worth every penny saved from salaries that barely paid the rent.

They were engaged within three weeks, but it took longer to find a priest who would marry them. Dad was not Catholic, and "mixed marriages" were discouraged. There's a story, more hinted at than told, of fists flying, or almost flying, or wanting to fly, in a rectory where their attempt at marriage was not only discouraged but maligned. Finally, after a thorough search of neighboring towns, they found a priest who agreed to marry them, but not in a church, and only if Dad would sign a document promising to allow his wife total control of their children's religious upbringing. He signed and, I can testify, abided by the promise, letter and spirit; Mike and I went to high schools where he was suspended for reading Darwin's *Voyage of the Beagle* and

I was publicly upbraided for a book report on *Anna Karenina,* thus ensuring his career in medicine and mine in words. Maybe Dad knew all along what a regimen of strict discipline and banned books would do for his children; after all, he went to a college that forbade dancing.

They reminisced tonight about the move from Perry to Des Moines, and the long drive on snow-covered highways from Des Moines to New York City, Mom eight months pregnant with Mike when they swerved off the road into a snowbank in western Massachusetts. They recalled their first apartment in Flushing, N.Y., and the couple next door, record-breaking flagpole sitters, who became their best friends. Mostly, though, they talked about that first meeting, the double take on the walk through the Montgomery Ward women's department forty-eight years ago.

They do not talk about that time as if it were terribly distant; they laugh at the low two-digit salaries they lived on or the primitive condition of interstate roads, but not at the attraction they built a life around. That hasn't dated. They would still dance if they could.

TUESDAY, MAY 6:

My leave-taking was eased by a call this morning from John and Sue, Mom's favorite nephew and his wife. When John left Fort Dodge as a young man to take a job in Chicago, Mom and Dad stood in for the big family he missed. Mom fixed Allie's pot roast and mashed potato dinner every Sunday for a year so John would feel at home, and when he met Sue, he brought her to Newt and Bea for approval. Sue wasn't Catholic, but she decided to convert, so Mom gave the shower and helped plan the big church wedding she never had herself. As their family and income grew, John and Sue kept moving one suburb farther north, but they never moved outside the radius of Sunday visits.

John called to say he and Sue have been in Fort Dodge since Allie's death and want to make a visit before returning to Chicago. Mom says they are "dropping by on their way home," but since Edina is five hours in the wrong direction, I know what John is thinking. He's lost his mother and he's not taking any chances.

GLENCO MILLS, N. Y.
FRIDAY, MAY 10:

The wren eggs hatched several days ago, but it took me a while to recognize that the shabby bits of fluff in the bottom of the nest were birds. They looked like the debris that floats down from cottonwood trees. The mother still spends most of her time sitting on her babies, the rest of it feeding them. She doesn't budge from the nest unless I press my nose against the glass panel that separates me from her brood.

The mourning dove that built her nest in the dogwood tree behind the Ancram house is even more tenacious. If I walk right up to the tree and stand within two feet of the nest, which is built at eye level, she fixes me with a lidless stare that seems to threaten death if I come an inch closer.

The robin in the lilac bush, on the other hand, abandons her nest the instant I set foot on the porch, which is a good twenty yards away. She flies to the top branches of the maple tree on the other side of the yard and sends up a screeching chatter when I approach the nest. Her flight impulse is held somewhat in check by maternal instinct, but she is no great protector.

SATURDAY, MAY 10:

Al died. Dad called with the news this afternoon. When Mom came to the phone, she sounded so defeated I wanted to cradle her in my arms and kiss her brow until she no longer cared about anything but the sensation of cool lips brushing taut skin. "I know it's wrong to think like this," she said, "but I can't help feeling we are being punished for something."

The doctors are attributing Al's death to a stroke, but apparently cancer had spread so widely in his body that the specific cause is moot. He had been treated for both a brain tumor and liver cancer in the past two years, and Mom grounded much of her hope for her own recovery in the belief that Al was doing well. Until now, she has not been cowed by the dread the very word "cancer" induces in most people, but I heard fright today, the admission that there might be something in the world stronger than her own will. Mom isn't able to distance herself from this death the way she distanced herself from Aileen's and Allie's.

After losing two brothers and two sisters in less than a year, how can she not feel marked? Even Mike is shaken. "There are too many cancer genes in this family," he said on the phone this evening. I reminded him that the previous generation had been too long-lived to presume a genetic plague, but I felt the chill nonetheless.

I remember how I felt the day Grandma Meyer died, three days before her ninety-ninth birthday. Without thinking about it, I had regarded her as the family's front line against death. As long as she was alive, the next generation was safe, and we grandchildren were a whole century removed from mortality. Suddenly, the battle lines shifted. My parents were now the vulnerable ones, the front line, and my own life span was called into question. As long as she was alive, actuarial tables didn't apply to me. With the vista of her ninety-nine years before me, I could believe I had two thirds of my life left. With her death I suddenly became middle-aged, half spent at thirty-five.

I made frightened love that afternoon, with shutters open to admit October light; but without my mind's armor, I became convinced that I would die, literally die, if I had an orgasm. I had studied the metaphysical poets, I knew the applicable conceits, but I had never connected sex and death outside the footnotes of undergraduate term papers.

By nightfall, I persuaded myself that Grandma Meyer had been in control of her own death, had actually chosen the day and time. She died quietly, sitting up in a chair, and was buried three days later on her ninety-ninth birthday—October 4, 1979—a day her nine surviving children, forty grandchildren and countless great-grandchildren should have gathered to celebrate her steady progress toward one hundred. She was proud of her age, vain enough to powder and coif herself into the picture of a bountiful matriarch, swathed in purple silk and surrounded by her progeny. I had long suspected she would die, sitting up, on her one-hundredth birthday, after savoring the full bouquet of adulation she could expect on that occasion.

I was sure she had changed her plans for death at the last minute, and I thought I knew why. She had lived in a house of her own until she was ninety-six, but the last three years were spent in a nursing home, where the days were long and a year interminable. She needed annual celebrations of her longevity to motivate herself through the tiresome slog of the next 364 days. But when I called home the week before she died to find out the specifics of this year's gathering, I was told there was nothing special planned. October 4, 1979, was the day the pope was coming to Iowa, to Living History Farms, for the first time ever, and Kate Meyer's good Catholic children intended to be there. The mother who raised them devout couldn't ask her sons and daughters to honor her above the pope, but she could arrange her own funeral to ensure their whereabouts on her birthday. There were no progeny of hers at Living History Farms that day to hear Pope John Paul II upbraid American Catholics for shirking their reproductive duties.

I arrived at this interpretation of my grandmother's death the day I learned she died; I still hold to it, but I no longer believe her prerogatives will be mine.

MONDAY, MAY 12:

When I first recognized the baby wrens, they were too small and weak to show any movement other than the rise and fall of their breathing, which looked like a gentle breeze blowing through cotton balls. But as soon as they were able to raise their heads, they kept them pointed up, beaks open to receive food, even when their mother was nowhere in sight. The same was true of the robins, so that all I could see from below were still, open beaks poking out of the nest. When Milena saw them like that one day, she rushed into the house shouting, "The birds are dead!" I assured her they were not, but later the same day, when she spotted a nest of robins in the rafters of Jodie's barn, she again said, "Oh, no, it's a dead bird." I teased her, suggesting something was awry in her unconscious if she kept mistaking newly hatched life for death. In fact, the motionless gaping does look like a last gasp frozen in place. At dinner tonight, with no prompting, Jodie's youngest son, Merc, mentioned that he was always thinking baby birds were dead when they weren't.

It is so hard to see straight. When I was in my twenties, friends often chided me for seeing the world through rose-tinted glasses. They claimed I was still, at heart, a good Catholic girl, Midwestern to the core, a demographically determined example of overweening innocence. I, of course, vehemently protested their version of me, and countercharged them with a facile cynicism born of East Coast provincialism. They granted me a certain sophistication of intellect, but insisted I had innocent eyes, incapable of seeing ugliness and brutality. One time I played into their hands by expressing my surprise at an Army recruiting poster mounted above the toilet in a friend's bathroom. Why, I asked, would an antiwar activist hang a rosy-cheeked, finger-pointing Uncle Sam on his wall? In the silence following the catcalls, I was asked to look again, but I still couldn't see what they apparently did. Finally an exasperated friend said, "Look, his cheeks aren't rosy, they're red." I literally hadn't seen the scraped, bloody cheeks and bandaged head that inflamed this apoplectic Uncle Sam.

Now, knowing how likely we are to see what we expect to see, I guard against seeing death where there is none. I don't want to turn nature into a private garden of metaphors, pruned and weeded to suit my moods. And so when I see the still, open beaks of baby birds, I don't allow myself to register the resemblance to death. Surely, I think, it is a projection, a pathos of my own making. It takes Milena's and Merc's uncensored response to alert me to the distortions in my corrected lens. The resemblance is there, the falsity nature's, not mine.

WEDNESDAY, MAY 14:

Mom has returned to Dr. Ye twice. She doesn't think much of the herbs he found for her, but the TENS machine has kept her pain at bay. Since Dr. Ye is not licensed to practice medicine in the United States, she asked the medical center to prescribe the $600 machine, so that she could be reimbursed by Blue Cross for its purchase. The anesthesiologist who performed both pain-causing nerve blocks on Mom was familiar with the device and happy to prescribe one. "They're very effective," he said, nine months too late.

There are several manufacturers of TENS machines, and Dr. Ye referred Mom to a St. Paul company that makes a particularly sophisticated one. Dad says that when he went to purchase the machine, he met the president of the company, whom he asked for advice on how best to use the machine, which can be set to emit electrical pulses of different frequencies that have different effects on various types of pain. The company president told him what he knew, but said that he in turn relied on Dr. Ye,

who had shown him ways to use the machine that were a rev-
elation to its designers. They've tried to hire Dr. Ye as a paid
consultant, but he doesn't seem to grasp the concept of information as private property.

FRIDAY, MAY 16:

I have finished painting the upstairs of the Ancram house, and
I am pleased, unequivocally, with the results. I found a paint
called Windchime that precisely matches the color of the new
growth on the spruce whose needles clog the gutter on the south
front corner of the house. When the branch tips of the spruce
mature and darken over the summer, their fresh spring color
will remain as window trim. I chose a minty off-white for the
walls, but when I began to apply it, the room threatened to take
on an undersea quality. Rather than apply two coats of paint and
let it dry overnight to confirm my fears, as I did downstairs, I
cut my losses immediately and switched to plain white. The mint
ended up on the walls of the adjacent bedroom, where, with
white trim, it conjures up gelato rather than aquarium water.
The foyer is white, with a trim called Italian Straw that looks,
yes, like straw, though I consider the color international.

My masterstroke, however, was what I didn't paint. When I
cleaned and scraped the upstairs window molding to prepare it
for Windchime, I uncovered several generations of previous
paint jobs—mostly browns and blues and creams. Not all of the
redecorators were fastidious; few had removed hardware before
painting, and some had not even bothered to remove the shades,
so certain pieces had stripes and patches of several different
colors. About halfway through my painting, when everything
was looking overwhelmingly new and clean, I began to miss the
motley. The solution was to leave the top pieces of window
molding as they were, a time capsule of earlier owners' efforts

at renewal. After all, mine is not the last word on this house; it's just the next word.

When I was finished, I was so dazzled by what I had wrought that I felt as I did on the beach in Vieques. I want Mom to see it. They talk of a visit this summer, but rather than wait on that hope, I drew a large, very precise floor plan of the house and pasted paint chips into the corresponding rooms. I did not send them a sample of RV092W. The soft palette upstairs induces such a feeling of calm and well-being in me that I can't stand walking downstairs into that gaudy riot of pink. I've found an off-white that promises me the color of magnolia blossoms, so I'll try again next week.

TUESDAY, MAY 20:

This afternoon, when there was a sudden drop in air pressure that lasted for about a half hour before a heavy rainstorm, the animals got weird again, as they did after the April snowfall. I had to slow or stop the car a dozen times between Glenco Mills and Ancram to avoid hitting birds, squirrels, rabbits, chipmunks, who were all behaving like chickens in the road.

On "Nova" the other night, there was a segment on Chinese seismology, on how they record observations of animal behavior and feed the data into computers to help predict earthquakes. I can see why. I don't know how far in advance the warning is, but creatures definitely sound an alarm when the sky is about to fall.

In the woods behind the Ancram house, I watched a blue jay chase a young squirrel from branch to branch of a tall elm until the squirrel finally lost its balance and crashed twenty feet to the ground. The thud was followed by a rustling of dry leaves, so I suppose the squirrel survived, no thanks to the jay, who deserves his reputation.

The painting is done at last. I broke the fever in the living room by applying an off-white called Magnolia, which may be the only well-named paint in the land. After six coats of paint, my new walls are an inch thicker than they were meant to be, but they no longer seem to be closing in for the kill.

The problem is the floor, whose boards are more splintered and cracked than I'd realized when they were under a carpet of plaster dust. Before I left for Edina last month, Bob persuaded me to let him lay a new floor in the renovated downstairs section of the house. He promised to complete the work while I was gone, but it's now one week before my rental in Glenco Mills expires, and he hasn't even begun. Each week, he says he'll begin next week, but after a month of broken promises, I no longer know what to expect of him. Bob worked so steadily all winter that I can't muster a satisfying degree of righteous anger now, but I do feel stranded. Today I called the company I hired to move my belongings from the city apartment to Ancram and told them I was postponing the move indefinitely. There's no point in trucking furniture to Ancram when there's no finished surface to set it on, and besides, I will have to live in the city until Bob lays the floor.

SUNDAY, JUNE 1:

Yesterday, after moving several carloads of bikes and sleds and books and clothes from Glenco Mills, I spent my first night in the Ancram house, sleeping on the new mattress I bought so I can camp out here until my furniture arrives from the city. When I woke up this morning, I had five exhilarating minutes watching the morning light filter through the silvery blue boughs of the spruce outside the bedroom window. Then I went downstairs. To wash my face, fix a cup of coffee, inaugurate the plumbing, introduce the basics of habitual life to my new house.

The faucets didn't yield a drop.

After a moment's panic, I rallied. Aha, I thought, the pump needs priming. I can handle that, astute home owner that I am, with the foresight to have asked Bob to show me how it's done. So I went to the basement and poured several coffee cans of bottled water through a funnel into the narrow pipe on top of the pump and screwed the pressure gauge back on with a wrench. Then I switched the pump back on and watched smugly as the needle on the gauge bounced up and down before settling in at thirty-pounds' pressure.

Enjoying a tingle of self-reliance, I climbed the stairs to the bathroom, turned on the faucets and waited for the clunks and groans of suddenly engorged pipes to turn into the soothing steady flow of tap water. But before the faucets even got to the spitting and coughing stage, the pressure died. I wanted a cup of coffee and I wanted Bob, but mostly I wanted the reassuring sight of water, if not flowing then standing. I decided to look into the well, not because I expected to find any answers there, but because I had exhausted my applicable home-repair knowledge and didn't know what else to do. At the very least, I thought, I can haul a few buckets of water from the well until I get the pump fixed.

Lifting the well cover is a two-person job, but I managed it without falling in, which is fortunate, because I would have tumbled to the bottom without anything to break my fall. When I've looked into the well before, the water has been within three or four feet of ground level, but today the sandy bottom of the well was clearly visible under only about a foot of water, enough for a sitz bath if the pump could be persuaded to draw it.

I called Clara, who professed amazement. She said her mother sometimes ran out of water in the middle of August if the house was full of well-showered and flushing guests, but never had such a thing happened in June. I called Bob, who promised to come see what he could do this afternoon, and then I introduced myself, bucket in hand, to my next-door neighbors, the Boyles.

"You run out of water already?" they said in greeting, without a shred of surprise in their voices. They filled my buckets and generously offered refills if I needed them, as long, that is, as their own supply lasted. Ancram, it seems, is notoriously dry. Even with a 400-foot well, the Boyles run out of water on wash days; the owner of The Grog Shop, they said, dug 800 feet and then dynamited before finding enough water to supply her home and business. There are rumors of 1,200-foot wells at The Oliver House Inn, where bed-and-breakfast guests are advised to check in clean and flush sparingly.

"Nobody told you?" the Boyles asked.

I devoted the rest of the day to learning the things nobody told me. Not all of Ancram is dry, just the village center, where washing machines are a rarity and daily showers a luxury. Watering the lawn is out of the question. Go a mile in any direction and your average 150-foot artesian well produces five to fifteen gallons a minute. In Ancram, the average artesian well is 400 feet deep and produces a miserly gallon or less a minute, which means one is always rationing. Well-diggers love to set up their rigs in Ancram, because they charge by the foot and so make as much money digging one well here as they do digging three or four wells anywhere else. And the deeper the well, the more powerful and expensive the pump they get to sell you. It seems, in short, that it will cost me as much to get a barely adequate water supply as it has cost me to renovate the entire house.

When Bob arrived at 2:00 P.M. I got my first sympathy of the day. He lives in Copake, eight miles north of here, and had never heard of Ancram's water problems; unlike the neighbors I talked to today, he did not seem to think I should have known better than to buy the house in the first place. He also advised me to try to make do with the old hand-dug well, at least for the summer, before undertaking the expense of drilling a deep well that might not produce much water either. He says I can install extra tanks to store water during times of plentiful rainfall for use during dry spells. What puzzles him is that this has been a wet spring—so where's the water?

His solution today was to lower the foot valve on the pipe through which the pump draws water from the well. The valve was above the water level today, which is why the pump could draw no water at all. He lowered it to within a few inches of the well bottom, which put it six inches under water. That will allow me to draw twenty-five gallons without losing pressure, and if I'm lucky, those twenty-five gallons will keep replenishing themselves as fast as I use them.

MANHATTAN
MONDAY, JUNE 2 :

It is strange to be living here again. When I arrived last night, I knocked on the door as if I expected the real owner to greet me. When I moved to Glenco Mills two years ago, I decided to rent my city apartment rather than sell it, because I was too attached to its quiet, airy rooms to let strangers fill them with noisy claims to permanence. Now there seems to be nothing of me here. I look at the furniture, found and refinished piece by piece over twenty years, and think how much more at home it will be in Ancram. I turn on the taps and hear something decadent in its unbroken wastrel's rush. I know it's crazy to prefer my bug-infested dry well to the generous abundance of New York City water, acclaimed the world's tastiest, but it's also convenient. I have no regrets about letting realtors traipse over the parquet floors, snoop in empty closets, fold back the white shutters to admire the rooftop gardens of the brownstones across the way. My territorial instincts are firmly attached elsewhere.

This month has left no mark on me. My Weekly Minder tells me I've had dinner with George and Kim at Claire's, lunch with Susie and Eden at Sagano's, drinks with Michael at The Museum Café, and a half dozen brunches on Columbus Avenue with friends and former colleagues. I've spent my time with people I like, but in ways I no longer enjoy, squandering money I don't want to squander on food I don't want to eat and drinks I don't want to drink. And I can't remember a thing that anyone said. Maybe it was the drinks. Or maybe I've become unfit for Manhattan, which, unlike a bicycle, requires skills that must be practiced.

I feel the way I did my first month in Manhattan, when I met so many people so quickly that by the end of a day I literally couldn't remember where I had been or whom I had seen. My brain circuitry was still attuned to Boston, to a leisurely life among a small circle of friends whose every word or act was registered in collective memory, subjected to group scrutiny and then mulled over privately. My Boston-trained synapses didn't know how to fire at Manhattan speed. If I couldn't reflect, I couldn't remember, and since there was no time for reflection, I became amnesiac for a month. I adjusted in short time, as every Manhattanite must, and even learned to relish the bombardment. In truth, I miss the stimulus of a wide acquaintance, but I seem to have lost my appetite for all the eating and drinking and rushing about it entails.

The only times I've felt at home in the city this month are from 10:30 to 11:00 each morning when alternate side of the street parking forces the city's harassed car owners out of their separate cells into the buzzing hive of block life. For a half hour we sit on our stoops or stroll the sidewalk, chatting about the weather as our eyes sweep the block for the telltale brown of traffic police uniforms. That mutual preoccupation prevents the true engagement of eye contact, but it allows for leisurely admiration of the block's dogs and baby strollers and window boxes. For a half hour, we are a small town. The rest of the day we are Manhattan's misfits, the people without offices, housewives and retirees and unemployed. We have no shoptalk. One woman whose last name I will never know went so far as to give me half a packet of her favorite morning glory seeds.

I am out of touch. I talk to Mom on the phone, but I don't know what she is saying. "I'm not too bad," she says. "Not much pain, really," she says. Usually I can hear or intuit or dream what she means, but not now. If she's sending me messages, I can't find the channel.

SUNDAY, JUNE 29:

I've opened my door to dozens of realtors who offer me the moon and deliver me not a single bid. I've dusted and packed the contents of six floor-to-ceiling bookcases, given away ten Hefty bags of clothes that I now admit will never fit again, severed my relations with AT&T and Citibank, postponed scores of decisions. Do I keep or toss the carton of research for my unfinished Ph.D. thesis, now covered with fifteen years of dust and gnawed at the edges by cockroaches apparently desperate for knowledge of the modern American novel? Do I keep or toss the love letters I once imagined posterity might weep over? What about the essays I wrote to earn my Marian Badge, the most-coveted award in Catholic girl scouting? Or the files from *Time* magazine for my never-written exposé of the way foreign news was manipulated during the days I considered Henry Kissinger my personal nemesis?

Should I cart those boxes of tarnished silverplate to the country for a tag sale? Is there still a market for lion-pawed butter dishes and monogrammed candlesnuffers, or should I get a quick divorce from these twenty-year-old wedding presents? Is it a sin to throw away engraved plaques and trophies one has been given in good faith for exemplifying the values of worthy organizations? What about the memorabilia from my days as the *Times'* historic first lady sports editor, my supposed claim to fame? Must I prize my honorary membership in The Touchdown Club of America, my expired press passes to locker rooms that nobody, including myself, wanted me to enter, except on principle?

I thought I had nothing to do here; I forgot how much I had to undo.

ANCRAM, N.Y.
TUESDAY, JULY 1:

Moving day. Bob's pegged pine floor looks great. The furniture looks like it was born here. Jodie's son, Zack, the self-appointed welcome committee, took it upon himself to tell the movers where to set down their burdens while Milena and I, blurry-eyed from an all-nighter of packing and tossing, sipped beer on the front porch and cursed the state trooper who caught us going seventy. Zack's fishing skills were well known to me, but nothing in his twelve-year-old deportment led me to expect his fine instincts for furniture arranging. Jodie was equally astounded and says his bedroom does not reflect the same discrimination.

I am trying not to dwell on the fact that there is still only a foot of water in the well.

MONDAY, JULY 7:

I drove to Taconic State Park today and lingered for an hour at the foot of Bash Bish Falls, dangling my feet in the swirls of its ice-cold pools and letting its spray bathe my upturned, worshipful face. I would gladly dedicate a lifetime of novenas to the water gods if only they would look kindly on my poor, poor well. Can't this county, crisscrossed by streams and dotted with ponds, spare one small seam of its aquifer for me?

I have learned to manage with my pittance, but it takes more time and ingenuity than anyone should have to expend on survival in an industrialized country in peacetime. During dry spells I eke about twenty-five gallons a day from the well, enough for six flushes or two five-minute showers or one dinner party. For a while I tried to recycle dirty dishwater for flushing, but the toilet tank began to smell like a salad bowl well rubbed with garlic, so I stationed four thirty-gallon garbage cans under the downspouts at each corner of the house to catch rainfall. From these I flush. Four gallons per flush. Men and boys to the bushes.

What water reaches my rain barrels doesn't stay clean enough for bathing, but I've found a secluded spot on the Roe/Jan two miles south of the house where the water is chest high and the streambed sandy. I've actually come to enjoy that fresh creek-washed feeling, despite my guilt for subjecting the fish downstream to occasional gulps of shampoo suds. I spare them on days when it rains by standing directly under the drain pipe that siphons water off the porch roof. My porches are front porches, which puts me in clear view of passersby, but I'd rather be clean than inconspicuous. Most of the village knows my plight and I presume their understanding.

FRIDAY, JULY 11:

I seem to have three regulars who visit the backyard—a cardinal, a chipmunk and a rabbit. Many of the other birds—mostly chickadees, house finches and sparrows—are probably also regulars, but they are not so easy to distinguish as individuals. The cardinal often perches on the dogwood tree and makes frequent use of the feeder I've hung from the lilac bush. At first he would take flight as soon as he spotted me through the kitchen window, but now he keeps on munching even when I'm sitting outside on the deck watching him.

The rabbit usually forages near the tree stump about twenty

yards uphill from the house. I've watched many times as he lets Merc get within two or three feet of him before quick-hopping into the brush. But whenever I approached him, he fled when I was still ten feet away. In the past I approached him very quietly, taking two or three slow steps, then stopping to show I meant no harm. Always at ten feet, he ran. Today I changed tactics. I simply strode uphill toward him as I would toward a person, talking out loud in flattering and reassuring phrases like "Don't worry, bunny, I won't hurt you, I just want to get closer because you're so beautiful." He let me get within three feet. My quiet, respectful approach must have seemed like a hunter's stealth. Flattery got me farther, but still not all the way.

The chipmunk hangs out under the bird feeder on the lilac bush and scarfs up whatever seeds the birds drop. Sometimes it seems like an active collaboration, with the sparrows scratching seed over the feeder's ledge to the chipmunk waiting below. I can't figure out what's in it for the birds, though. Maybe it's sheer extortion—I'll leave your nest alone if you kick me back some seed.

Anyway, when I came into the yard the other day, the chipmunk kept on feeding after the birds had scattered, so I approached him. At two feet, he retreated to the base of the lilac bush, where two main branches form a V. He stood his ground there and stared at me. I took one more step and he dematerialized. I blinked, looked again and saw an inch-wide hole at the point of the V. I crouched on my knees to peer into the hole and saw a chipmunk snout twitching at me. He had retreated only a couple inches into his burrow. I stood up and he stuck his head out. We both seemed pleased to make acquaintance, but since I didn't know where to take the relationship, I left after a few moments and returned to the house.

When curiosity brought me outside again fifteen minutes later, the chipmunk stopped eating and struck a prairie dog pose in front of his hole. I walked right up and crouched down in front of him; he backed half of himself into the hole but left his head and forepaws out, like an Italian lady taking in the street from her window. After a while, he backed all the way into his burrow, but without haste, much, I imagine, in the same spirit as I had earlier returned to my kitchen. We had run out of things to say to each other. I poured a small mound of seed outside his front door and left him alone.

THURSDAY, JULY 17:

I am beginning to notice the differences among sparrows. Most of the time, I see them as a blur of browns and grays, but if I force myself to concentrate, I spy a black mask on one, a yellow eye patch on another. Some wear rusty caps and others prison stripes on their heads. I can't yet match their marks to names— say which is a song sparrow and which a field—but I do begin to respect their variousness. And yet I am not such a democrat that my attention is not easily drawn from them to more glamorous species. While watching the sparrows at the feeder this afternoon, I heard a racket in the sky and looked up to see a crow dive-bombing a red-tailed hawk. The hawk's wing span was at least twice the crow's, and he could cover more sky with one tilt than the crow could with a dozen flaps, but the crow was the attacker and after a half dozen strikes, he drove the hawk out of Ancram and the sparrows out of my mind. If I ever found a religious order, I will make the novices practice the moral discipline of fixing their eyes on sparrows while hawks soar overhead.

MONDAY, JULY 21:

Most of the rainfall this month has been in the form of light showers, but this afternoon we had a sky-ripping thunderstorm. I was so excited at the prospect of replenished rain barrels that I ran from one corner of the house to the next inspecting the flow from the downspouts. Three of the four gushed, but the spout on the left front side of the house was withholding its bounty. I rushed inside and upstairs to check out the situation from the bedroom window. A solid wall of rain was spilling over the front side of the gutter onto the porch roof, bypassing both the gutter downspout and the siphon hole in the porch, which was clogged with needles from the spruce. I climbed out the window onto the flat porch roof to see what I could improvise. Two gutter straps were pulling loose from the angled house roof, but when I tilted the gutter level and pounded the straps back into place with my fist, a fifteen-foot length of water-filled gutter emptied itself straight down the spout and into my barrel.

Drenched but happy, I turned my attention to the porch drain on the outer edge of the porch roof. Kneeling with my back to the just-fixed gutter, I poked a stick into the siphon hole to clear it of needles, but before I could finish the job, I was knocked flat and nearly washed off the roof by a sudden blow of water to my back. The two fist-pounded gutter straps had broken completely free of the house roof, sending an enormous weight of water down on me. I crawled to the window and stood up against the house, my back pressed against it for safety as I watched a virtual waterfall of rain splash in front of me. I wanted that water in my barrels so badly that I stepped forward and lifted the sagging gutter over my head, holding it level. Once again the water rushed smoothly on its appointed course to the downspout.

I was prepared to stay in that position all day if it would bring me a week of anxiety-free flushing. I knew how ridiculous I must look, a flesh-and-blood caryatid supporting her crumbling temple, braving the lightning and thunder of more powerful gods. That train of thought, and a sudden blinding flash, brought me to my senses. How stupid can I be? I'm willing to be a human gutter strap but not a human lightning rod, my outstretched arms and legs a conduit between metal roof and metal gutter. I let the gutter go, dumping another several gallons on my head, and climbed back through the open window into the house that isn't worth dying for.

I am having trouble explaining trout fishing to my city friends. They think it either idleness or blood lust, and can't imagine why I spend so much time in its pursuit. When they visit, I equip them for the stream, but they are bored within twenty minutes and look at me very strangely when I return home hours after they've resorted to more fail-safe diversions, like porch sitting, book in hand.

They don't feel the fascination of a stream, but then, neither did I before I began fishing. Oh, I was dazzled by the flow and sparkle, but that can be taken in at first glance, and unless you're in the mood to be hypnotized, it's not enough to hold one's attention for long. I only began to see things when I tried to think like a trout. The game of hide-and-seek we play is so stacked in the trout's favor that I must be as alert and wily as my inferior senses allow just to catch sight of him. When I approach the stream, I must step softly or he will pick up the vibration of my footfalls on the bank, sent express from my boots through the water to him. On sunny days, I must notice where shadows fall, so I can hide my own among those cast by the trees, or he will know a large, ungainly creature has darkened his shimmering world.

Before entering the stream, I sit on the bank for a while to see what insects are swarming above the water. I turn over rocks in the streambed to see who's living there. I am not a strict imitationist, but if I can't approximate the size and shape, color and movement of something above, below or on the surface of the water, I might as well surrender my hopes for the day. I have tried expressionist flies, but they work only on expressionist fish, like bass, who will leap for any gaudy bauble when they're in the mood. Trout have more refined tastes.

Even a finicky trout must eat, though, and he can't expend more energy getting food than the food supplies, or he will waste away to nothing; he must find some quiet spot and let the food come to him. This knowledge is my only edge, so once in the stream, I scan the surface of the water for variations in its flow. I look for large boulders above and below the surface, for fallen logs and indentations in the bank, anything that interrupts the flow of the stream, creating pockets of still water on its down-stream side where a trout can rest without struggling against the current. I approach such places with great stealth, staying in the shadows when possible, inching my boots along the slippery, moss-covered rocks of the streambed, checking in all directions for overhanging branches that might snag my fly before it reaches its target. Wind permitting, I try to cast my fly just upstream from where I suspect the trout will be so my tempting morsel will float right past him.

If my fly lands on the water more indelicately than a gnat would, the older, wiser, larger trout will let it pass and I'll never know what I've missed. There are no second chances with an experienced trout; the merest suspicion of a predator in the vicinity and he will not risk revealing his hideout by taking any insect, hand-tied or God-made, for hours. I might trick a six-inch native trout or even a ten-inch stocked trout, a newcomer to the stream raised in the sheltering walls of a hatchery, but to catch a veteran trout, twelve inches or more, I must be perfect and I seldom am. I may move soundlessly through the water for twenty yards, stirring not a ripple as I approach a likely spot, and then stumble just as I'm about to cast, sending a tidal wave of warning to even the most innocent stockie. Or my wrist may betray me and shoot the line out so fast it slaps the surface of the water or lands in a spiraling jumble, as if I'd cast the web as well as the fly.

When I'm fishing well, my concentration is so intensely fo-cused on the surface of the stream that I enter a kind of trance, from which I emerge startled by some sudden sound or change in light. I'll look up, as if just awakened from a dream, and see a great blue heron taking flight at my approach, the tips of his spindly legs lagging three feet behind his crested head, curled claws still skimming the surface of the water. One hazy afternoon, I looked up, reentered time and felt a sudden searing stab of fear. Day had departed unnoticed by me and the last rays of the setting sun shot horizontally through the woods toward me like the beams of a motorcycle gang waiting in silent ambush.

Often, on clear days, I'll see a cardinal fly across the stream ahead of me, a streak of red against blue sky for an instant before he's lost again in the green world of the other bank. Every time, I think of the passage from Venerable Bede about the flight of the sparrow through the mead hall. Bede likened the sparrow's flight from door to door to the brevity of man's life on earth. I too am reminded of mortality, but, midstream on a sunlit day, I have no complaint. If the cardinal's flight from bank to bank were less fleeting, it would also be less glorious. Midstream, it seems all right to die; sickness is the sin.

FRIDAY, AUGUST 1:

There is too little news from Edina. I know that Mom is out of pain, thanks to Dr. Ye's continued ministrations. She returned to him in June when the TENS machine had reduced but not eliminated her back pain. He stuck two needles in her back and sent an electrical charge through them. Two weeks later, he repeated the sticking and Mom has felt no pain since. In July Mom went to the medical center for a routine round of tests and the doctors there found nothing to alarm them. I have let these facts lull me into a convenient complaisance, which our daily phone calls reinforce. Mom and Dad sound no alarms, but they are probably too worn down by the tedium of their daily struggle to raise their voices above faint complaint.

Mom's distress is not dramatic, just a slow, steady erosion of weight and energy—"Not much zip" is how she puts it—that the doctors say they can't account for. The conclusion she draws, without saying so, is that she is to blame for her own physical worthlessness.

MONDAY, AUGUST 4:

My forty-first birthday. I spent the day alone, by choice. If I had made the occasion known, Jodie and the boys, who have adopted me as sibling to both generations of their makeshift family, would have been eager to celebrate, but I wanted a day as minimal as Mom's seventy-fifth, which passed quietly one month ago on the Fourth of July.

I got the present I wanted though. At five o'clock, a realtor called with a firm bid on my city apartment. The buyer is a lawyer, and, with the realtor as intermediary, we negotiated the first dozen details by phone this evening. Their bid is 20 percent below the asking price, 10 percent below what I told realtors I would accept, but I am so desperate to get that apartment off my mind I have entertained night thoughts of simply walking away from it and the $1,000 a month I pay to own its empty rooms. My sense of relief may be premature, but I called Edina with the news and made plans to visit as soon as contracts are signed.

EDINA, MINN.
FRIDAY, AUGUST 15:

Mom is a wraith, ninety-five pounds of bruised flesh and spirit. Last week she fell several times, which the doctors say is nothing to worry about. It's probably just the side effects of Elavil and prednisone, two drugs they prescribed to elevate her mood and appetite. Elavil causes changes in blood pressure that make her light-headed when she rises from a seated position, and when she crashes dizzy to the ground, the prednisone causes huge blood bruises to form on her skin. Her legs are splotched black and magenta from ankle to knee.

The fear of falling naturally makes her hesitant to walk any more than is absolutely necessary, which weakens her muscles further and makes her prone to more falls. She has so little strength in her thighs that she has to inch herself forward to the edge of a seat and then push against the chair arms as hard as she can to raise herself. There is a precarious moment between sitting and standing when she looks like she is going to pitch forward, and sometimes she has. Her walk is wobbly, any slight unevenness in surface a hazard, but she doesn't want help and she refuses to consider a cane. She won't even use one of the hickory walking sticks Dad made for their mushroom hunting.

She spends most of her time on the green chair in the living room just staring into space. Sometimes she seems to be reading, but I've seen her fix her eyes on an open magazine for an hour without ever turning a page. It's just a prop, probably for my benefit. Today I asked her if she got bored sitting so much, and she said, "No, not really. Oh, sometimes I do, but I don't let it get to me." I asked her what she thinks about when she sits and gazes. "Oh, a lot of things," she said. "Mostly I think about all the things I'll do when I'm well again."

Her desires are not born of regret for missed opportunities. She just wants to do ordinary things, go window shopping at Southdale's, take a walk around Lake Cornelia, have lunch out with her neighbor Verna. She doesn't want more out of life than it's given her; she just wants more life.

MONDAY, AUGUST 18:

I bought a pair of khaki pants and a matching jacket for myself this afternoon. When I modeled the outfit for Mom, she liked it so much she asked me to get her one just like it, "for the fall." I thought the safari look would seem odd on a very, very frail, ninety-five-pound, seventy-five-year-old woman, but I returned to Southdale's and bought a size 5 version of my new clothes. The pants look fine on her. The heavy cotton material is substantial enough to hold its own shape on her whippet-thin legs, lending the appearance of muscle to her flesh. The jacket, however, which has pads that extend Mom's shoulders a good six inches, looks like it's wearing her. I thought the effect was ridiculous, and under the circumstances, pathetic, but Dad loved the look of Mom in the jacket, the illusion of the jaunty and robust woman who climbed the hills of Tuscany with him last summer.

THURSDAY, AUGUST 21:

Mom is starting to talk funny. Tonight, as I was leaving to pay Freya a visit, she said, "That's a straight shot out Route One Hundred, isn't it?" Yesterday, when I inquired about a friend's drinking problem, she said, "He's better now, but he still gets pretty tanked up sometimes." When Dad brought news of a storm warning last night, Mom said, "How do you know? Did they run a crawl?" How did she know? Even I, a former media maven, didn't know the term for those messages that scroll across the bottom of the television screen.

Mom has always been a woman who knows more than she lets on, but I never suspected she was hoarding a cache of slang. Iowa colloquialisms, yes, like "I'll be there in two shakes of a dog's hind leg" or "It's raining pitchforks and hammer handles" or, her highest accolade, "You look clean as a bandbox." But slang, never. Maybe she's using it now as a way of reminding us not to underestimate her. She may look out of it, lost in her gaze, but she is still a woman of this world, however constricted her sphere.

I was slow to appreciate Mom's intelligence but not as slow as she was. Whenever anyone praised Mike's and my school records, Mom would always say, "Well, I guess they inherited their dad's brains." She confuses intelligence with a college degree, and her lack of one is her sorest, perhaps her only, regret. She graduated from high school in 1930, a bad year for aspirations of any sort. Two of her three older sisters were already in college, but that year her father announced he would find money to send his sons to college and any daughter who promised to become a schoolteacher. Mom couldn't make that promise in good conscience, and even if she had, her father could not have made good on his. A year later he was pumping gas in Fort Dodge, his farm foreclosed by the bank that had lost his life savings in its bust. A local family who knew my mother's reputation for winning spelling bees offered to send her to college, but my grandfather's pride couldn't accept another bruise.

I know Mom left the farm at eighteen to seek her fortune in Chicago, but I don't know what she found there. She holds that time as a very close secret. My most persistent prying has yielded only vague outlines of a Dreiserian tale. As I understand it, Mom and a new friend were taken up by the friend's rich uncle, who offered them rooms in his luxurious home and introduced them to a world outside the reach of most salesgirls. Something burst the bubble and sent Mom back to Iowa, where she worked her way up from salesgirl to buyer, waiting for a man who could provide safe escort to big cities. There's a suggestion she discovered that the rich uncle made his money in an unseemly way, most likely from bootlegging, but not a word about the enticements he must have offered two beautiful young girls.

Newt is her college man, her visa to a wider world, and we children are his inheritors, our achievements nurtured by her but reflections of him. She still believes this.

Once, when I had absorbed the merest rudiments of palmistry to enhance my party skills, I looked at Mom's hand and exclaimed over the length of her head line, palmistry's index of native intelligence. She took such clear delight in this small confirmation of her value that I told her how much of my academic ease I attributed to her genes. She blushed with pleasure before handing the compliment to Dad, in her mind the rightful recipient. To her, the fact that she read every book Mike or I ever brought home from school, through his medical training and my graduate studies, was no compensation for her lack of documentation.

I still send her copies of the books I am reading; it's been one of our lifelines, linking us with words and images that fill our heads and inform our eyes.

SUNDAY, AUGUST 24:

It was a beautiful summer day, all cloudless blue sky and soft breezes. Mom spent the morning in her easy chair with the Sunday paper, doing a simple leg-lift exercise I suggested to help strengthen her thighs. After lunch, Dad left to take a walk round Lake Cornelia, and Mom, openly envious, said she would like to go outside for a while. She wanted sun, not shade, so I moved two lawn chairs from their station under the tall oak near the kitchen door and set them deeper in the yard, beside a bed of dahlias in full scarlet bloom. I watched as she struggled out of the easy chair and walked from the living room through the kitchen with the concentration of a drunk determined to prove his sobriety. She let me help her down the short step-off from the kitchen door to the yard, but she wanted to negotiate the fifteen yards from door to lawn chairs by herself.

We sat side by side, and I watched her, eyes closed, face upturned to catch every particle of sunlight. She was rapt, as pure a portrait of contentment as she had been last summer when I watched her taking the sun on the villa patio from my perch in the open arch of the loggia above her. After an hour, she said she thought she had better go in. She stood with difficulty, and took my right arm for support as we walked slowly toward the house. I kept my eyes fixed on her every step, and yet I didn't see her fall. One instant she was clamped to my side; the next she was sprawled on the grass looking up at me with shock and confusion in her startled eyes.

Time stopped as the image sank deep into the part of memory that stores a moment photographically, forever. The exact shadowless green of the grass, the light-filled blue of her wide-open unflecked eyes, the flatness of her back against the ground, the bend of her knees. My mind registered horror and my eyes a strange beauty. I saw my mother, helpless, and I saw a woman lying in the grass on a clear summer day.

She was not hurt but she was pinned in place by her weakness. "How will I ever get up?" she asked in genuine consternation. She couldn't imagine that anyone but Dad was strong enough to lift her. "That's not a problem," I said, and then I bent down, lifted her to her feet in one effortless movement and gave her my arm for the walk to the door. I became her hero for a moment, bold and strong. I wished for a cape to lay at her feet.

TUESDAY, AUGUST 26:

I return to New York tomorrow, my departure excused by problems that have arisen in the sale of the apartment. The buyers are concerned about several lawsuits brought against the building by former owners who are challenging the 15 percent profit tax the board exacted from them upon sale. We—Mom, Dad and I—are pretending my presence in New York will somehow allay the buyers' fears about a possible costly settlement from the building's coffers. In truth I am leaving because I don't know what else to do. I feel useless, as I always do by the end of a visit here.

There are few ways I can be of genuine help, other than as a morale booster, and my own morale sinks so low after a week that I become part of the problem. At first my arrival is uplifting, a change, diversion, occasion for rallying, but within days, I am struggling against my own depression. I have no world of my own here, and so cannot bring the stimulus of other lives to their cloister. If they still lived in Evanston, I would renew old friendships, frequent old haunts and bring back stories to entertain them. But in Edina, removed by a thousand miles from everything that occupies and sustains me, I become as confined as they are. I lose what resources I have to withstand the grimness. If I could walk in the stream for an hour, or rest my eyes on a beloved landscape, or sit silently with a close friend, maybe I would feel replenished. As it is, I am all inadequacy, a helpless bystander to their feats of endurance.

Tonight I cooked dinner, hoping to add an ounce to Mom and please her palate with the kind of sauces I know she enjoys. I broiled lamb chops and steamed fresh asparagus, as I have done to perfection countless times. She came to the table expecting a treat. I gave her tough meat, stringy asparagus and flavorless sauces. I have never served such a meal in my life; I couldn't repeat the performance if I tried. I apologized but I can't forgive myself.

OPEN EYES

ANCRAM, N.Y.

THURSDAY, SEPTEMBER 11:

The well has been dry all week. I have not had a drop of water from my faucets for eight days. I bathe in the creek. I flush with the little water left in my rain barrels. I finally found a man who agreed to go down into the well and dig it a little deeper. This afternoon he went down into that dark hole and came up with a dead rat.

On the six-o'clock news, I learned that the stock market fell eighty-six points. I panicked and sold everything.

I laughed a lot today and then went to sleep and dreamed this dream.

I dreamt that Mom and Dad and Mike and I were supposed to be leaving for a long car trip, but that a series of delays had pushed back the hour of our departure until the wee hours of the morning. I was concerned that Dad was going to be too tired to drive safely and was trying to find Mike so that we could get going at last. I found Mike in a barn and was urging him to hurry up when I saw Mom and Dad waiting in a car on the country road that went by the barn. As we walked toward the car, it began moving away from us, which puzzled me for a moment, and then I realized that Dad was asleep at the wheel.

I grabbed Mike by the arm and said, "Look, Dad's driving in his sleep. We've got to do something before they get hurt." Mike didn't respond, and I could now see that Mom was awake and pounding on Dad but she was too frail to rouse him. I was still trying to mobilize Mike when I saw the car go crashing through a wooden fence and enter a field.

I started running toward the car with superhuman speed, desperate to reach it before they were killed. As I gained on the car, I saw that it had been transformed into a pickup truck, and Dad, awakened by the crash through the fence, was driving it like a bucking bronco. The truck was lurching into the air and crashing down again, wheels skidding and spinning. Dad was grinning at his stunts like a drunken cowboy, and Mom, terrified and in pain from having her wracked body tossed around in the truck, was beating her fists against Dad, trying to get him to stop. The look on his face was bullheaded and sadistic, as if he had lost his mind.

Racing after the truck, I leapt onto the running board and tried to wrest control of the steering wheel from Dad. Mom was crying, "I can't take it anymore. I can't stand it. I can't stand it." There was a look of extreme physical pain and despair on her face, as if this last, cruelest blow, her protector turned tormentor, had broken her spirit utterly. As I struggled with Dad for the wheel, I looked at her and said, "It's going to be okay. I'm here now. I'm going to take control. It will be okay." She looked straight at me, her face streaked with tears, our eyes locked, and she let me see she had no hope. She knew I couldn't make it okay. I woke up screaming. And I knew she was right. Her suffering cannot be borne. It is insupportable, obscene. The horror is not death. The horror is pain and disintegration.

I called home today and Dad said he had driven Mom to the emergency room in the middle of the night. She had been unable to urinate for forty-eight hours and was in such extreme discomfort that they went to have her catheterized. On the way home from the hospital, she vomited all over herself and the car. Dad described in detail how he had spent the morning cleaning the car and Mom's clothes and the blanket that had covered her. He spoke in a loud voice, sounding impatient, disgusted, and I imagined Mom, in earshot, eyes steely with pride and suppressed anger.

I was so depressed by my dream and the call that seemed to make it true that I was unable to summon the energy demanded by another day without water. Finally, about four in the afternoon, I forced myself to drive over to a friend's vacant house for a shower. Tears ran down my face as I drove, and they continued running as I showered. I didn't will them and I couldn't stop them.

When I got back in the car to drive on to Hudson, the sun came out, the county road turned west and I was given a glorious view of the Catskills in clear September light. The tears stopped. Seconds later, I saw a long black snake twisting in the road ahead of me. I swerved, not because I didn't want to hit the snake, but because I didn't want it to hit me. It felt like a vicious attack, and I was stunned, scared, then angry. Why, why, why was I being confronted with my phobias now? Why on this road, at this moment, when I needed to find the courage to face so many real fears?

SATURDAY, SEPTEMBER 13:

Dad says Mom refuses to eat. She will only take enough liquid to get her pain pills down.

TUESDAY, SEPTEMBER 16:

I'm on a People's Express flight to Minneapolis. Mike thinks Mom has only a few days left, and I can't tell whether his sense of emergency comes from a doctor's trained judgment or a son's panic. It seems to me he periodically stirs up a false sense of crisis to break through his own neglect of the ongoing agony. He may be doing that again, but I can't take the risk of discounting his warning. Besides, it's clear that whether these are the final days or not, Mom's medical needs have become too complicated and demanding for Dad to handle alone. Mom has not eaten solid food since Thursday, and last night she threw up the water she drank to take her painkiller. Dad sounds exhausted, demoralized, without the energy to exercise good judgment. Yesterday morning on the phone, he said, "I think it would be good if you could come out in the next day or two." That's the closest he has come to asking for help since this ordeal began a year ago.

Sunday night was the first time anyone suggested to me that Mom's latest symptoms might signal the return and spread of cancer rather than the continual shifting side effects from drugs and radiation. Mike drew this conclusion from Dad's description of Mom's condition and a phrase Mom's local oncologist apparently used when Dad consulted with her on Friday—"That's typical of this cancer." Dad was unsure what she meant by the phrase, and despite repeated calls from both Dad and Mike, the doctor has not explained herself, has not returned calls.

On Sunday Mike said that unless he got information that relieved his anxiety, he planned to fly to Minneapolis on Wednesday or Thursday. Yesterday I waited all day for a call from Mike that never came, because he was waiting for a call from Mom's doctor that never came. About 2:30 in the afternoon I called Dad and that's when he said, "I think it would be good if you came out."

About 9:30 last night I called Mike, and he very calmly said he had moved his flight up to today, because he didn't want to risk arriving "too late." He said he thought Mom might die within the next twenty-four hours and Dad thought so too. The doctor had still not returned his calls, so there was no new medical information, but Mike had been alarmed when Dad told him that Mom had slept all day.

I called Dad immediately and his first words were "Mom had a much better day today. There's no need to rush out here." He was relieved because Mom seemed more "comfortable" today; the long, deep sleeps, which alarmed Mike, reassured Dad.

After talking to Mike and Dad I tried to sort out what I had heard. Mike thinks Mom could die within days or hours. Dad seems to think there is no immediate danger. Mom's doctor, the only one with certain medical information, isn't answering calls. Common sense tells me that if Mom hasn't eaten in five days and can't even keep water down, some remedy has to be found fast. I could have advised Dad to take Mom to the hospital for intravenous feeding, but I didn't. I was afraid that if Mike were right and she were taken to the hospital, she might never return home again. So I did not disturb Dad's sense that Mom's sleeping means improvement.

Since talking to Mike last night my mood has been eerily calm. My energy has been channeled into the logistics of "getting there," and since I really do not know what to expect, I don't want to exhaust myself with anticipatory mourning. I also think my mood may be calm now because I went through this crisis last week, when I woke up screaming in the night. That dream has stayed with me. It made me feel that the time of denial is ending, the time of death approaching.

Yesterday Dad greeted me at the airport with the news that Mom was much improved. She had eaten solid food—toast and a boiled egg—so the sense of immediate crisis had abated while I was in flight. Whatever was obstructing the movement of food into and out of her stomach has relented for the time being, which means it isn't a tumor. The intestinal turmoil of the past two weeks may have been caused by the antibiotics they mistakenly gave Mom the first time she went to the emergency room to be catheterized. They tested her for a urinary tract infection, got a positive result and prescribed antibiotics. A few days later, when the doctor questioned the diagnosis, they retested her and determined that she had not had an infection; the urine sample had been contaminated in the hospital.

Whatever caused her distress, the change in Mom is marked. When I was here three weeks ago, Mom was becoming too weak to get into and out of a seated position by herself, but once she was standing, she could walk from room to room by herself. She was wobbly, and falls were a constant danger, but she could move around on her own. Now she is virtually bedridden, with moves from the sofa to the bathroom or bedroom a major joint effort by her and Dad. Mom is physically incapable of standing on a scale to weigh herself, and there is no motive to do so now that the results could only be discouraging, but I would guess she weighs ninety pounds or less.

She spends most of the day asleep on the small sofa in the den. The room is small and dark, and the sofa is too short for her to extend her legs fully. Yesterday I asked her if she wouldn't be more comfortable on the longer, living-room sofa, where she could stretch out and look out the window. "No," she said, "I don't like the living room. It's too big."

Reducing the space and light around her seems a way of gradually shutting down, letting go. She doesn't seem to want much stimulus of any kind. She does not look at the newspaper anymore and the sound of the television, even on low volume in other rooms, annoys her. A little bit of conversation goes a long way.

Now that her intestines are functioning again, she says that she does not have any chronic discomfort, but at times she is stabbed by sharp pains near her ribs. The jabs take her breath away and contort her face, but they come and go so fast that she almost seems not to mind them. If she is talking when one jabs her, it turns her speech into a kind of stutter ("I—*wince*—would like—*wince*—some—*wince*—co—*wince*—Coke"). She responds to the pain as a polite person would to a rude interruptor. She doesn't let it stop her sentences from proceeding, she doesn't let it change her train of thought, she just waits for the opportunity to reassert herself.

Last night, about 6:00 P.M., when Dad and I were in the kitchen exchanging news of what had happened in the last week, Mom suddenly piped up from the den and expressed a desire for Swanson's Chicken à la King on biscuits. Since this was the first time she had expressed an active desire to eat, her wish was our command. Earlier in the afternoon the three of us had drawn up a long grocery list of things Mom might want to eat, but as soon as she stated this preference, Dad suggested I go immediately to the nearest supermarket, forget the other items and rush back with the chicken à la king. The fire drill began.

I literally ran to the car, broke speed limits getting to the supermarket, endangered several innocent shoppers as I whizzed my cart to aisle 6—canned meat—only to find the shelves devoid of chicken à la king. There were a couple dozen cans of Swanson's Chicken and Dumplings, and I grabbed three of them as poor substitutes before charging cart first after a young man putting cans of beans onto the shelves of aisle 8. Breathlessly, I asked him if there might possibly be more cans of Swanson's Chicken à la King in a back room. He looked at me coldly and let it be known that there was no back room with hidden cans of chicken à la king or anything else. Everything they had was on the shelves for the whole world to see. I found that hard to believe, so I rounded the corner into produce and asked the man stacking green peppers if he knew where they kept the extra chicken à la king. He gave me the same answer as the first fellow but seemed more sympathetic to my unexplained but clearly desperate need for chicken à la king. He suggested I try the Country Boy Supermarket on York Avenue and gave me directions for getting there by the shortest route.

Belatedly realizing that I didn't need a cart for three cans of chicken and dumplings, I ran to the express check-out and waited impatiently as the three people in front of me wrote checks for their items. I muttered something about how, where I come from, check writing is not allowed in express lines. When my turn came, I gave the check-out clerk exact change and, without waiting to have my cans bagged, ran to the car and burnt rubber getting out of the parking lot exit nearest York Avenue and the Country Boy.

When I had parked, slammed the car door shut and begun my sprint toward the store's open doors, a man in the Country Boy parking lot shouted, "Hey, lady, you left your lights on." I gave him an annoyed look, but rather than explain I was in a big hurry to get a can of chicken à la king before my mother lost her appetite again, I ran back and turned off my lights, cursing myself all the while for whatever character flaw was making me respond to this stranger's directions. When I entered the store, instinct led me straight to the right aisle, saving me the usual twenty minutes of reconnoitering an unknown supermarket. I beamed at the sight of those blue and yellow cans, grabbed three and made it home by 6:30 P.M.

Dad, seeing the three back-up cans of chicken and dumplings, said, "Oh, that looks good. Let's have that." Too incredulous to protest, I simply said, "I don't think it will be as good as the chicken à la king on fresh, hot biscuits." Dad said, "Oh, I think it might be good," and took a can of dumplings into the den to show Mom. "Doesn't this look good, Bea?" he asked, clearly trying to tip her decision. Mom, acquiescent, said, "Oh, that'd be fine, I guess." So I shrugged my shoulders, heated up some chicken and dumplings and served a small plateful to Mom. After sampling it, she said, "It's not too bad. The biscuits would have been better." I felt a keen pang of failure, and fury at Dad, who sat in a chair at Mom's side eating a plateful of the soggy, doughy dumplings. "Very tasty," he said, as I silently steamed.

I did not eat any dinner, but at midnight, after picking Mike up at the airport, I heated a frozen pizza for him to snack on. It was a plain cheese pizza, so I doctored it with onions, green peppers, garlic salt, hot red pepper and Parmesan cheese. I offered Mom a piece. To our amazement, she ate it, red pepper and all.

THURSDAY, SEPTEMBER 18:

This afternoon Mike and I used a trip to the rental car agency at the airport as a way to talk privately. He says he thinks Mom has a month or two to live, that there is no immediate medical crisis, but he expects a gradual weakening and diminishment to take its course. He could be wrong, of course. He could also be right.

Dad told me that one of the young emergency room doctors, when told that Mom had been treated for pancreatic cancer a year ago, opened his eyes wide, looked straight at Mom and said, "Gee, I've never seen anyone living a year later." Dad told the story with pride, as proof of Mom's durability.

This afternoon, while Mike and I were discussing Mom's likely life span, Dad was bathing her, dressing her and helping her apply makeup for a surprise appearance at the dinner table. She joined us for a meal of spaghetti with meat sauce, which seemed a stunning accomplishment for a woman who only yesterday had trouble raising her head by herself.

After dinner, she went to the living-room sofa rather than the den. Did she really want this change of venue or was she just putting on a display of getting stronger for Mike and me? At one point, while she was napping and I was reading in a chair across the room from her, I heard groaning and looked up. Her right leg had slipped off the sofa in her sleep and she was struggling to raise it back up. I went over to help her, and Mom, looking sheepish, said, "That's pretty bad, isn't it?"

Tonight, when Mom went to bed, I noticed that she put her dentures on the night table. I remembered how this time last year she balked at removing them even for surgery, saying that no one, including Dad, had ever seen her without teeth and she wanted to keep it that way. But now she has lost so much weight that the dentures don't fit well. The loose fit irritates her gums and makes eating difficult, but she is not strong enough to undergo the process of getting fitted for new ones. When I talked to Dad about this problem, he said he had to repowder her dentures a dozen times a day now because the fit is so bad. This indignity must have altered their relation more than any other detail of her illness. This spring Mom was willing to endure extreme pain in order to go to the beauty parlor "for Dad." She has fought hard to maintain her vanity throughout this ordeal, and now it is being wrenched from her. That, more than any other loss, puts her and Dad in different worlds. Dad is among the living. Mom belongs to the dying. I think they have each accepted that in the last two weeks.

Mom doesn't talk about dying though. She talks about getting better and is dismayed that it is taking so long. Mike thinks that if her stoicism and denial have lasted this long, through such extremity, they will last to the final moment. She will believe that she is going to be fine, that bad things don't really happen to good people, that she is not going to die, right up until the second of her death. I don't believe that. But neither do I understand how she can maintain hope as she does in the face of such assaults upon her well-being.

Mom felt lousy today. She did not sleep well and started the day weak and depressed. The fact that she felt worse rather than better than the day before shook her already very fragile confidence that she was rallying from a temporary setback. The problem with denial is that each day her only goal is getting better, and most days she fails. Today, especially, it was clear she felt worthless. Several times, when I encouraged her to rest, she said, "I might as well sleep. That's all I'm good at anymore."

Dad looked more haggard and depressed this morning than I've ever seen him, his face all gray sags and folds, his eyes small and lost in the bleak geography of his face. Over breakfast he told Mike and me that he would like to have a wheelchair in the house, because he worries about what might happen if he tripped while guiding Mom from room to room. They walk together like parent and toddler. Dad stands behind Mom and virtually supports her entire weight while she unsteadily places one foot in front of the other. It is physically taxing and dangerous for both of them.

After talking with Dad, Mike and I broached the subject of a wheelchair with Mom and her eyes glistened with tears. She doesn't want to hear of a wheelchair or a walker or any other kind of hospital hardware. Later, independently of that exchange, she told me that in her dreams last night she was riding a bicycle around the block. What's strange about that is that she has never ridden a bike and has claimed since Mike and I were kids that it was too late for her to learn.

Mom had a long-standing 11:00 A.M. appointment with her local doctor this morning, but she was too weak even to contemplate leaving the house, and since she can't safely be left by herself anymore, Dad stayed behind while Mike and I seized the opportunity to talk privately with this elusive woman. Although she is not affiliated with the medical center in Rochester, she was recommended to Mom by doctors who trained her there, and we carried some of the resentment we felt toward them into her office.

We arrived unannounced and scowling, but she immediately recognized us as our parents' children and extended her hand. "Hi, I'm Margaret McCrae," she said. Despite the unanswered phone calls, her direct gaze and voluntary surrender of title gave me hope. If she offers her name, bare, like a fellow human being, maybe she feels some accountability for being one. Maybe she treats patients as well as their tumors, which, I guess, is the responsibility the medical center tries to pass on with its referrals.

She apologized for failing to reach us last week, saying that she had tried calling Mike at his hospital several times, but that he had never been available. Since he didn't challenge her version of events, I presumed it rang true. They began speaking doctor-to-doctor and I noticed that Dr. McCrae kept checking to see if I felt represented in the conversation. When she confessed her discomfort at being responsible for handling Mom's emergencies while the medical center doctors were still in charge of her overall treatment, Mike assured her that he regarded her as Mom's primary physician. He said that he wanted nothing more to do with the medical center, that Dr. McCrae was completely in charge of Mom's case. From the look on her face, I could tell she was thinking what I was: Mike may regard her as the only doctor on the case, but that doesn't stop Mom and Dad from regarding the medical center as the godhead, especially when the doctors there tell Mom she is cured and Dr. McCrae thinks otherwise.

Dr. McCrae was very straightforward about Mom's condition. She said she thought Mom had taken a very serious turn for the worse in the last two weeks. For the first time tests showed that her liver function was impaired, and she thought the symptoms Mom presented last week were probably due to the "progress of the cancer." I asked her if she had used that exact phrase to Mom and Dad, and she said she had. In her judgment Dad had shown less resistance to accepting that news than Mom. Dr. McCrae feels Mom has been given the information she needs to understand her situation but chooses to reject it, for better or for worse.

I asked her if she agreed with Mike's assessment of a likely one-to-two-months' survival, and she said that one or two months was likely but six months was also possible. In either case, she said she felt "very uncomfortable" with Dad's being totally responsible for Mom's day-to-day needs. She said home nursing care was available through Medicare hospice benefits, and she would be happy to see it in place. If we agreed, she would write a prescription that entitled Mom to receive home services. She paused after making this offer and exchanged a glance with Mike which made me wonder if I had missed something. Dr. McCrae read my expression and explained that a doctor can "prescribe" Medicare hospice services only if he officially designates the patient as terminal, with six or less months to live. "Does Mom have to accept that diagnosis?" I asked. "No," she said. "I will write the prescription now if you want me to." She also, with Mike's agreement, wrote a prescription for a higher dosage of prednisone, a drug that is supposed to increase appetite and "feelings of well-being" in cancer patients.

Dr. McCrae arranged for us to meet with Evelyn Hammond, the head of hospice services at Fairview/Southdale Hospital, and we went straight from her office to the hospital. Mrs. Hammond, a sweet-faced woman in her sixties, with a halo of white, curly hair, exuded an air of professional solicitude when she found us wandering among the wreckage of the hospital's eighth-floor renovation. She led us into her office, asked a few questions about Mom's insurance coverage and then said she'd like to wait until the chaplain arrived before we had further discussions. I took that as a bad sign. We didn't want religious counseling; we wanted practical help.

A few minutes later we were joined by Johnny, a red-haired boyish-faced man of indeterminate years who wore a powder-blue leisure suit with white piping and the smile of a television evangelist. He didn't claim any particular church affiliation but he did mention, several times, that he was a member of A.A. Mike and I offered him empty smiles of greeting and then, without further ado, Mike started presenting the facts of Mom's case. Diagnosis. Treatment. Current condition. Prognosis. Patient attitude. Family circumstances. When he was through, I said, "He's a doctor," meaning that's why he talks this way. Evelyn said, "I know, Dr. McCrae told me," meaning either "I expected him to talk this way" or "Yes, isn't that nice." I couldn't tell which.

Then I explained the situation my way. I said that Mom was desperately ill but she was no way near accepting her condition as terminal, in part because of her own temperament, in part because the doctors at the medical center continually misled her. Mike added that Mom was a very proud woman and that any hospice workers who entered the house should understand that before they set foot through the doorway. Evelyn explained that hospice workers were trained to help patients accept their situation without trying to dismantle their defenses or undermine their hope. She said in her experience patients often use denial to handle day-to-day difficulties while at the same time, in some other part of themselves, they may be facing their situation with profound realism. She reassured us that no one would try to force Mom to accept the prospect of dying. At this point Johnny chimed in and said, "We at hospice say there is no such thing as a terminal patient. Train stations have terminals. Airports have terminals. Hospice has no terminals." He finished and smiled broadly as if awaiting applause for a surefire crowd pleaser.

Evelyn gauged our reaction and quickly began explaining the practical services available to us: twice-weekly visits from a registered nurse who would keep in touch with Dr. McCrae as needed; three visits a week from nurses' aides who could do things like give baths, wash hair, change linens; once-a-week visits from trained volunteers who would keep the patient company or simply be there for four hours so other members of the household could take a break. Plus twenty-four-hour, seven-day-a-week nursing on call for emergencies. Plus equipment: wheelchairs, hospital beds, over-the-bed tables, respirators, IVs for morphine. Costs of all the above covered by Medicare.

I looked at Evelyn and Johnny with new eyes. I forgave Johnny his white piping and Evelyn her unctuous manner. They were angels of mercy. If Mom and Dad could be persuaded to accept these services, many of the strains working on us could be relieved. All our energies wouldn't have to go into amateur, inadequate efforts at nursing. We could try to help each other in other ways, maybe even enjoy each other again. I can hardly remember the last time any of us have talked about anything other than Mom's medical condition. She's becoming our "case" and that must demoralize her as much as anything.

I also think it would be good to open up the household a bit. Mom is in hiding now, too ashamed of being sick to allow herself to be seen by anyone but the family. If nurses come into the house, Mom will charm them, become the favorite patient as she did in Rochester, and perhaps regain some self-esteem.

After leaving the hospice office, Mike and I drove straight to a hospital supply warehouse in Saint Louis Park to pick up a wheelchair and over-the-bed table. We chose the lightest, least gleaming wheelchair and were very careful to not let Mom see it when we brought it into the house for Dad's inspection.

We told Mom that Dr. McCrae had introduced us to some people who could provide free practical help at home, but we did not mention equipment and we did not use the word "hospice." "Oh, I don't think we need any help," she said.

We left the discussion at that, but Mom was more depressed this evening than I've ever seen her. I know the arrangements Mike and I tried to make this afternoon are going to be essential for all of us, but I can't help feeling guilty, more betrayer than loving daughter. The wheelchair sits in a corner of the dining room for all to see, all but Mom, who isn't able to walk around the house to discover the wheelchair she insists she doesn't need.

SATURDAY, SEPTEMBER 20:

This morning I awoke with a sense of dread. Would Mom feel as badly in body and spirit as she did yesterday? If she did, could she stand it? Could I stand it? I stayed in bed, anxious and depressed, listening to the sounds of Mom and Dad's slow shuffle between bedroom and bathroom. I knew much attention would be focused on Mom's bowels. They didn't function yesterday, and by evening Mom's stomach was becoming swollen and hard, as it had been during last week's crisis. It was one of the symptoms that had alarmed Mike, who told me yesterday that a bowel obstruction is a real danger now, one of the many possible complications that could lead to hospitalization and a gruesome death.

Yesterday, on the way home from the hospital supply company, Mike spelled out for me some of the possibilities there are to dread in the next several weeks. Mom could develop jaundice, accompanied by terrible itching; ascites, with grotesque distension of the stomach; pneumonia; opportunistic infections. Mike, like Nancy, hopes for a pulmonary embolism as the quickest and kindest of several possible deaths. The term both he and Dr. McCrae use for her current condition is "the dwindles"— the stage of cancer during which there is no specific crisis, just a gradual diminishment and weakening unto death.

So this morning, armed with this information, I lay in bed and wondered what symptoms and what spectres the day would bring. Mom has been coughing a lot lately and complaining of a "bad feeling" in her chest. Is that the beginning of pneumonia? Mike says that in her virtually bedridden state, the lower lobes of her lungs will fill with fluid if she doesn't make more of an effort to get off her back. I feel resentment rising in me against Mike, who is returning to Philadelphia this afternoon. He teaches me what there is to fear and then leaves me alone with his dread knowledge. I begin to understand the burden Mike has been bearing all along, but I don't feel like exercising sympathy now. My sympathy is exhausted on Mom, and myself.

When I finally came out of my room, Dad promptly, proudly announced that Mom's bowels had moved. He was clearly greatly relieved, as was I, by this fact, but I also resented the infantilizing of Mom that comes with talking about her bodily functions as if they were public, or at least family, rather than personal matters. Dad has adopted a parental tone toward Mom since my last visit, and it makes me cringe, particularly when it is used in her earshot. Increased weakness has made Mom utterly dependent on Dad, her body cannot function without his help, and so she has lost all privacy, all bodily integrity, but not all shame.

Mom doesn't mind us talking about her body medically, but when Dad sounds as if he's talking about an infant in his charge, I see her face stiffen and go blank. There is a look in her eyes— resentment? contempt? defeat?—I can't tell which, but it's there. Why doesn't she protest? Because she is too weak to summon the energy to challenge him? Because she is afraid to challenge the man who now has complete control over her? Because she realizes she has completely controlled his life by her illness and feels she cannot criticize a husband who devotes his every energy to her care, twenty-four hours a day?

I at least have the escape of sleep. Dad has to be prepared to tend to Mom all through the night, to administer pills, walk her to the bathroom, listen to her sleep or wake or groan in pain. He is never unaware of what is happening to her. They sleep in the same bed.

See, I've already talked myself out of my anger, as Mom no doubt does too. We all need somebody to get angry at, but the targets are both too easy and too hard to fix on.

Mom seemed in fair spirits when I left at 11:00 A.M. to take Mike to the airport, and she seemed fine when I returned. She had eaten a bowl of Dad's homemade vegetable soup, which pleased him, and although she did nothing but doze on the den sofa, she didn't seem plagued by any of the discomforts I've seen since Thursday. The pains that made her wince and stutter are gone, a pain near her bottom right rib disappeared after one session with the TENS machine, her stomach feels all right. Dad felt reassured enough to leave the house this afternoon for the first time since I've arrived.

While Dad was taking a walk around Lake Cornelia, I was in the kitchen making custard when I heard Mom calling from the den. "I think I need to go to the bathroom," she said. The look on her face reminded me of the time she had fallen in the backyard and couldn't imagine that anyone but Dad would be strong enough to help her up. In the past few days I had watched carefully when Dad maneuvered her, and so I was able to get Mom into a seated and then standing position without much fumbling, and support her as she walked shakily down the hall to the bathroom. I helped her sit down and then stayed a moment, unsure whether she was able to support herself in a seated position. "I'm sorry," she said. "Go now." Her head was bowed but I thought I heard tears. My heart broke with hers. As I stood before her, torn between leaving as she asked and fearing that she might get hurt if left alone, I heard the back door open and knew that Dad's arrival could spare us both.

She has learned to accept her weakness before Dad, but she could not face the defeat of seeming abject before me. She does not want these to be our roles. She wants to be my mother. She wants to be Dad's wife. She wants to be the one who gives. And right now I think she feels she is nothing. She feels she can't be mother or wife or friend if she doesn't have her body, her pride, her strength. Her personality, her existence as Bea, is under assault and she has no defense as long as she remains identified with the fate of her body. She has to detach spirit from body. But how? And how can I urge her to find truth in the old catechism of body and soul when I don't believe in it myself? I counted on her to believe in the church and its consolations.

I needed to get out of the house, but I waited until Dad returned Mom to the den, waited until he finished his loud announcement of her bowels' progress, waited until I thought Mom had time to gather herself back together, and then I went in to offer her a bowl of custard. She accepted and ate it with greater relish than she has shown for anything in these past several days.

A little later, I said that I was going to Southdale's to buy earrings, which sounded plausible, since they knew a box containing all my jewelry had been stolen from my baggage on the flight here. The sun was making its first appearance after several rainy days, so, once outside, I drove to Lake Cornelia, parked the car and began walking the wide trail that circles the lake. I just wanted to stroll and smoke and think, all activities that made me feel criminal in the eyes of the right-minded Minnesota joggers who clogged the trail. Desperate for privacy, I took a detour onto a narrow path that led into a densely wooded area between the joggers and the lake.

Mud crept up the sides of my Cherokee sandals, but I kept taking paths that forked off paths, each narrower and more overgrown than the last. I was determined to find some sanctuary for my troubled soul, but there was no pleasure in the search. Trees blocked out the sun, mud took the spring from my step, the fear of getting lost kept me from sorting out the thoughts that had driven me into this maze, and though I had lost all sense of direction, I never escaped the sound of traffic. This might have been reassuring, but wasn't, because I knew there was no quick way to reach the roads except by wading through marshland. After forty-five minutes of morose wandering, I found my way out and back to the car.

I went on to Southdale's and made myself look for earrings, so that I could return home with my cover story intact; there is no excuse for returning empty-handed from the nation's historic first shopping mall. I was so depressed by this time that I could only stare blankly at the racks of baubles before me, and whenever another customer came close, I would move to the next counter to protect myself from scrutiny. Devoid of consumer impulses, I felt criminal again, the target of suspicious glances from sincere shoppers. After a while, though, I found myself genuinely engaged in the niceties of earring selection. My spirits lifted and I even started a conversation with the clerk who wrote up my purchases. I left Southdale's marveling at the restorative power of shopping. Is it possible that costume jewelry has the power to penetrate my darkest moods?

I returned home, made dinner and spent an evening marked by nothing worse than boredom. By the time Mom went to bed, I realized the day had hope in it. A day limited by Mom's extreme weakness yet a better day than some others, with fewer pains, less coughing, more eating. While I was at Southdale's, she had allowed and enjoyed a visit from Verna, the first break in her shut-door policy toward neighbors.

At dinner tonight Dad attributed the improvement in Mom's appetite to the increased dose of prednisone, which irritated me. Why not give Mom the credit? Why take that small victory from her? She needs praise more than the pill. Why not let her feel she's getting stronger rather than remind her she is being jerked around by another drug, another dosage?

SUNDAY, SEPTEMBER 21:

A day remarkable only for its tedium. Mom awoke feeling "not too good"—no specific complaints, just a general malaise and depression, which soon filled me as well. When I brought her breakfast, I noticed that the face on her digital watch had gone blank. Batteries dead. I got a chill the moment I saw its dull, gray window—like a screen that will never show images again or a monitor of some crucial function that is registering no more activity. When clock hands stop, one feels only that time has stopped. When a digital face goes blank, it makes you feel there is no more time. Mom didn't react as I did, though. "Better not to watch the time anyway," she said.

About noon Dad decided Mom would feel better if she were bathed. I was in the kitchen trying not to hear the grunts and groans of exertion coming from the bathroom when Dad called me in to help him "do her backside." This entailed Mom's standing up, but she was of course too weak to support herself, so while she steadied herself by gripping a chair back with both hands, I held her under the arms in case her strength should give out. Head bowed while Dad washed her from behind and I supported her from the front, she said, "No pride." The bathing destroyed what little was left of her strength and morale.

I think these tasks would be less demoralizing for all of us if they were performed by a nurse. Sickness is humbling, but I think it would be less so for Mom if her husband and daughter weren't always the nurses. There's a part of nursing—providing food and physical comforts—that is best done by us. But the more invasive parts of nursing might be more easily accepted from a professional.

A few minutes after writing the above, I asked Mom if she would like to have a nurse help her with bathing, and she said, "No. Until I'm on my feet again, the less intrusion from the outside world the better."

"Is that your vanity speaking?" I asked. "No," she said. "It's just a feeling."

Later Dad brought up the subject of the wheelchair again and told Mom that we already had one in the house. "Get rid of it," she said. "I don't need it and I don't want it." Despite Dad's and my most persuasive arguments about her safety and his, she remained very, very firm. In fact, I have never seen her so vehement about anything.

The only piece of hospice-issued equipment we have been able to introduce into the household is the squawk box, a small wireless intercom with a two-hundred-foot range. We place the transmitter near Mom and the receiver near whoever else is in the house. Before we set it up on Friday, Dad had been afraid to spend time in his basement workshop for fear that Mom would need help but not have the strength of voice to shout for him. The puttering he does there is what keeps him sane, so the deprivation was a serious one.

The squawk box lengthens Dad's leash, but there is a price to pay. We hear every noise coming from Mom's room; every cough, groan, shifting of position is magnified over the receiver, which heightens and exaggerates our awareness of Mom's discomforts. Since Mom can't hear what comes over the receiver, she doesn't know she is emitting a continual symphony of distress calls. In effect we have her under total auditory surveillance. We've become eavesdroppers, violating her privacy in yet another way and undermining our own as well.

Sitting in the kitchen watching the late news, I hear the box sigh, then say, "Oh, to be well."

MONDAY, SEPTEMBER 22:

This morning I was awakened by the sound of Mom calling, "Pop, Pop." Dad was already up and apparently out of intercom range, so I threw off my covers, rushed into their bedroom and saw Mom, toothless, her eyes round with fright, the entire length of her tiny body half off the mattress and sliding toward a crash landing on the floor. She looked old, miserable, helpless, disgusted with herself and unhappy to see me. She had been trying to get out of bed by herself and got stranded halfway. I yelled for Dad, and when he came, I returned to my room, shut the door and crawled back into bed. Then I cried.

The tears wouldn't stop flowing, so for an hour I just let them roll down my cheeks and into the corners of my mouth. I tried to be quiet, and I kept my facial muscles still, so that I wouldn't emerge from the room looking the way I felt. Several times I tiptoed past Mom's bedroom into the bathroom to wash my face and blow my nose, then climbed back under the covers to let the storm run its course. I couldn't get the image of Mom's toothless face out of my mind.

Without teeth, Mom looks ancient, pathetic, wasted, beyond help and without pride. The image is so strong it makes me feel she is those things. With teeth in, there is nobility and extreme beauty in her face, now more than ever. She looks stoic, indomitable, her wide brow and cheekbones set in high relief, a triumph of strong bones over weak flesh. But now I can't tell which face is the truer mask. And I don't know whether she can either.

When I finally ran out of tears and left my room, I was surprised to find myself feeling strong and calm. I didn't need to rearrange myself for Mom's or Dad's benefit. Maybe I am beginning to learn how to weather the changes each day brings. Until now Mom has led the way, showing us by her sustained hope and good spirits that what she is suffering is tolerable, that she is able to bear it and remain intact. Now it is time for us, for Dad and me, to demonstrate by our response to her that what is happening to her is still tolerable, that she is still Bea. But our responses have to be genuine, she can't be fooled, and that means we have to discover her, rediscover her, under the shifting layers of symptoms.

Yesterday, during one of Mom's rare waking hours, I asked her if she was sleeping out of exhaustion or boredom. "Oh, probably both," she said. I asked her if she would like me to rearrange the room so she could look out the window, which is now behind her. "No," she said, and after a pause, added, "I'd rather see the action there." She nodded toward the door that opens on the hallway running between the kitchen and the bathroom. The occasional sight of Dad or me walking past the den to the bathroom is her "action."

Today, for the first time, Mom stayed in her bedroom all day. I think she wanted to stay put, because we were expecting a visit from a home-care nurse (an arrangement made acceptable to Mom by our saying Dr. McCrae wanted the nurse to do some testing). But perhaps it represented some resignation to a bed-ridden state.

The nurse, Virginia, called in the morning to say she would come by about 2:00 P.M. I asked Mom if she'd like me to help fix her up for the visit, and was amazed once again to see what transformation can be wrought by lipstick and a hairbrush. At 3:30 Virginia arrived, stocky, cheerful, dowdy, with a broad, round chin and a no-nonsense look in her eye. I admit wishing she were better-looking, because I know Mom is easily seduced by beauty.

After we brought Virginia up to date on Mom's condition, she went into the bedroom and introduced herself to Mom. Dad followed Virginia, but I stayed behind in the kitchen, where I could hear everything that was said over the squawk box. My eavesdropping was unabashed. I wanted to know what information was exchanged between Mom and Virginia, but I didn't want my presence to affect Mom's presentation of herself. After a few minutes Dad came into the kitchen and suggested I take his place in the bedroom. I was hesitant but walked down the hallway to check on them. When I reached the doorway, I saw that Virginia was seated very close to Mom and the eye contact between them was intense. I quietly retreated to the kitchen and listened over the box as Virginia deftly won Mom's trust.

At first she asked the questions Mom most likes to answer, questions about me and Mike, where we lived and what we did. She complimented Mom on her appearance and her home and let her dwell for a while on the sources of her pride. And then, without the slightest change of tone, she asked Mom what problems she was having, implying by her evenness that she saw no difference between the woman who was proud and the woman who was sick.

Mom began by describing herself as a person with few problems, "just weakness, that's all. No real pain or discomfort." When Virginia asked if she used the wheelchair, Mom said, "No. I don't need it. I can walk." It was an easy bluff to call, and Virginia called it by asking Mom to show her how she walked. I heard the sounds of Mom trying to come through on her claims, and then I heard Virginia say, very matter-of-factly, "You're not going to make it. You can't walk." Part of me wanted to rush into the room and save Mom from Virginia's candor.

I inhibited that impulse and listened as Virginia began talking about how hard it must be for Mom to lose her independence. "Yes, it is hard," Mom said. Virginia was compassionate but also very firm. She told Mom the most important thing was her safety, and if that meant swallowing her pride to accept a wheelchair, as she had accepted a catheter, then she just had to do it; the alternative was the very real danger of falls, broken bones and hospitalization. Mom promised to be sensible and use the wheelchair, but her capitulation sounded forced and unconvincing to me, as if she had her fingers crossed behind her back. I considered going into the room, taking Virginia aside and telling her not to believe Mom, but that quickly proved unnecessary. As soon as Virginia changed subjects, Mom reverted to talking about how she expected to be out of bed and on her feet any day now. "I'll greet you at the door next time, Virginia."

Before leaving the bedroom, Virginia asked Mom if she'd like a visit from a nurse's aide, who could help her bathe and wash her hair. "No," Mom said. "That won't be necessary." But she did accept Virginia's offer of a visit from a physical therapist.

When Virginia came into the kitchen to confer with Dad and me, it was clear she didn't think physical therapy could help, but it might teach Mom her limits and wean her from her "illusions." Suddenly Dad and I were on Mom's side, insisting that she would be able to walk again, with time and therapy. Virginia backed off, allowing that it was, of course, possible that Mom could walk again, but her face betrayed total skepticism. What I read between the lines of her studied, open-minded expression was "Sure, anything is possible, she might walk and the sun might shine in Minnesota tomorrow, but don't count on it. And I see I have to contend with your denial as well as hers."

Dad helped Virginia into her coat and we walked her to the front door. "There's one more thing I should tell you," Virginia said. "You don't need to call 911. You can call us and we'll inform the coroner's office. If she should stop breathing, and you call 911, the police will come with flashing lights and sirens." Dad looked stricken. After a pause, Virginia continued, "And the police will bring a respirator." It took me a second to realize what she was saying. If we call the hospice office, they will let her die. If we call the police, they will try to revive her. What a choice. Let the fingers do the snuffing.

Virginia held us in a steady gaze until she saw that we had registered her meaning. A certain stiffness had entered her voice, as if she were required to read us our rights by some medical Miranda Act. More likely she had been required to say what she said by her employer, Fairview-Southdale Hospital. Since Reagan's cuts in Medicare spending have made long hospital stays a money-losing proposition, the last thing a hospital wants is a terminal patient on a respirator. Not long ago, the medical establishment regarded the hospice movement as quackery, like home birth and chiropractic. Now every major hospital has a hospice program, apparently to ensure that terminal patients are allowed to die as quickly and inexpensively as possible.

After dinner, Dad made a trip to the drugstore to buy some denture liners Virginia had recommended, and I took the opportunity to talk privately with Mom about the afternoon's visit. She called Virginia "a great gal" and said nurses like her are "real angels of mercy." I reminded her how much she had liked the nurses and nurses' aides at the medical center, like Kim, the Cambodian refugee whose smile lit every room he entered and whose personal history had been as dark as Pol Pot could make it. "Yes, they were all great," she admitted. "But I don't need nursing now."

"God, you're stubborn," I said. She smiled. It was an opening and I entered it. Echoing Virginia, I said it must be terrible not to have the use of her legs and yes, the very sight of a wheelchair was depressing, but she mustn't spite herself. If, for instance, the sun ever shone again and she wanted to feel its warmth on her body, she should not let anything stop her, not even her vanity. "Well, yes," she said. "I'd go out on a beautiful day, but you and Dad could walk me out."

I wanted to talk about dying, acknowledge its possibility, stop pretending that recovery is assured to those who hope. I wanted her to stop desiring the body she had lost.

"Mom, your body can't make you happy now. But maybe there's a way to free your spirit. I don't know how."

"It's not easy," she said.

"I know. But even when your body is so weak, your spirit comes through strong. Dad and I see the beautiful woman and you should never forget that."

It was lame, clichéd and half true, but I tried. I made a start.

After dinner I drove to Freya's for a visit. When I arrived she and the twins were watching the end of *Old Yeller* on the VCR, the part when the old dog gets rabies in a fight with a wolf and has to be shot by the boy who loves him. Freya was sitting propped up by pillows on her king-size bed and the boys were sprawled on the floor with blankets wound around them. When rabies turned lovable Old Yeller into a snarling beast, Bly started whimpering. "Oh," he moaned, turning around to Freya, "I don't like this part. I'm scared. Can we come up there with you?" Freya nods her okay and both boys hop onto the bed with us. A few minutes later, Bly says, "I'm going back down there. I'm not scared anymore." Bly slides off the end of the bed onto the floor, but Rowan stays huddled between Freya and me. Seconds later, when it becomes clear that Old Yeller is going to be shot, Bly panics and yells for his brother. "Rowan, Rowan, come down here with me. I'm scared again. ROWAN, PLEASE! Come here with me." Reluctantly, Rowan leaves the bed and joins Bly under the blanket on the floor. Bly calms down and begins enjoying the movie again; Rowan quietly rolls on his side, buries his head in the blanket and cries. Bly, all smiles, tries to jiggle Rowan out of his tears. Freya intervenes and tells Bly to leave Rowan alone. Bly obeys.

I watch the boys intently, fascinated by their responses and interaction. Mostly I watch their beautiful six-year-old bodies, their long, lean bare backs and slender arms, the sweet spot at the back of their necks where silky hair meets silky flesh.

TUESDAY, SEPTEMBER 23:

I awoke with apprehension. Not dread, just apprehension. Dad had an appointment to get his hair cut at 10:00 A.M., which meant that I was responsible for meeting Mom's morning needs. Morning is not a good time for Mom. She looks terrible and feels worse. Usually she is groggy from sleeping pills or a poor night's sleep, slightly nauseated and demoralized by awakening each day to rediscover her helplessness. Each morning begins with a trip to the bathroom, and, as she becomes weaker, the five-yard trek between bedroom and bathroom becomes even more treacherous. It takes tremendous effort on her part to keep her legs from buckling, and I've found that ninety pounds can be extremely heavy when you have to support it with two hands held in front of you at chest level.

We got through it though. I was able to hold her steady while she washed her hands in the sink, and when she was back in bed, I brought her a warm washcloth for her face. She let me experiment with the waxy denture liners bought last night to see if we couldn't sculpt a better fit. Then I brought her a break-fast of tea and toast. She has appetite only for a few bites and sips, but when she was through, she looked relaxed and re-freshed, more rested than usual. Only two days ago it made her unutterably sad to have me tend her in these ways, but this morning she accepted my care without shame. And I gave it with greater confidence.

When Dad returned, he seemed relieved to find the first, hard part of the day over. He cheerfully took on the next tasks, moving Mom from bedroom to den, fixing her another snack and bathing her as she reclined on the sofa. Mom looked fine and had few complaints—a sore tongue, stiff legs and, of course, weakness.

The sun came out in the afternoon, so about 2:00 P.M. I drove over to a nature preserve on the Mississippi that Freya told me about last night. As soon as my sneakers hit the damp earth of the trail, I felt a thrill of expectation and a grin spread over my face, stretching muscles I forgot I had. It was a good path, wide enough to let some sun shine through, but not so wide it tamed the wildness of the surroundings. The path led down a steep incline, then turned left across a small brook and into a more densely wooded area. I paused for a long moment on the wooden plank that spanned the brook, storing up the warmth of the sun before setting off on the shady part of the path.

Two strides beyond the brook and a thin black snake slithered onto the path in front of me. I jumped and it whiplashed under my feet and into the brush before I landed. "Shit," I thought. "Do I have to face my irrational fears today as well as my rational ones?" I remembered the snake that crossed the road in front of me that last Friday in Glenco Mills. I hadn't seen a snake all year, so why two in two weeks? Why in these two weeks?"

I continued along the path thinking about snakes, my spirits sinking fast. I heard the sounds of scurrying all around me and became very attentive. Who knows what might be lurking here? When I parked the car at the entrance to the preserve, I'd seen a large, black furry animal bound away in the distance. I had presumed it was a dog, but it's a strange dog that leaps through the air like a wild beast.

Alert, I caught sight of several birds and a squirrel; then, as I walked slowly uphill on the narrowing path, I heard a loud crashing that made my heart race. I spun left toward the noise and saw three deer running away from me, white tails held high. In that instant I realized where the phrase "hightailing it" came from, and felt foolish for not having known it before.

Two of the deer bounded from sight, but the third about-faced and stood his ground. We stared at each other across a distance of about ten yards. The ground was wet enough that I could walk silently over soggy leaves, so I backtracked out of his line of sight and then, keeping tree trunks between him and me, sneaked a few paces closer. At twenty feet I showed myself. The deer made one step sideways to hide himself behind a tree. I did the same, and we peered through leafy branches at each other. After a minute of stillness, I took another step, to show myself and get a better angle of vision. He took one step into the open and, staring straight at me, raised one hoof and stomped the earth. I didn't move. He raised the other hoof and stomped. His look was now a glare. I waved. He stomped. I flashed a peace sign. He stomped. I raised my right hoof and stomped. He whirled to his left, ran three steps, whirled back around to face me and snorted. I stood still. He sent me a quick volley of snorts and stomps and looked like he might charge. I took three steps in a direction that kept me the same distance from him, showing him, I supposed, my wariness but also my lack of fear. He snorted. I waved. He tossed his head high to one side, the other two deer came running from their hiding place and all three hightailed it through the woods and across the path I had strayed from.

The whole encounter lasted about ten minutes, and I had been exhilarated every second of it. For the first time in my life, I had felt an animal was treating me like a fellow creature. These deer aren't tame, but living in a preserve they apparently haven't come to know humans as hunters with an unfair advantage. Here we're just big, not very talented, not very good-looking creatures on hind legs.

I returned to the path and followed it round a curve and down a hill toward a flat stretch of thickly wooded land that bordered what looked like a large pond in the distance. A wide strip of huge cottonwood trees went right up to the water's edge, and I came within a few feet of its bank before I realized I was looking at the Mississippi. I'd become used to the streams of upstate New York, streams that twist and rush and swirl and tumble, noisy streams that announce their presence at every turn. And here was this silent, smooth-surfaced, steady-paced, wide, wide river reminding me that I was back in the Midwest. The trees caught in its current after these many days of rain looked like they would be carried all the way to New Orleans without a snag.

The river calmed me and I walked north along its flank, stopping to admire the cottonwoods, some of them eight and ten feet in diameter. I wanted to walk along that bank forever, but the path turned inland along a swampy inlet. I was trying to figure out how to cross the inlet and keep walking north when I got distracted by the sight of turtles basking in the sun at the edge of a pond up ahead. As I approached, they dove off their logs, one by one, and I continued along the path only to find myself back at the point I'd started from an hour ago.

Disappointed that I had already come full circle, I decided to backtrack to the river, but when I reached the turtle pond, I saw another snake in the path ahead of me, this one black with a yellow racing stripe. I stepped back a few yards, scraped the earth with my feet to scare it off, but the snake didn't move. I wanted another sight of the river but not so badly that I was willing to step over a snake. I chose retreat.

It was close to four o'clock, but the sky was still clear and sunny, and I returned to the car thinking that if I went straight home, I might be able to persuade Mom to let me take her outside. Or maybe Dad would like to visit the preserve before night and rain returned.

As I neared the house, I noticed that every lawn in the neighborhood was being mowed. Apparently that's what Minnesotans think gorgeous days are for. Five days out of six, it rains or snows, and on the seventh day, they mow or shovel, filling the air with the drone of their beloved machines. You need nature preserves to escape the shrill sounds of Minnesotans being tidy.

When I reached home, the sun was streaming into the den, where Mom was sitting with her back to the window. She could not be persuaded to go outside. Dad said he had to mow the lawn. I thought evil thoughts and called them both Minnesotans.

Early in the evening Mom mentioned that her lower legs were stiff, and I offered to massage them. I cupped my hand around her calf and was shocked to feel the flesh yield. There is almost no muscle left. No wonder she can't walk! Three weeks ago, her calves still had their normal size and strength. Radiation and a year's inactivity had weakened her thighs but not her calves. How could so complete a deterioration have happened in three weeks?

I immediately suspected prednisone. Earlier in the week I had read all the material that came with the various medications Mom is taking, and I had noted that the possible side effects of prednisone include loss of muscle mass. I've never understood what benefit Mom is supposed to be deriving from this drug. All I know is that it affects her circulation so that she bruises badly and easily; her shins are still discolored by large purple blotches, which appeared when she first started taking prednisone in August. It also increases water retention, which has caused her feet to swell to almost twice their normal size and which may have contributed to her bladder problem. Why did Mike and Dr. McCrae decide to increase her dosage from 20 to 40 milligrams a day?

Suddenly, I began to entertain an entirely different interpretation of Mom's condition. What if there is in fact no recurrence or spread of cancer? There is no clear evidence to support Dr. McCrae's assumption that cancer is causing Mom's decline—only inferences from statistical probability and Mom's constantly shifting symptoms. But all the symptoms can theoretically be accounted for as side effects of either prednisone or Elavil—both antidepressants that were supposed to enhance her appetite and "sense of well-being."

Elavil lowered her normal blood pressure, causing dizziness and falls. The falls resulted in dramatic bruises because of the prednisone, which was also weakening her muscles. Together, the drugs made her more fearful, less active, which in turn accelerated her loss of strength. At the same time, the prednisone was causing a painful degree of water retention, which led to her catheterization, the prescription of penicillin for a non-existent infection, the consequent intestinal problems and the five days without food. So now we have a depressed, bedridden patient, and the easiest explanation is to say that the cancer, in abeyance for a year, has now returned and she is terminal.

The only way to get nursing help from Medicare is to accept the diagnosis "terminal." But once that label is attached to a person, everything conspires to make it true. What if prednisone, which is supposed to save her from depression in her last weeks, is making it impossible for her to regain strength? What if we are robbing her of her last chance to walk again? What if there is no recurrence of cancer and she lives for another year, bedridden and miserable? What if, after her brave struggle to survive, she dies from the side effects of unneeded drugs?

I became so convinced of the plausibility of my interpretation that I decided I should talk to Dad about my suspicions of prednisone. His reaction was immediate. He grasped at my explanation as if it were a rope dangling above an abyss. His entire demeanor changed. I could see the energy surging through his body, straightening his back, squaring his slumped shoulders, pinkening his sallow cheeks. He said he never believed that Mom is suffering from a recurrence of cancer. Is this denial or the considered judgment of the man who has followed Mom's daily fluctuations far more closely than anyone else? Whichever, he began talking disrespectfully about doctors, Mike included, and became more respectful toward Mom. "Mike's suggestions haven't been very helpful, have they?" he said. He went into Mom's room and talked to her in a tone I hadn't heard for a month— he was talking to his wife again, not to his dying ward.

I was encouraged by his response but also wary, and a bit guilty that it had swerved into an attack on Mike. Each day, it seems, each one of us decides who will be the villain in this family drama. Is it Mother, Father, Sister or Bro'? Often, of course, it is the doctors, but having one in the family complicates that antagonism.

Last week Mike said to me, "The medical center doctors aren't interested in Mom. They're interested in her disease. She's just the host for the tumor." He sounded bitter, vengeful, and said he planned to write a damning letter to the ethics committee at the medical center about their handling of Mom's case. I didn't doubt the sincerity of his anger but his words carried an echo for me. I remembered the day several years ago when he gave me a tour of his hospital's radiology department. He rifled a patient's file to show me "the beautiful color picture" of a brain tumor he had been able to get with the latest technology of those pre–CAT scan days. I was shocked to hear him call a tumor beautiful and said so. He laughed and said, "C'mon, patients are just hosts for beautiful tumors like these."

That mentality seems to prevail among doctors, at least among fancy doctors, and Mike has certainly been party to it. Now, I think, Mike is disgusted with that cavalier cynicism, with himself, with medicine. And yet it is his life, his livelihood, his brotherhood. And his mother is dying.

I called Mike about 10:00 P.M. for a consultation on prednisone. He said prednisone is supposed to work as "a general tonic" for body and spirit and is usually prescribed for terminal cancer patients. He explained that it is easy to put a patient on prednisone and easy to raise the dosage but tricky to reduce it, because prednisone provides the ACTH normally stimulated by the adrenal gland. When ACTH is provided by the drug, the adrenal gland begins to shut down its output, and if you withdraw the drug too quickly, the adrenal gland may not be ready to go into action.

In his opinion Mom's muscle loss is due to inactivity rather than prednisone. He acknowledged that my interpretation of Mom's problems was possible, but he thought it unlikely and clearly suspected I was succumbing to another bout of denial. I don't know whether I am or not. I only know that when so much is uncertain, I don't want to deny Mom the possibility of walking again.

About midnight I called Candace. I reached her as she was rushing to catch a flight to Los Angeles. Her healthy, non-smoking, non-drinking stepfather died this afternoon of a stroke while he was burning weeds in his backyard. When Candace's mother came home from work, she found her husband lying in the grass looking peaceful.

WEDNESDAY, SEPTEMBER 24:

This afternoon I went to a florist's to send flowers to Candace and her mother. When I returned, a physical therapist was putting Mom through a workout. I distrusted her at first sight. She was very young, very overweight and full of false jollity. When I entered the bedroom, she chuckled nervously and said that Mom had already "hit the floor" once. She actually said things like "C'mon, c'mon, you can do it, atta girl" as she clumsily worked Mom's arms and legs. She seemed dangerous to me. At one point, while showing Mom how to exercise her legs from a prone position, the therapist smelled her fingers, screwed up her nose and said, "I've got this terrible smell on my hands. Another patient had an accident, and I can't get the smell off. I've scrubbed and scrubbed." Mom looked as if she would have liked to strangle that girl and I knew she was thinking, "A year ago, I was in twice as good shape as you are and I'm three times your age, you snip. Get out of my house."

I exchanged glances with Mom, read her clear meaning and told the therapist I thought Mom had exercised enough for now. I escorted her out of the room, assured her I would be able to help Mom with her exercises from now on and that no further visits from her would be necessary. Although my regard for this woman's judgment was close to nil, I asked her if prednisone would diminish the effect of exercise. "Oh yes," she said. "I don't like prednisone at all. It can slow recovery quite a bit." I asked her if inactivity could have undone Mom's calf muscles in three weeks. "No," she said. "That was prednisone." I didn't know whether to feel reinforced or undermined by her support of my position on prednisone.

I spent the evening with Trish Hampl exploring the book shops on Grant Avenue in St. Paul. I was too preoccupied with what might be happening at home to give myself over to browsing, but one title finally caught my attention. I pulled a slender paperback called *The Invention of Solitude* from the shelf and, not knowing what to expect, turned to the bold print of the back cover: "ONE DAY THERE IS LIFE . . . AND, THEN, SUDDENLY, IT HAPPENS, THERE IS DEATH."

I felt slapped, as I did again when I read the first paragraph, which tells of the author's response to news of his father's death. "Death after a long illness we can accept with resignation. Even accidental death we can ascribe to fate. But for a man to die of no apparent cause . . ." writes Paul Auster, whose father died without warning or apparent cause. It seems we are two camps, those who survive sudden deaths and those who survive slow deaths. Each thinks the other has been spared; maybe each of us wants to believe in the possibility of some other, easier ending. I bought his book, prepared to accept his loss, not mine.

Later, over dinner, Trish and I talked of many things before we reached the subject of "How is your mother?" When I described much of what I've recorded in these pages, Trish said, "You are with her. That's the most, the best you can do for her. That's as good as it gets." She was speaking from her experience as a hospice volunteer. I thought, "Oh no, that can't be true. There's got to be something more I can do, something better that can happen between us."

THURSDAY, SEPTEMBER 25:

I awoke feeling guilty this morning, because after spending a night out with Trish, I was now planning to spend most of the day with a friend from New York who was arriving in Minneapolis this afternoon. I know I am entitled to some portion of a life of my own, but now that Mom requires such constant care, time out of the house feels like desertion, not of her but of Dad.

I was also worried about bringing Milena to the house for a visit. Over the years Mom had met and charmed most of my close friends from New York, and since learning that Milena would be in town for a convention, she had looked forward to meeting her. The anticipation was mutual, because Milena was eager to meet the woman who had endeared herself to such an unlikely assortment of hard-to-please New Yorkers. But now that the day had arrived, Mom, who had assumed she would be "on her feet by then," was clearly afraid that she would make "a bad first impression."

When I returned from the airport with Milena, I went into the den to see how Mom was feeling. Cosmetically, she looked fine, hair combed, lipstick applied, face arranged to win friends. But there was something very visibly wrong. There was no energy in her body. She looked almost erased by exhaustion, as if she were in a waking faint. She said she felt "terrible." I asked her if there were any specific aches and pains. "No," she said, "just a general malaise." I asked her if she meant she hardly had enough energy to breathe, and she said, "Yes, but I want to see Milena."

Only the briefest visit was possible, and I think that disappointed everybody. But Dad, who has been virtually housebound for weeks, was delighted to have a guest to entertain; he showed Milena his paintings and fossil collection, and walked her through his garden, teaching her how to harvest seeds for next year's annuals. The three of us sat around the kitchen table cracking open dried seed pods, listening to the silence of the squawk box.

Later I took Milena to the nature preserve, where we walked the path to the river. Few critters stirred, but it was a gorgeous, summery day, clear, eighty degrees, with a soft, steady breeze touching everything. We sat on a log at the water's edge, letting the wind and the water do all the moving. A turtle poked up its head to look at us and discreetly ducked under water again, leaving the log to us. I didn't feel the need to say anything. I was just glad that someone from my former life had come and seen my present one.

After driving Milena to her hotel in downtown Minneapolis, I returned home for dinner. Mom's energy and spirits were at their lowest. "When will I get out of here?" she asked me, ostensibly referring to her cramped position on the den sofa. All day there were tears in her eyes, not flowing, just pools of sadness, a film between her and the world.

About eight o'clock Mike and Nancy called. When I described Mom's mental and physical condition, Mike became very concerned that someone tell her she is dying—me, a priest, a hospice worker, anyone. He doesn't want her to die without knowing what is happening to her, and he is blaming himself, among others, for never having encouraged her to face the prospect of death.

I felt he was ordering me to tell Mom she is dying, and I resented the pressure and the presumption. None of us want Mom to end her life in confusion and depression, but do any of us have the right to strip her of hope? Mike and Nancy seem to think her hope is some kind of personal failure or deficiency of character. I reminded them that until very recently she had good reason for hope, or so the doctors led us to believe, and that if she had not been able to summon hope, she would never have been able to withstand the sufferings of the past year. Suddenly she is being confronted by defeat, and it is not easy to adjust, not easy to abandon the stance that has allowed her to endure as long as she has.

At first Mike responded to my defense of Mom as if it were just another instance of the irksome denial that besets me, Dad and Mom. Then he stopped mid-sentence and asked, "Is Mom taking any thyroid supplements?" I passed the question on to Dad, who said she wasn't. "Oh, my God," Mike said. "Why didn't I think of that? She's almost certainly hypothyroid, and that could be what is destroying her energy."

About twenty years ago Mom was diagnosed as hyperthyroid, and the treatment given her was an oral dose of radioactive iodine that destroyed part of her thyroid gland. This treatment for hyperthyroidism is apparently very effective, but fifteen to twenty years after receiving it, most patients develop the opposite problem, hypothyroidism. Again, the treatment is simple—thyroid supplements in pill form—but if the condition goes untreated, the consequences can be very dangerous.

Instead of blaming Mom for her denial and me for "making prednisone the enemy," as he had been doing only minutes earlier, Mike began blaming himself and Mom's doctors for overlooking this crucial part of her medical history. He thought it very likely that "thyroid supplements might turn things around for her" and made me promise to have the nurse take the necessary blood tests when she came tomorrow.

Dad got on the kitchen phone with Mike, and the prospect

of recovery Mike held out to him made him jubilant, just as our discussion about prednisone had the other night. Receiver in hand, he pranced back and forth between sink and fridge, stretching the coiled phone cord to the point of disconnection.

After saying good-night to Mike, we immediately called Dr. McCrae's answering service and left a message for her to call us first thing in the morning.

FRIDAY, SEPTEMBER 26:

I was awakened earlier than usual this morning by the sound of Dad cheerfully bustling around the house. He was still high on the thyroid theory and seemed to expect Mom to show immediate signs of recovery. Mom, innocent of her thyroid's new place in her life, was not obliging. When I entered their bedroom, Dad had Mom propped up in a sitting position and was urging her to summon strength for the move to the den, where he would bathe and ready her for Virginia's visit. Mom's body was bent into an S-curve of defeat, head falling kneeward and slippered toes jammed against the floor in a losing battle with gravity. At the sound of my entrance, she turned her head toward me and said, "Le Anne, I'm sad."

It was the most open expression of emotion she had ever allowed herself in my hearing. It was not a plea; nothing in her tone suggested she was asking me to make her happy. It was as if she had recognized a pure, unmixed, thoroughly transparent state of emotion in herself, perhaps for the first time in her adult life, and she wanted to communicate it to me. She was able to utter something entirely true and she trusted me to hear it. I felt chosen, blessed, forgiven, loved. "Le Anne, I'm sad." I didn't know it, but I think I have been waiting to hear those words all my life.

I wanted to be alone with her, but the rite of bathing took precedence and the opportunity was lost. Much later in the day,

I asked her how she was feeling and she said, "Not bad . . . not too good really." I asked her what she was thinking about. "Not much," she said. "Just how much I'd like to be well." She paused, then added, "No heavy thoughts. Nothing deep." I thought she was saying, "Don't ask me to talk about dying. Not now."

Milena arrived by cab to spend the afternoon with us at exactly the same moment Virginia pulled into the driveway. Milena sat in the backyard, chatting with Dad and sorting seeds, while I went back and forth from their sides to Mom's, checking to see what Virginia was doing and discovering. Mom looked better this afternoon than she had on the day of Virginia's first visit, and I think the illusion of improvement helped draw Virginia into greater sympathy with Mom's situation. When we told her about our conversation with Mike last night, Virginia was very eager to do the necessary testing, but she had to have authorization from Dr. McCrae, who had not returned our calls.

While we stood in the kitchen waiting for the phone to ring, Dad and I talked to Virginia in greater detail about Mom's medical history and treatment. She seemed to open up to the possibility that Mom may not be a typical "terminal" case, if there is such a thing. When she left to see another patient, Virginia promised to reach Dr. McCrae by one means or another before the afternoon was over and return to do the testing.

She did as she promised, returning with authorization to do tests for potassium, hemoglobin and blood sugar levels, as well as thyroid function. But when she tried to draw blood, Mom's veins were so tiny and her blood so dehydrated that the needle came out empty. Virginia said the major veins in her hands and forearms looked less than one-sixteenth of an inch in diameter. After twenty minutes of sticking, probing and apologizing, Virginia succeeded in drawing only 3 cc's of blood, not enough for all the tests, and said she would return tomorrow to try again.

About 10:00 P.M. Virginia called to say she had results for the potassium test—Mom's level was high normal—and blood sugar—normal. Virginia was astounded by the results, especially the blood sugar level, which is typically very high in patients whose pancreas is not functioning properly. In Virginia's opinion, the tests just did not make sense for someone who is supposed to be in the last stages of pancreatic cancer.

I talked to her at length about the possibility that the tumor was still quiescent, that other factors were depleting her, and Virginia seemed much more receptive to this interpretation than she had been earlier. She seemed very engaged, so much so that it was hard to get her off the phone. "She'd make a real interesting autopsy," Virginia said, and I knew, despite her phrasing, that she meant well. She was in Mom's corner now, ready to challenge conventional medical wisdom.

Maybe denial is catching, and we've infected her, but hospice nurses should be occupationally immune. They're prepared to see death, resistant to seeing signs of anything else.

Milena became similarly engaged today after witnessing the hour-to-hour, minute-to-minute fluctuations of this battle. When I took her to the airport, she asked me to call her more often, let her in on the dailiness. I would like to draw the links between my New York life and my life here tighter, and it should be more possible now that someone has seen the stage, met the cast and knows what scene we're in. But there is still the problem of privacy. I have none. My only link to the outside world is the kitchen phone, and I can't talk freely on it until Mom and Dad go to bed, which has been happening at a later and later hour. Even then I feel I must keep my voice low, which leads to long-distance calls full of "what-did-you-say's."

I wouldn't need so much privacy if I could bring myself to describe Mom's ailments in her earshot, as Dad does routinely, but I can't. And Dad and I so often have different perspectives on what is happening that I don't feel comfortable talking in his earshot either. The only place where I can speak what I see is in this journal.

The day began as usual. Mom was extremely weak but without specific complaints other than stiffness in her very swollen legs and a painful sore on her tongue. Mouth ulcers are a common side effect of radiation, and this one, which appeared on Wednesday, has made eating a torment for her. Given the other impediments to eating—virtually no appetite and poor-fitting dentures—it has become very difficult to motivate her to take any nourishment. She subsists on sips of milk and water, pills her only solid food.

The morning was spent waiting for Virginia, who said she would come by about 10:30 A.M. to draw blood for the other tests. By noon, I was crazed with tedium. In the house my only diversions are reading and writing, both activities Dad feels no hesitancy to interrupt, often, this morning at intervals of approximately thirty seconds. I timed them. If he washes a dish, he comes into the living room, where I am writing, to tell me he is about to wash a dish, then again to say he is doing it now, then a third time to tell me he has done it. With each interruption I build a stronger case in my head about the male sense of entitlement to female attention, the oppressive male need for an approving female witness to every act, however insignificant.

My better self knows that Dad is also crazed with tedium, lonely, bereft of the companion who was a willing, loving witness to his daily cares and pleasures. He is exhausted, scared, taut from the effort of repressing the magnitude of his present and impending losses. He needs me to care that he is washing a dish, drinking a glass of milk, thinking of mowing the lawn. But his need for my attention so violates my need for solitude that I am beginning to dread the sound of his approach. And to hate myself for feeling that way.

At 12:30 I decided it was better to leave the house than poison it with my anger. I drove west toward the river, and then north to another spot Freya had told me about. I parked the car and walked on a rutted tractor path through a wheat field to a thin stretch of woods bordering the river. The midday air was still and hot, near eighty degrees. After my walk at the nature preserve, I was prepared (braced is more like it) to see things slither. In fact nothing slithered and very little darted or stirred, but each step was made hazardous by my anticipation.

When the path turned south along the riverbank, there were twenty feet of dense, high brush between me and the water, placed there no doubt to thwart my desire for a view of its soothing expanse. I might as well have been walking a hot, dusty, inland road through scrub, except the dusty road had deep, wide ruts of mud that could only be avoided by stepping gingerly through high grass, heart pounding. I was wound more tightly now than I had been before I sought this escape.

I decided to cut my losses and return home, but as I approached the car, I saw Freya jogging the road toward me. She waved a greeting and rasped an invitation, so I followed her in the car as she finished the last half mile back to her house. She and Tom asked me to go apple picking with them and the boys, but I told them I was too foul-tempered to be allowed near innocents and proceeded to unload my wagon of complaints. Tom responded by offering to evict the tenants from their guest house and letting me live there in blessed solitude for as long as I wished. Freya, as generous but less impulsive than Tom, was clearly wondering how the tenants would react when I thanked them for an offer I couldn't accept. Not now, when my twenty-four-hour availability in the house is all that stands between Dad and the potentially calamitous strain of Mom's incessant need for care.

I returned home about 3:30 to give Dad a chance to get out, but he didn't take the opportunity. He told me that Virginia had come by but that she had been unable to draw blood again; what little blood she did extract from Mom's tiny veins was so dehydrated it immediately clotted in the tube, making it unusable for testing. Virginia said she would send another nurse, "an expert sticker," tomorrow.

When I entered Mom's bedroom, she was lying dispiritedly on her side. "Being sick is terrible," she said. I asked her if she felt the same as yesterday. "Yes," she said. "No zip. I don't care about anything . . . I don't care if school keeps." There was a pool of tears in her eyes, as there has been for the past few days, either from sadness or the constant pain of her mouth sores or both.

I told her that without energy she couldn't possibly "care if school keeps," and won a weak smile for my use of the phrase she must have heard from her own mother's mouth. I explained, truthfully I think, that no one really knew why her energy was so low, that it could be her pancreas or dehydration or hypothyroidism or lack of nourishment or, most likely, some combination of all those factors. I told her the only thing she had to do was drink water so that we could test her blood and get some answers.

As I spoke to Mom, I was sitting in the wheelchair, which now rests, unused, in the bedroom. I sat there because it was the most comfortable place to perch, but I also thought that if Mom got used to seeing me sit in it, she would regard it with a little less distaste.

About 6:00 P.M. I was sitting at the kitchen table writing when I heard a bird cry three times over the squawk box. For a split second I imagined the bird was heralding my mother's death. I went to look in on her and saw that she was sleeping soundly despite the bird's shrill crying from the evergreen outside her bedroom window. I went outside, spotted the offending jay and chased it out of the tree with a stone. I didn't want her sleep disturbed by a jay. She deserves a better birdsong.

There is still some fire left in Mom, a spark at least. Tonight, when Dad brought Mom a cup of tea, she looked him up and down and said, "Change your shirt. I'm tired of looking at that same dirty shirt." Earlier she told me to buy her some new sheets. The bed needs changing, and she doesn't want to see "any threadbare old ones" around her.

SUNDAY, SEPTEMBER 28:

The same. Mom slept all day except when she was awakened to take milk, water, prednisone, milk of magnesia. What a diet! Virginia suggested we try alum as a home remedy for Mom's mouth sores, and it seems to be helping but it burns terribly. Mom sticks her tongue into the spice box and winces as if she's been made to eat fire.

The expert sticker came this morning to draw blood and succeeded. Not long afterwards Virginia called to say that Mom's red and white blood cell counts and platelets were normal. We called Mike with the information and he admits these test results are extremely unusual for someone with a recurrence of cancer. He is as puzzled as we are and clings to the hypothyroid theory as a plausible explanation for her ever-waning energy.

We should have the thyroid test results tomorrow and Mike says if they show Mom to be severely hypothyroid, she may need to be hospitalized and put on emergency life support systems to prevent her from slipping into a coma before the thyroid supplements take effect. Unlike prednisone, thyroid supplements are slow-acting, and may take two weeks to show effect.

The irony will be bitter if she dies from a benign, easily treatable disease after surviving this cancer. Even if the problem proves to be hypothyroidism, and her energy can be restored, there is still the terrible ravaging of muscle that has come from her being treated as a terminal cancer patient in these last weeks. Will she have the strength and will to undergo physical therapy if her energy is restored? All idle speculations, I suppose. Much hinges on tomorrow's answers.

It's hard to believe Mom can survive much longer in her present state, and unless we know what is causing her decline, it will be very hard to make decisions about life support systems. If cancer has spread to other organs, we would not choose to prolong her life by what they call "heroic measures." But if she has even a slim chance of recovering from a treatable ailment, we will have a very different decision to make. We must have the best possible medical information, because once a hospital places a patient on life support systems, it cannot legally suspend them.

I was just interrupted in my writing by loud moans from Mom's room. When I went to check on her, she said she was having sharp pains under her right breast. About an hour ago, she had two spells of severe coughing, caused by the sensation that she was choking on her saliva. The chest pains are probably from pulled muscles and can be soothed by the TENS machine, but she is so frail that violent coughing could easily lead to broken ribs as well.

Her whole body is sore now from muscular weakness. When she is awake, Dad or I have to help her change her position in bed several times an hour to relieve the pressure of bed against bony back and shoulders and hips.

There were no tears in Mom's eyes today, just a look of profound discouragement and distaste for her helplessness. Several times she said, as she has often this week, "It's awful to be sick." But today she didn't have that look of innocence surprised when she said it.

It's 1:30 A.M. and I hear Dad snoring loudly. Is Mom lying next to him with her sore mouth, sore shoulders, sore legs, sore ribs, listening to him snore? Does she have the strength to wake him? Is she angry at him for not saving her? Does she realize he is the only one who never gives up, who never wants this to be over? He won't leave the house now even for a ten-minute trip to the drugstore. He is afraid, I think, that he might not be there to save her from some accident that might have been avoided.

MONDAY, SEPTEMBER 29:

I awoke with dread again this morning. So much can happen in a night. If Mom were worse, it would be a day of urgent measures and difficult decisions. Each morning I lie in my narrow bed and try to decipher the sounds I hear coming from the bedroom and bathroom. Are bowels moving or not? Is food being taken or not? This is the basis on which spirits lift or crash.

This morning I feared the worst and had to force myself to get out of bed. Mom and Dad were in the bathroom, so I went into the kitchen and made coffee while waiting for the day's first progress report. Virginia called to say the thyroid results would not be ready today, maybe tomorrow. A few minutes later Dad wheeled Mom into the living room. She was in the wheelchair under duress and wanted to be taken back to bed, but Dad insisted she sit up for a while. He was chipper, convinced that Mom was better today. The grounds for this conviction were not immediately apparent. Mom looked as miserable and agonized as ever.

As the day progressed, however, it did seem as if her level of energy was higher. She slept less, seemed more alert. This did not make it a better day for her, because consciousness is not a blessing in her situation, but she seemed a little farther from death than she did yesterday, less comatose but just as distressed. And more demanding.

Several times an hour, every hour, she asked me to massage her calves, which she said felt "like wood." Her right leg and foot were very badly swollen and seemed dangerous to touch, because the dark purple bruises caused by prednisone are covered by paper-thin skin that looks as if it would tear at the slightest pressure. The bruising is worst on the fronts of her calves, so usually I massage only the backs of them, but today she kept saying that the fronts of her calves were "so stiff," couldn't I do something.

I tried to massage them very gently, working carefully around the discolored areas, but when I touched a spot near her right ankle, the skin tore and she began to bleed. I doused it with hydrogen peroxide and prayed, "Please, Lord, don't let this get infected." Mom wasn't upset, the raw spot didn't hurt her, but I worry about her capacity to heal. I was almost afraid to tell Dad what happened. I wanted to hide the evidence the way I used to hide the cuts and scrapes I got as a child doing things I wasn't supposed to do.

By the end of the evening I was exhausted by Mom's wakefulness. She became a fretful child, calling for help, comfort, attention every five minutes all evening, a massage, a change of position, a cup of tea, more covers, less covers, a light on, a light off. "She'll be harder to take care of now that she's getting her energy back," Dad said with conspiratorial cheer in his voice, as if it were a challenge he couldn't wait to meet.

There was one good moment today. One of Dad's rosebushes produced the most beautiful bloom I've ever seen—the Platonic ideal of rose, the Platonic ideal of pink. I clipped it and brought it to Mom, whose eyes widened in disbelief. It was that gorgeous, and for an instant she was transported beyond herself to a realm of pure pleasure.

TUESDAY, SEPTEMBER 30:

Candace arranged a four-hour layover in Minneapolis on her return flight from California to New York today. She arrived by cab about 1:00 P.M. and, after indulging Dad and me in a few minutes' conversation, asked if she could see Mom right away. I tried to warn her not to expect much of this visit, but Candace, who has shared a special rapport with Mom since they first met several years ago, seemed unwilling to believe my mother could be as diminished as I described her. I led Candace into Mom's room, watched two sets of matching blue eyes spark with pleasure, and left them alone.

In the kitchen I turned off the squawk box and set the table for a lunch I expected to serve in fifteen minutes. When half an hour had passed, I walked down the hall to make sure Candace was not overtaxing Mom's strength. I saw Candace on her knees at Mom's bedside, crying. Mom held both of Candace's hands in hers and spoke softly. I returned to the kitchen without intruding and wondered if Mom had finally allowed herself to speak of death.

After almost an hour had passed, Candace emerged from Mom's room and went into the bathroom. Curious and concerned, I ducked in to see how Mom had survived by far the longest visit in months. Relaxed and smiling, she said how good it was to see Candace again. Later I learned from Candace that she had not expressed her sympathy for Mom but asked it of her. She placed the burden of her sadness over her stepfather's death in my mother's hands and she had been ready to receive it. "That's why I came," Candace said. "To get her comfort, and to let her give it." I was thankful, but also jealous, that Candace had found a way to let her be a mother again. I wanted to be the one kneeling at her bedside, but how can I ask her to comfort me for her sufferings?

WEDNESDAY, OCTOBER 1:

I awoke unsuspecting to one of the worst days so far. When I came out of my room, I saw Mom resting on the sofa in the den, usually a good sign, because "bad days" are spent in the bedroom. But when I went into the kitchen, Dad said Mom was too weak to get back into bed after her trip to the bathroom. He said that her right leg and foot were badly swollen again and that her bowels had not moved in three days, a fact that seems to obsess him.

When I went in to see Mom, she looked very pallid and frightened. "I'm worried," she said. "About what?" I asked. "My legs." She sat huddled against pillows in the corner of the sofa and her eyes didn't meet mine. "I'm worried," she repeated. I asked her if she was worried about the cancer returning, and she said, "Oh, no. Nothing like that. I'm worried about my legs." I asked her if they hurt, and she said, "They're stiff."

It didn't make sense to me that she was more concerned about stiff legs than spreading cancer, but when I tried to elicit more of a response from her, she kept going around in the same tight circle. She held her body very still and her eyes darted around the room focusing on nothing while she kept saying, "I'm worried, I'm worried," as if intoning a mantra. She was clearly getting no relief from talking with me. Finally I asked, "Are you worried that you will never walk again?" She looked at me for the first time and said, "Yes."

Meanwhile Dad had become fixated on his idea of a cure-all. He left the house for the first time in days and returned with a Fleet enema, brandishing his purchase like a warrior with a new weapon. He made elaborate preparations for battle, enlisting the aid of the wheelchair and me. I knew how demeaned Mom would feel and suggested we wait until the nurse arrived this afternoon, so that Mom would not have to undergo this torment at the hands of her husband and daughter. But Dad was adamant. It must be done now.

The ordeal that followed so depleted Mom in body and spirit and so enraged me that I felt hate enter my heart and dislodge every other emotion my father had ever engendered there. I knew he had acted out of concern for Mom, out of a panicked fear that if he didn't do something there might be a repeat of the five-day crisis that began this gruesome phase of Mom's illness. But still he acted irrationally, cruelly, heedless of everything but his own fear of death. As if death could be controlled like a dutiful wife and daughter.

When we returned Mom to the den and covered her nakedness, she wanted the blankets pulled up to her chin. Several times during the day and evening, she asked me to pull the covers higher, a task her arms were too weak to accomplish. I think the reason she worries more about her legs than her pancreas, stomach, colon, liver, kidneys or any of the organs that can kill her is because, without the use of her legs, she is our prisoner, and that is a more frightening state for her than death. Her depression today was deep and inconsolable.

Father Mahon, apparently alerted by the neighbors to the seriousness of Mom's condition, called yesterday and arranged to make a visit today at 2:30. Whenever Mom would remember his impending arrival, she would groan and say, "Oh, I wish he weren't coming today. Can't we cancel it?" She also asked me to call her sisters and tell them not to make the trip from Fort Dodge tomorrow, as they had planned after talking to Mike yesterday. For months, the relatives in Fort Dodge had accepted Mom's version of herself as a cured but still recuperating patient, but Mom's sisters became worried in the past few weeks when she was no longer able to come to the phone to reassure them, as Dad did, that everything was fine. Yesterday they called Mike, who told them Mom might not have much longer to live, and the five of us—me, Mike and the three sisters—conspired to get them up here as soon as possible.

It makes me feel guilty to refuse Mom's requests, especially requests to do simple things she would do herself if she had the strength, like make a phone call. But I didn't want to dissuade her sisters from coming and I thought a visit from Father Mahon might also do some good, so I stalled. I told her if she let me comb her hair and apply a little makeup, she would look so good Father Mahon would wonder what her trouble was. And the strange thing is, it's true. With hair combed and lipstick on, her face is so beautiful it is impossible to imagine the wracked body hidden under the blankets.

So Father Mahon came, admired her appearance, prayed for the recovery of her body "if that was God's plan," forgave her her sins and delivered communion. Dad went into the den to receive communion with Mom, but I stayed out of the room, too angry to join them, the ministering men. Father Mahon stayed no longer than ten minutes, offered no words other than those prescribed by the ritual of prayer and his habit of cajoling "the ladies of the parish" with a bit of sly flattery. As he was leaving, I heard Mom say, "God can plan whatever he wants for the rest of me, but I want my legs back." Afterward, Mom said it was "good to see Father Mahon again," but it was not so uplifting that it prevented her from slipping back into a deep depression within minutes of his departure.

By the time Virginia arrived, Mom was almost autistic. She would not speak or make eye contact with anyone while Virginia examined her. Blood pressure—normal. Rate of respiration—normal. Mom remained expressionless when Virginia told us the results of the thyroid tests we had been awaiting—her T-3 and TSH were normal, her T-4 slightly hypo, definitely not results that could account for her symptoms.

Virginia, visibly saddened by Mom's mental anguish, signaled a retreat to the kitchen for a conference. There, she told Dad and me that she was mystified by the discrepancy between all of Mom's test results and her very marked deterioration. How could someone so sick keep producing test results a healthy person might well envy? The only symptom she thought she might be able to relieve was the fluid buildup in Mom's swollen legs, which she said was probably caused by circulatory and kidney problems. The antidote, however, was a diuretic and Virginia was hesitant to use a diuretic on a patient already so severely dehydrated. She called Dr. McCrae for advice, miraculously reaching her on the first try, and told us the doctor would call in the prescription for a diuretic, but we must make sure that Mom drinks as much water as possible while on this medication.

Before leaving, Virginia went back into the bedroom to talk with Mom. She returned fifteen minutes later and told us that Mom said she "wanted it to end," which Virginia interpreted as Mom saying she wanted to die. I said I thought Mom meant she wanted the sickness to end, not her life, but Virginia felt certain that Mom had confessed her readiness for death. This confused me. Why would she say that to Virginia after telling me this morning that she only thought about getting well again? Something stirred in me that felt suspiciously like jealousy. Had Virginia won more of Mom's trust in two weeks than I had in my entire life? Did Mom find more solace in her presence than in mine?

I went into Mom's bedroom, turned off the power on her squawk box so we could talk without Dad's surveillance and tried to fathom her state of mind. She greeted me with a heartfelt "It's awful to be sick," one of the expressions that has become a refrain in the past two weeks, and I responded with "It sounds as if you're more worried about being sick than about dying." It was the first time I had used the word "dying" to her, and she rejected it like a bad skin graft. "Oh, no," she said, "I'm not worried about dying. I know I'll get up again." I wanted to know if she really didn't understand that she was in very immediate danger of dying, but before I could say anything else, Dad entered the room and said, "Is something wrong with the squawk box? I was listening and it went dead."

The rage I had felt this morning flared up to full heat, and I decided to leave the house rather than risk explosion. I am paying the price now for a lifetime of not challenging the family ethic of keeping the peace at all costs. I have learned, through other relationships, that anger can be expressed and survived, but I have never brought that knowledge back to my soft-spoken family, and now it seems too late. How can I bring anger into this home, to parents who have barricaded the door against it for as long as I can remember? How can I raise my voice against my mother who is sick and dying, my father strained beyond his understanding?

It was 5:30 P.M., too late for a drive to the river, so I got in the car and headed in the direction of Highland Park, a nature preserve I'd been told about that is closer to home. A wrong turn brought me to Normandale Lake instead, but rather than risk spending the rest of the daylight driving in circles, I parked the car and began walking the path round the lake. Like many of the area's much-vaunted lakes, this one was a large duck pond surrounded by busy highways and featureless high-rise apartment complexes. The pond was ringed by a two-mile path, with exercise stations of tastefully weathered wood telling you what muscle to flex every one hundred yards, and providing the necessary rings, balance beams, and parallel bars to do so.

As I walked, at least one hundred grim-faced Minnesotans ran or marched by me, gazes turned inward as they monitored their pulses, their breathing, their virtue. Apparently their lawns were already mowed. Or perhaps they were high-rise residents, free to do the next best thing on a rare, beautiful day. Halfway round the duck pond, I about-faced and sprinted against the flow to get back to my car and head on to Highland Park, where I hoped nature could be found with better aspect.

I discovered that Highland Park is only a quarter mile from Normandale Lake, incomparably more peaceful and beautiful, and because this is Minnesota, I had it all to myself—three miles of trails that wind through woods and fields, along high ridges and low marshes, with spectacular fall vistas and without the roar of traffic in the near distance. I chose a trail that went uphill on a wide, soft dirt path cushioned by fallen leaves and chips of bark. There were dense woods on both sides of the path and a loud chatter from creatures flitting, scurrying and leaping all around me. The sound of leaves falling and rustling into place added to the chorus. There was so much movement that I didn't need to stop and listen and search it out the way I usually do. My footsteps just added another note to the general racket, not distinct enough to alarm the birds and squirrels and rabbits who crisscrossed the path in front of me, on the ground and in the air. The higher the path went, the more of a mob scene it became. Then, as the path sloped downhill and curved back toward the starting point, the woods became stiller.

I didn't want this walk to end, so when I saw a small side path, I took it. The side path led uphill to an overlook, where a deck had been built for viewers' convenience. The deck was deserted, but its weathered wood creaked with civic virtue, so I looked around for a more pastoral vantage point and saw a very narrow path, made by and for animals rather than Minnesotans, leading up through chest-high brush to a clearing. I climbed up through the brush, stepped into a narrow strip of grass and found myself five yards from a startled fawn.

The fawn looked me over but didn't run away. I stood very still and told him how beautiful he was and how much pleasure it gave me to come upon him like this. When I finally took a step, he bounded several yards into the brush on the other side of the grassy swath. There he stopped, looked to see if I was going to follow him, and seeing that I wasn't, calmly began munching leaves. He was so small I knew his mother had to be nearby, so I began walking downhill on the grassy strip. Ten paces brought me within yards of the doe. She looked at me, I explained I meant no harm, which she already seemed to know, and kept on walking. She didn't move when I crossed her path, nor when I recrossed it a few minutes later.

I walked the short distance to where the fawn was still munching and gave a little whistle. He looked up, seemed uncertain of my intention and bounded through the brush toward his mother, as I had hoped he would. I followed to get a look at doe and fawn together. The mother continued to chomp leaves without alarm and baby followed her cue. I felt a twinge of guilt for toying with the fawn, but only a twinge. I had just wanted to see them together. I said good-bye and left them to their meal.

On the way back I picked up the prescription diuretic that is supposed to help Mom's legs. By the time I got home, my anger was long gone. Not resolved, just gone. I stayed by myself as much as possible for the rest of the evening.

THURSDAY, OCTOBER 2:

I was awakened at 8:00 A.M. by the usual assortment of dismal sounds, the most disturbing of which was Dad's coughing, violent and prolonged. Unready to face another day like yesterday, I pulled a pillow over my head and willed the morning back into darkness and silence.

About 10:00 A.M. I was forced to get up by the ringing of an unanswered phone. It was Nancy, wanting to know if Mom had accepted the fact she was dying. The pressure she and Mike are placing on me to create "a good death" for Mom is hard to take, particularly after yesterday, and after my many abortive attempts to fathom Mom's state of mind. It is easy for someone at a distance to think there is some abstract state called "acceptance of death" and that you can maneuver a sick person into it at your convenience. Here, on location, Mom is not cooperating.

That I came to the phone half awake, without benefit of coffee or even a splash of water on my face, made me less patient than I might have been, but patience, which used to come too easily to me, is getting harder and harder to muster. I told Nancy I'd call her back.

Twenty minutes later, when I was awake and awash with coffee but not yet dressed for the world, a carful of aunts pulled into the driveway, two hours earlier than expected. I asked Dad to entertain them in the living room while I prepared myself and Mom for company. I had not seen my aunts since Grandma's funeral in 1979, and I didn't want to look as if I'd aged twenty years in seven. I dressed and put on makeup, combed Mom's hair and applied a little color to her lips and cheeks; then, just as I was ready to greet my aunts, the phone rang. Nancy again, wanting to continue our conversation about Mom's reluctance to welcome death. She seemed irritated when I explained I couldn't talk because I was getting Mom ready to welcome her sisters.

I hung up the phone, willed the ill temper off my face, and walked into the living room. Anna Marie, Katherine and Veronica were sitting together on the sofa, shoulder to shoulder and hip to hip. They were a delight at first glance, more immediately endearing as a threesome of sisters than they are when flanked by their husbands and children, as they usually have been in my presence. Their faces radiate a sweet innocence that is not in the least insipid. They look so inherently benign it is impossible to imagine them wishing anyone harm.

This innocent look is more marked in Anna Marie and Katherine, the two youngest sisters, than it is in Veronica or Mom, who pride themselves on a degree of worldliness. The two oldest sisters, Alice and Sister Innocentia, had none of it; their faces were stern and judgmental, cracked on occasion by forced or pious smiles.

Looking at the three of them sitting side by side, I had a sudden insight into the sisterly economy that must have been at work in their family: the two eldest sisters made stern by early responsibility for the younger ones, the two middle sisters made mischievous and worldly in rebellion against the older ones, the two youngest made sweet by the doting of so many older brothers and sisters as well as a mother who now had so many helpers.

Anna Marie, the youngest, must be in her early sixties but she could easily be mistaken for my slightly older sister. She looks the most like me, or I should say, I look the most like her, but Mom is the one with the piercing eyes I inherited. The others have twinkling eyes. Katherine's are just slits in her smooth, round cheeks. Her face, open and unlined, seems to register a constant state of effortless ecstasy. It's a remarkable face for a mother of eight who has worked on a farm all her life. "We may lose the bean crop this year, because of the rain," Katherine says when I ask how the farm is doing. "But the corn'll be okay even if we can't harvest it. It'll take the freeze." I see distant fields of soggy beans and frozen corn warmed by the light of her beatific smile.

After chatting for ten minutes, I go into Mom's room and ask if she is ready to see her sisters. "Not yet," she says. "I'm afraid I'll cry if they come in." I tell her we will visit some more in the living room and she can summon us over the squawk box whenever she wants. A few minutes later, Mom signals her readiness and all three enter the bedroom for a joint audience. Then Veronica and Katherine come out, while Anna Marie stays, and they all take turns seeing Mom one by one, youngest first and oldest last, with breaks in between. A minuet of sisters.

They all say how relieved they are to see Mom isn't in pain. And they are happy to see she still has "her pride," a quality they identify entirely with wearing makeup. "Allie didn't do that," Veronica says. "She lost her pride. Well, it was . . . she was so depressed." Katherine, playing chorus to the main commentator, interjects a "Ya, she was so depressed," before Veronica continues: "Now Bea is just the opposite. She still wants to look good. Several times I went to visit Allie determined to get makeup on her, but then I'd get there and I just couldn't do it."

"Always the older sister," I say. "Ya," they all agree. "But Sister Innocentia is the worst," Veronica adds. "Oh ya!" comes the chorus, with an emphatic nodding of gray heads. "She's always calling and telling us off," Veronica explains. "She told me off again yesterday, I won't even tell you what for." Veronica starts laughing into her hands at the thought of her most recent scolding, and Katherine, the next oldest, takes over: "She treats us like we're still children. She calls to tell me something and says, 'Now go get a pencil, Katherine. Have you got it? Good.

Now write this down. Did you get it all? Good. Now read it back to me, Katherine.' Can you believe it!"

About this time they started feeling guilty for talking disrespectfully about an eighty-three-year-old nun who just happens to be their overbearing older sister. The talk turned to more practical matters, like preventing bedsores. Veronica boasted that Aileen never had a bedsore during the entire six months she was in a coma. The mention of my aunt Aileen was an opening I had been waiting for. Keeping my voice casual, I said, "You know, I've never understood why Aileen was institutionalized."

Veronica winced. Then she began her reply with the prolonged "Oh" all the sisters use to buy a little time, just a few seconds to recollect the facts or maybe rearrange them. It's the kind of "Oh" that usually precedes a slow "I don't know" and means "I'm not sure I want to say anything about this right now." This time Veronica decided to talk.

"Oh," she said. "I don't know. Nobody's sure. I guess she was slightly retarded." Each short sentence is halted by a long pause. "You know, she lived at home until she was twenty-seven. But she couldn't do the things the rest of us did, and, well, I guess that became a problem."

"A problem for whom?" I asked. "For Aileen?"

"Yes," Veronica answered. "For Aileen. I guess it's supposed to be best, when that happens, to be among other people like yourself."

She said this tentatively, glancing sidelong at Katherine. One of Katherine's daughters is retarded, and after living on the farm for twenty-five years, she recently moved into a community home for retarded adults, where Katherine says she is very happy.

Seeing Veronica's discomfort, Katherine took over the task of reminiscence. "Aileen was beautiful," Katherine said. "Have you ever seen a picture?" I told her I had seen one picture of

Aileen, taken when she was about four years old, and that I had been amazed by her beauty. I didn't say that what most amazed me was Aileen's eyes, the almost scary, laser-beam look that shows up in some pictures of Mom and of me, but which I had not expected in Aileen.

Katherine said there was another picture of Aileen that I must see, one of Mom and Aileen taken when Aileen was a teenager. The offer of a picture showing is the Fort Dodge equivalent of a free ticket to a sold-out Broadway show. On Christmas Eve, 1925, when my grandfather's farmhouse burnt to the ground, all but a very few photographs of the sisters burned with it, so the remaining ones are jealously guarded by whoever managed to gain possession. I said I would like to see that picture when I next came to Fort Dodge, and then we all fell silent, acknowledging that my next trip to Iowa would be for my mother's funeral.

The silence was broken by more talk of how beautiful Aileen had looked, in that picture and in her casket six months ago. I tried to move the conversation back to what exactly had been wrong with Aileen. "Well," Veronica said, "she had a stroke when she was fourteen, they think. We didn't know it was a stroke at the time, but she was never the same afterward."

Katherine and Anna Marie exchanged astonished looks and said they hadn't known about the stroke.

"Oh yes," Veronica said, "she was completely normal before that."

"This is the first I've known that," Anna Marie said, her tone slightly accusatory.

"Well, how do you think she got through eighth grade?" Veronica rejoined. "You knew that."

"Yes," Anna Marie said, "but I thought they had just, well, pushed her through, the way they do with kids now."

"No," Veronica said. "She was a regular student. She used to stay all night over at Eileen McMahon's. They were best friends."

The fact that Aileen had a best friend, a woman whom they knew, a woman like themselves, seemed to stun Anna Marie and Katherine.

I was astounded that they knew so little about their sister, that they had never exchanged this information, that they had never been curious enough to ask these questions, or just to gossip among themselves about how Aileen got to be the way she was, however she was. Grandma must have imposed a virtual vow of silence upon the subject of Aileen, but even if that were so, it seems incredible such a vow should be honored.

I wanted to keep pumping Veronica for information, but the talk veered back to bedsores and eggshell mattresses, and soon it was time for them to begin the five-hour ride back to Fort Dodge. They said their good-byes to Mom, respecting Veronica's place as the one closest to Mom in age and intimacy. She emerged from the bedroom last, alone, and lingered at the front door, wordless. She seemed to be waiting for something and then, with a look of immense physical effort, she pushed the door open and walked out of her sister's house.

"It was so good to see them," Mom said. Afterward, exhausted, she slept for most of the afternoon and evening. Whenever she awakened, she would say, "It's so awful to be sick" or "When will I be well?" or "I'm so worried."

About 7:30 P.M. I returned Nancy's call. Mike answered and I told him of my conversations with Mom, my use of the words "cancer" and "dying," my attempts to commiserate without offering false hope. He was relieved to know this much had been spoken and seemed to think it enough.

A little later Dad announced he was going to Southdale's to buy a new pair of "dress" pants. It seemed a strange mission. Why should the desire for a new pair of pants get him out of the house when nothing else had for the past many days? And why was he so elated when he returned an hour later, mission accomplished? He modeled his new pants for me and extolled their virtues at great length—he hadn't worn a size 34 in years, the textured polyester had a nice little stretch to it, the color was perfect, the inseam all he had hoped for. I was writing when he began to expatiate on his pants and quickly became impatient with the interruption, but I did my best to compliment his shopping skills and his figure before moving to the den for privacy.

The third time he opened the door to the den to tell me how pleased he was with his purchase, I became murderous. How can he be so impervious to my need for some privacy? And why does he need a new pair of dress pants anyway? What occasion does he have to wear them? Is he preparing for a new life, a life after Mom? Later, when I heard him enter Mom's bedroom and wake her to tout his new pants, again at great length, it occurred to me that he had gone crazy. Finally, he interrupted me for a last time. "You know," he said, "she must get awfully tired of seeing me in the same old clothes."

FRIDAY, OCTOBER 3:

We were all up early to be ready for Virginia's visit at 10:00 A.M. The diuretics had slightly improved the swelling in Mom's right leg, but otherwise she was the same as when Virginia last saw her. Again, all the vital signs were good but the patient was miserable, and Virginia was at a loss for what to do to help Mom feel better. Her only suggestion was a variation of pillow placement to relieve the stiffness in Mom's legs.

Mom keeps telling Virginia that she wants to get up again, which Virginia takes literally and so suggests to Mom that she spend more time sitting up in the wheelchair, joining us in the kitchen for meals. Mom gives her a "sure, fine, good idea" response, but Dad and I know such feats are out of the question. In the past few days, Mom has eaten only a few spoonfuls of soup and she resists any movement; she is so weak she even has trouble getting her hands out from under the covers by herself.

Virginia, unable to penetrate the dense fog of depression that settled into the house this morning, succumbed to it herself and left feeling useless. I hadn't stepped out of the house in two days and was counting on a lunch date with Freya to restore my equilibrium. At noon Freya called to say she had wrenched her back last night and couldn't get out of bed. Desperate for at least a change of sickbed, I insisted upon visiting her. Her mood matched mine, nerve for frayed nerve. Yesterday, on her tenth wedding anniversary, her back gave out and her cat got run over by a car, both of which events she took as messages about her marriage. She shared her thoughts with Tom, and so the anniversary they had planned to celebrate with a trip to Paris— canceled after last week's terrorist bombings—was spent getting hysterical together in Bloomington. We each tried to enter the other's trouble as an escape from our own, but neither of us succeeded.

I returned home to learn that Dad had lost patience with Mom's depression and yelled at her. She responded to his anger by going into a deep sleep, which he interprets as a "peaceful slumber," the beneficial result of "a good scolding." I seethe. And I call Blue Cross/Blue Shield to find out how we can arrange for the twelve-hour-a-day home nursing care we are entitled to by Dad's supplemental insurance policy. Blue Cross/Blue Shield puts me on hold, then transfers me to Medicare, who puts me on hold, then transfers me back to Blue Cross/Blue Shield. While I'm waiting for answers, I hear Mom groaning and, between groans, chanting, "I'm so worried. My legs. My legs. What's wrong with my legs? I'm so worried."

I call Southdale Hospital's Hospice Office to see if they can help me get information from Blue Cross/Blue Shield. The hospice social worker tells me that despite the contract I have in hand, which promises to supplement our Medicare coverage with 180 days a year of home care by a licensed practical nurse, we are in fact only entitled to Medicare's six hours a week of nurse's aide services. She cannot explain why this is so. I want to scream or kill or run away.

Instead I cook dinner. Roast chicken, dressing, gravy, sweet potatoes, cranberry sauce. I make this dinner for Dad, because I feel guilty for feeling so angry at him, and for Mom, because it is soft, easy to chew and full of good tastes, and maybe, just maybe, she will be tempted to eat. Dad loves it. Mom takes a bite of dressing, a nibble of cranberry sauce and then lowers the fork to the plate that rests on her chest. As always, Dad and I eat at the kitchen table, listening to the sounds of Mom's discomfort over the squawk box.

I hear her say, "I'm so sad," and leave the table to go to her. "What's making you so sad?" I ask. "My condition," she answers. My ears prick. This is a new word, a change in the refrain. For days she has fixated on her legs as the source of her misery. Does the word "condition" mean a change in her recognition of what is happening?

"What do you think your condition is?" I ask.

"I don't know why I am so sick," she says. "Why?"

"Because you've had a very dangerous disease and a very dangerous treatment."

"But I thought I was about to be better."

We are both quiet for a minute while Mom looks sad, thoughtful, as if she is sounding the depth of her belief, in God, in medicine. Finally, I say, "I know. It's rotten."

"Why me?" she asks, allowing herself that question for the first time in over a year.

"There's no good reason," I answer. "Why anybody? It could be me or Dad or Mike and probably will be."

"Oh, I know," she says, seemingly unperturbed at the thought of her family sharing her fate.

I tell her she should try to think about something besides getting better, about other times and parts of her life. I acknowledge how hard it is for her to stop focusing on that prospect, after a year of using it to motivate herself to withstand the ordeal of treatment.

As we talk, her face changes. Her eyes become clearer, her

pupils less dilated. She looks at me as if she sees me, as if she is looking through instead of at the film of tears that have covered her eyes for days. She seems to be listening to me, hearing my words instead of the refrain that has been playing in her head, drowning out the rest of us for days. She looks intelligent again. Sad but sound of mind. And, miraculously, relaxed. Soon she becomes very drowsy and falls into a deep sleep.

I survive the rest of the evening. In bed at 1:00 A.M. I try to read, but the words scatter at the quick gasps and slow, undulating groans of pain that come across the hall and slip under my closed door. I cry soundlessly until 3:00 A.M. and then, depleted, fall asleep.

SATURDAY, OCTOBER 4:

I am awakened at 8:30 by the clang of chrome against porcelain, wheelchair colliding with tub or toilet bowl. Her groans. His coughing. If I don't get up and help, there may be disaster in this house. It is all too plausible that their fifty years together will end in the grotesquerie of simultaneous death, he of a heart attack trying to lift her slack weight from wheelchair to toilet, she hemorrhaging from the fall. I get up.

This journal is turning to trash. There is too much riot of bodies and souls to bring into ordered telling, too little time and privacy to do the telling, and everything is changing so fast there will be no way to reconstruct each day's extremity later. Why am I keeping this journal anyway? Do I really want to remember this? Is it possible that I am hoping for a happy ending?

This morning Mom suggested we take her to Rochester. "Maybe there's something more they can do for me," she said. "Maybe they can make me well, find out what's wrong with my legs; I know it isn't cancer."

Dad caught a full-blown case of denial from Mom and fixated on getting another CAT scan, which Mom is probably physically incapable of undergoing. How can she drink the sixteen ounces of bilious fluid she needs to ingest for a scan when she has only been able to take a few sips of water a day? And, with so little flesh on her bones, how can she lie still on a hard surface for forty-five minutes? They seem to think of the CAT scan as a big pill that will make her better.

I think it is crazy to subject Mom to more testing when she is so weak. I've finally come to share Mike's perspective. There is no doubt in my mind that she is dying; the fact that we don't know precisely why is irrelevant. To my mind the only virtue of another hospitalization is to get professional nursing care, which we desperately need. Apparently the only way to get home care is to hospitalize a patient, because once a patient is admitted, the hospital is responsible for providing sufficient care for survival at home when the patient is discharged.

I'm not challenging Mom's hope for a last-minute miracle, but I am trying to get her to worry less about her body, tend more to her spirit. I spent more time today just sitting at her bedside while she slept, so that when she opened her eyes, she would see me. Several times she awoke and said, "I feel so sick," but once, as she was falling back to sleep, she said, "I see stars." I asked if that was good or bad. "I don't know," she said. "I just see stars." I asked if the stars were colored. "No, bright and clear," she answered, and my eyes lit with pleasure.

Later, she tried to repeat the performance. "I see mice," she said. "What are they doing?" I asked. "Running," she said. "And I suppose there's three of them?" I coached. "Oh, yes," she said and fell back to sleep. Other times she would awaken and say, "You're so good" or "You're such a faithful daughter." It was the first time in weeks that I felt my presence was a consolation.

About 4:00 P.M. I left the house to take a walk in Highland Park. The afternoon was gray and the park silent—only a few twitters and scuttlings as I retraced the route that had taken me through such a cacophony of critter sounds on my last walk here.

Heading down a trail toward the marsh, I spotted an ancient robin feeding on the ground, his fat breast a weathered rusty gray. Startled by my footsteps, he flew up toward the nearest tree branch, wings flapping so slowly and laboriously I thought he might not stay airborne. Looking more closely at the robin, I saw one of his legs was hurt, drawn up under its fat belly. When he tried to fly from one branch to another, he seemed to free-fall for several feet before getting enough wing action to move forward and up. The injured leg made it hard for him to land on the new perch, and when he did land, one wing was caught on a twig in a spread-open position. He finally flapped it free and stayed put long enough for me to write this.

A few minutes later, the robin did an open-winged free fall from the branch, grabbed a berry in its beak on the way down and crash-landed in a bed of leaves at my feet. Again, his right wing was caught, spread open, on brush. He freed it and stayed still for several minutes while we eyed each other. Crows cawed overhead and I wondered how much longer the old robin could survive by his wits. The analogy to my mother crossed my mind, but not sentimentally. I just wondered if the bird had anyone to help him, any family, any friends.

When I returned home, I learned that Dad had called Dr. McCrae and scheduled a CAT scan for Mom on Tuesday at Fairview-Southdale Hospital. I cursed myself for being out of the house when he made the call, because he arranged the scan on an outpatient basis, which means we will not be entitled to any professional nursing care, as we would have been if she were hospitalized and then discharged.

I also learned that Milena had called while I was out. She drove upstate today to check on the house and was pleased to find water in the well. But when she tried to prime the pump to get water flowing through the pipes, the hot water heater exploded and flooded the basement. I have to go home while I still have one, but I can't leave this house even for a day unless Dad has someone to help him. I'm also worried about the sale of my city apartment. The closing is scheduled for November 3, but my lawyer tells me the buyers have still not secured a mortgage and the co-op board has still not given its approval to the buyers. If this sale falls through, I'll be about as solvent as my well.

SUNDAY, OCTOBER 5:

The ordeal of bowels too weak to move, the painful transfer from bed to wheelchair to toilet of a body too weak to support itself in a seated position ended last night at 2:00 A.M. and began again this morning at 6:00 A.M. I am forced to participate, because to remain apart is to let Dad endanger himself as well as Mom. This morning Dad was exhausted, irritable, insensitive to Mom's panic and despair, and so his anger at her body's inability to function gets added to the blows she suffers. Dad's arms and back are sore from the hoisting of dead weight, his heart strained by physical and emotional stress to the bursting point. Each morning, when Mom is finally returned to bed, she lapses into a deep, depressed sleep, and Dad's loud coughing rumbles through the house for hours. This has to stop.

The morning convinces me that Dad is no longer capable of sound judgment about Mom's care. I don't suggest, I demand that Mom be hospitalized on Tuesday and then, if she wishes, be returned home with full-time professional nursing. Dad capitulates. I call Dr. McCrae and tell her this is what we are going to do. I call Mike and tell him this is what we are going to do and warn him that he better visit soon. I stride into the bedroom and tell Mom this is what we are going to do. I tell Dad to take a nap and I stay with Mom.

For the next several hours I change the position of her body when her right shoulder or left shoulder or right hip or left hip gets sore from the pressure of mattress against unpadded bone. I massage her stiff, swollen legs. I look into her eyes whenever she awakens. I promise her that something will get better, either her body or her spirit, I don't know which. She says it is good to see my face when she opens her eyes. In sleep, she looks more calm. The furrows on her right temple are gone.

I notice that there has been no urine in her catheter bag for hours, which signals a dangerous level of dehydration, and so every time she opens her eyes, I give her a sip of water but I don't tell her why. Dad makes the mistake of talking too much about every function or malfunction of her body, which only causes futile worry because there is nothing she can do about it anymore. I am trying to coach him out of the habit.

For lunch Mom tries to eat some potato soup, but after a few spoonfuls, she says, "You know, I'm not at all hungry." She doesn't say it like a penitent child expecting a reprimand; it's just a simple statement of fact, delivered and received as such. Progress.

After removing the uneaten food from the room, I put more covers on her, and before I leave, she says, "I'm snuggly." She has had a good sensation. I feel triumphant.

Dad spent most of the day napping and watching football games. And he ate voraciously. "I must need to catch up on calories," he said as he munched his way through the refrigerator's entire contents. Since he has eaten normally all week, I can only guess that he felt the need to indulge himself. He seemed to like it that I insist he take care of himself today, that he not even think about hefting Mom's weight ever again.

Mom seemed more peaceful today than in the past week, and more concerned about other people. "Am I wearing Dad out?" she asked me. "I'm glad he's taking a nap." Her face seemed composed, relaxed, without fret lines or furrows. When she opens her eyes after drowsing, they sometimes have that very wide, startled look I first saw when she was on morphine after her operation last September. At those moments she looks like she has returned from another world and is very disoriented by her surroundings. She's not on any painkillers now except for an occasional Darvoset; I wonder if the body produces its own morphine in its last days.

I just hope hospital admission will not be an ordeal, that she can be transported comfortably, her needs attended to. If she is neglected or otherwise mistreated, which is always a danger in hospitals, it could undo the fragile beginnings of peace we've managed to establish today.

MONDAY, OCTOBER 6:

Last night, as I was falling asleep, I heard a high-pitched whimper that sounded like a small animal's last gasp. I bolted upright in bed and heard the sound again. It was coming from my stomach.

Without the usual clash of steel and porcelain, of Dad's strong will and Mom's weak flesh, the early-morning hours are quiet. But at 10:00 A.M. the silence is broken by loud moans. Gas pains are rippling through Mom's intestines every few minutes. We were supposed to receive an early-morning visit from a nurse's aide who could teach us how to use a bedpan. At 11:00 A.M. I call the hospice office to complain about the delay and urge them to send us help as soon as possible. At 1:30 P.M. I call the Home Care Nursing Center; the administrator hears Mom's shrieks over the phone and says she understands our desperation but two of her nurses' aides called in sick and she is having trouble locating someone for us. It is 2:30 P.M. now, Mom's pains are intense and uninterrupted. I am trying to stay sane by writing, but Dad walks into the den every few seconds to say, "I think we need another carton of milk" or "Oh, I just thought of something else, cheese." I am clenching my teeth, trying not to add my screams to Mom's.

At 3:30 Virginia and a nurse's aide arrive. They bathe Mom from head to toe, brush her hair, change her pajamas, arrange her pillows and bedcovers so that the patient makes a pretty picture, but they can do very little to ease her discomfort.

While Virginia is tending Mom, I call the hospice social worker, who tells me that yes, she has checked again with Blue Cross/Blue Shield, as I asked her to, and no, we are not entitled to any home care services from them. With a jaw so tight the words have to fight for exit, I say that I already know that, what I want her to find out is how they can justify their position when I have a contract clearly stating that we are entitled to 180 home visits a year. Will she puh-leez get them to explain what circumstances will activate this clause of our policy while the patient is still alive?

About 7:00 P.M. Mom's pains disappear for no apparent reason, and calm is restored for a few hours while both she and Dad sleep. I turn on "Cagney and Lacey," hoping for escape, and find myself watching an episode in which Isbecki mercy-kills his cancer-ridden mother because he can't stand to hear her moans in the night. I start framing a letter in my mind to the producer, but before I can decide whether to protest this method of dispatching Isbecki's mother, I am interrupted by moans from my own very real mother.

I rush into the bedroom and she starts crying, "My legs, my legs." In fact her legs look good; there is no swelling for the first time in three weeks. And her stomach looks good, flat, quiet, no distension. Suspecting she just wants attention, I stroke her forehead rather than massage her legs, and her pains vanish. For the next several hours, however, she develops a new complaint every time I try to leave the room. She seems full of ploys to hold my attention, and it is almost funny. It is also exhausting. Perhaps she is behaving this way now because she is afraid that once she enters the hospital tomorrow, there will be no one to indulge her until she returns home.

Mom's restless calls for attention continued all through the night. Dad says she wakened him every five minutes with shifting complaints—her back, her arm, her legs. She would ask him to change her position, but when he tried to move her, she would scream. Occasionally the screams wakened me. Then, about 4:30 A.M., I heard Dad up and coughing. He prowled till dawn, coughing so loudly sleep was impossible for any of us.

At 7:45 A.M. the Medi-Bus came for Mom. The two young men who moved Mom onto a stretcher and carried her to the van were very gentle and competent, so the transfer from home to hospital was much less arduous than I had imagined it would be. The hospital, however, was a much worse experience than I expected. There will be no private rooms available on the hospice ward this week until someone dies. Mom's roommate is a pleasant, quiet woman, in robust health compared to Mom, but she is hooked up to a lung-cleansing machine that makes a loud, steady gurgle. It isn't a bad sound—one can pretend a brook is babbling on the other side of the curtain—but it drives Mom crazy.

Within minutes of admission, she began shouting, "Stop that sound. I can't stand that sound." I went down to the pharmacy and bought earplugs, but even with plugs in and towels pressed against both ears, she kept complaining. I told her we would try to get her room changed, but in the meantime, she should not protest so loudly, because the woman on the other side of the curtain needs the gurgling machine to breathe. "Okay," she'd say, and then thirty seconds later begin again: "Oh, that noise."

About 5:00 P.M., we were moved to another room, but there Mom complained about another sound—this time, the slight tick of her IV monitor, which had not drawn her notice in the first room. I didn't try to talk her out of her peevishness, because I noticed that once she fixated on an annoying sound, she stopped worrying about other, more serious discomforts. She only asked us to change her position a few times all day and she never mentioned her swollen legs. Once, as I watched a nurse prick her bruised flesh in a futile search for blood, Mom looked up at me and said, "This is so hard on you."

At mealtimes, Mom acted as though her arms were too weak to lift fork to mouth, so Dad spoon-fed her lunch and I spoon-fed her dinner. Her behavior was very infantile, more regressive than circumstances demanded. After allowing enough time to pass so that my words would not automatically be associated with our giving and taking of food, I told Mom I was upset by the way she acted at times today. I told her that even if she didn't have much control over her body, she still had a mind and soul to save, and I expected her to do it. She looked as if she were taking in what I said, as she had when I asked her to be more considerate of her roommate, but it's harder than ever to tell what she is thinking. I don't want to challenge her beyond her capacities, but I don't want her to abandon her intelligence.

Later I cornered Dr. McCrae during her evening rounds and asked if there could be any organic cause for the personality changes we've seen in Mom since last night. She said it was unlikely but she would check for metabolic explanations of her behavior.

After seeing Mom for the first time today, Johnny, the hospice chaplain, and Fran, the hospice social worker, tried to convince me that Mom should be put in a nursing home—or, as Johnny said, "We like to call it a 'care center,' that's a nicer term." After getting over the shock of hearing "hospice" workers recommend a nursing home, I told them their time would be better spent helping me wrest home care benefits from the insurance bureaucracy. At my insistence, the social worker called Blue Cross/ Blue Shield once again, and this time used the words I put in her mouth while standing over her shoulder.

It turns out that we are indeed entitled to 180 home visits, as

Dad's contract stipulates; the hitch is that it is virtually impossible to qualify for them. The visits have to be deemed "medically necessary and requiring the services of a skilled nurse." A year ago, a bedridden patient was by definition someone who required the services of a skilled nurse. But the Reagan administration, in its efforts to cut health care costs, has redefined what requires skilled nursing, and all the private insurance companies have adopted its guidelines.

A year ago there used to be a long list of skilled nursing tasks and a short list of custodial tasks. This year Medicare has simply shifted most of the items on the skilled list to the custodial list and therefore rationalized not paying for them. For instance, a patient with a catheter used to require skilled nursing. Now even patients on home respirators are deemed ineligible for skilled nursing. Family members are supposed to learn how to operate the respirators, and if they kill the patient in the process, so much the better.

Another nicety of the revamped rules is that if you need the services of a nurse's aide for more than the six hours a week Medicare provides, and you can't get home benefits from your private insurer because of the above regulations, and so in desperation you purchase extra hours of private nursing out of pocket, then Medicare revokes your free six hours.

How, I asked, can Medicare justify cutting off the care they are giving because a patient needs more care? The social worker had no answer. And how, I asked, would the federal government know whether a family had purchased additional nursing care? Well, she explained, most hospitals and private nursing care agencies have contracts with the government to provide Medicare and Medicaid services, and rather than risk their relations with the federal government, they will report the work they do for private clients.

What if, I asked for the sake of argument, what if I hired a nurse who did not have any association with a hospital or a home care agency? Well, she said, in that case, the nurses' aides providing the six hours of Medicare-financed care are supposed to find out what goes on in a home and report it. "So you are telling me that hospital-employed hospice workers are supposed to spy on families for the federal government?" I asked. "Yes, you could say that," she answered.

I thanked the social worker for her candor and asked her to find out what services Mom might need that would require skilled nursing, as defined by Medicare. I felt certain she would find a way to crack the system. The information she pried from Blue Cross/Blue Shield today was news to her as well as me, and she seemed sobered by her new understanding of her role as a government and insurance industry apparatchik. She is, I think, like Virginia, a good woman trying to function within a very cynical, profit-motivated health care system. But she has been less savvy than Virginia, less open-eyed, more innocent and therefore more cruel.

When I returned to Mom's room, I found Dr. McCrae and Dad in earnest consultation. Mom's platelet count had dropped to 20,000—it had been 182,000 when tested last week. If it drops any lower, she will need immediate transfusion. Even now the slightest mishandling can cause internal hemorrhaging. Several times today Mom asked to go home and we promised her that she could leave the hospital after she gets her CAT scan tomorrow, but this information calls our assurances into doubt. If we had remained home today, Dad or I would probably have killed her through ignorance and ineptitude. And yet we are not entitled to professional home care.

When we got ready to leave the hospital about 9:00 P.M., Mom seemed scared. We showed her the call box for the night nurse, but she said she couldn't reach it. We attached a remote switch to the call box, which she could hold in her hand, but she said she was too weak to depress the button. We asked the night nurse to look in on her frequently and she promised she would. We left Mom's room, exhausted and guilty.

I arrived at the hospital about 9:00 A.M. and learned that Mom had already been taken down for her CAT scan. When she was returned to her room at 10:30 A.M., she was still stupefied by the sedative they had given her to make the hard scanning table tolerable to her bony backside. Her face was calm and she mumbled that she was okay, but her speech was otherwise incoherent.

By noon her voice was returning, and she said, when asked, "I feel better" and "My legs don't hurt anymore." Yes, she had slept well and, yes, the night nurses had been good to her. Yes, it would be fine to stay in the hospital some more, "There's no place I'd rather be." No, she wasn't sad. She wasn't worried about anything. "Everyone here has been so good to me."

At first I was relieved, even though I suspected her contentedness was sedation-induced. By midafternoon, however, she was still saying she felt much better than yesterday, despite no apparent grounds for feeling that way. Her platelet count had dropped lower, to 16,000, and a transfusion was ordered for tonight. Her arms are now as purple and blood-bruised as her legs, and her chest is flecked with red spots—signs of internal bleeding from injections and mere touching.

It occurred to me that she was simply displaying the flipside of yesterday's regression; instead of being a bad child, cranky and demanding, she is being a good child, cheerful and obedient. In both states of mind, her hold on reality is tenuous.

Mom's new roommate has a daughter about my age who spent the night across the hall in the visitors' lounge. She says that Mom was restless all night long and that she began moaning very loudly about 4:00 A.M. Her cries went unheeded for a long time; finally the daughter, concerned for her own mother's sleep, cornered a nurse, who tried to ease Mom's pains.

I can't bring myself to describe the incident that led to this information, but this afternoon I was forced to hold Mom on her side while a nurse inflicted excruciating pain on her. As I

clutched her in my arms, she screamed, "No, no, Le Anne, no."
I pressed my skull against hers, hard, as if I could make us one
brain, one nerve center, one scream. I would say it was the
hardest, saddest, most painful moment in my life, if I didn't
know that superlatives are meaningless now, when each day's
extremity is equaled by yesterday's and tomorrow's.

I insisted on Mom's hospitalization to spare us such moments,
but there seems to be no escaping them. It takes at least two people to physically maneuver a person without muscle, so instead
of Dad and me as a team of tormentors, there is a nurse and
me. Mom's state of mind yesterday and today makes me think
of hostages and concentration camp prisoners who at first resist
their captors and then try to appease them by good behavior.

Freed from my grip, Mom fell into a deep sleep. Two hours
later, when the nurse came to administer a platelet transfusion,
it was very difficult to rouse her. Dad, who had left the room
during our ordeal but who had no doubt heard Mom's screams,
chose to interpret her sleep as peaceful. I interpreted it as a
willful obliteration of consciousness after an experience too trau-
matic to be borne. The discrepancy between Dad's and my response to crucial moments is hard to take. I don't care if he sees
what I see; I'm glad he doesn't see any more trauma than he
does. But after such moments I need time and privacy to heal
my wounds, and he is often full of a garrulous optimism that
makes my head feel it is being squeezed with a barbed-wire
tourniquet.

The image branded on my mind today is the most violent yet
and I pray it will not be my last. I am afraid if I leave for New
York tomorrow as planned, Mom will die while I am gone and
I will be left with the sound of my screamed name ringing in
my ears. The only hope left to me is that she experience some
brief period of peace before her death and that I be able to
witness it.

Once I was afraid of being present at her death; now I am
afraid of not being there.

All day we had assumed Dr. McCrae would contact us by phone or in person with the results of the morning's CAT scan. The radiologist's report on the scan had arrived at the nurses' station by early afternoon, but it couldn't be released to us without Dr. McCrae there to interpret it. At 6:30 P.M. I went to the nurses' station to ask when they expected the doctor to arrive for night rounds and was told she was not coming to the hospital tonight. At 9:00 P.M., I returned to the nurses' station and persuaded the nurse on duty to make a Xerox copy of the report for me.

The only sentence in the two-paragraph report that was intelligible to me said that the tumor in Mom's pancreas had not grown in size since last year. That seemed so implausibly positive that I was tempted to rush into Mom's room and share this information with Dad, but better judgment prevailed and I decided to take the contraband report home, read it over the phone to Mike and get his interpretation of it before raising anybody's hopes.

Mike listened without comment until I had read the entire report, then with the studied calm of a doctor bearing bad news to the patient's family, which incidentally included himself, he explained: The tumor in the patient's pancreas is unchanged; it has not grown or become active. The radiation treatment last September effectively "killed" it. The cancer, however, has now spread to her stomach, liver and chest cavity.

Mike sighed and changed his voice. Now he was the son who happened to be a doctor. He told me that on the day of surgery last September, the surgeon had seen fluid leaking from the pancreatic tumor into Mom's abdominal cavity during the operation and had included that information in his report. Mike knew from that time that Mom's chance of recovery was virtually nil. The five weeks of external radiation had been a very against-the-odds effort to destroy whatever malignant cells had escaped from the tumor. "They succeeded in killing the mother tumor, but the daughters are flourishing," he concluded.

My neck stiffened at his metaphor, but I ignored the anger trying to rise in me. I needed to register what he was saying. He had never shared our hopes for Mom. He wanted to, but couldn't; he knew too much. And he chose not to undermine our hope with his knowledge, even at the risk of estranging himself from us. All this time, he has been on the outside looking in. That's why he and Nancy kept burying her all these months, kept hoping for a pulmonary embolism or some other quick end to her suffering and their estrangement.

I handed the receiver to Dad and left the room. I presume Mike told him what he told me, but Dad has been oddly cheerful ever since he got off the phone. "Well, your mother is still a mystery," he said and then opened the refrigerator to browse for snacks. I was silent and sought refuge in the living room, where I sit writing this, wondering what was said and what was heard.

THURSDAY, OCTOBER 9:

This morning I packed my bags, loaded them in the car and arrived at the hospital about 9:30 A.M., hoping that Dr. McCrae would make an appearance in time for me to ask questions that would determine whether I would board my plane for New York at 4:00 P.M. I found Mom in a sound sleep, but wakened her long enough to say hello and find out how she was feeling— "Not too bad." Were the nurses taking good care of her? "Oh, yes, I'm getting the best of care." Her speech was not slurred, as it was yesterday, but her voice was so small that I had to get within inches of her face to hear her and even then it was necessary to clarify the sounds by lipreading.

About 10:00 A.M. Dr. McCrae entered the room to give us her assessment of Mom's condition. Dr. McCrae looked directly at Mom as she spoke, and Mom, who had opened her eyes at the doctor's entrance, looked alert. Dr. McCrae told her the CAT scan confirmed that her cancer was advancing, which was to be expected. In addition there were two surprising changes— her low platelet count and a low sodium serum level, which might account for some of her drowsiness. Transfusions and a sodium IV were necessary and it would not be wise to leave the hospital until these conditions were stabilized. Nothing more could be done about the cancer, unless Mom wanted to start a course of chemotherapy, which, in any case, would further lower her platelets.

It was hard to tell exactly what Mom understood and how she was taking it. Her eyes seemed to tear slightly, as if she were stoically absorbing a blow. There were tears in Dr. McCrae's eyes as well when she met Mom's steady gaze. As soon as Dr. McCrae left the room, Mom closed her eyes and seemed to sleep.

I followed the doctor into the corridor and asked her if it was safe for me to leave for a few days. She said Mom was not in crisis now, but at this point it was impossible to predict what might happen when. The odds were that Mom would live another couple weeks, but she added, the odds don't mean much anymore.

I also asked Dr. McCrae if Mom's stomach pains could be due to ascites and she said yes, that was likely, and she could ease them by having pancreatic enzymes administered through her IV. Since that has been the main source of Mom's distress the past few days, maybe she can have a few days free of pain.

About 11:30 Dad left the hospital to meet Mike and Nancy at the airport. I had counted on having this time alone with Mom, but when it came, I spent most of the hour sitting at her side watching her sleep. When a nurse awakened her for a pill, I took the opportunity to talk. I told her I was leaving for a few days while Mike and Nancy were here, but I would return on

Tuesday. She said that was "fine," that she would be "fine," but tears trickled from both eyes. I told her I loved her, I would miss her and I would hurry back. And the truth is I will miss her, even if she is no more than a sad, sleeping face above a body so spare it doesn't even make a contour in the blankets that cover it. She said she would miss me too, and then she fell asleep.

I took a picture out of my purse, a picture of Mom and me looking eternally young in Rome last summer, and placed it on her bedside table. It was not for her to see, but for the nurses and aides who would tend her in my absence, the strangers without memory, perhaps without imagination. I wanted them to see that she had been like them, is still one of them, even now, when she is so nearly invisible. I hoped to seduce them into kindness, with her beauty and her life.

When Mike and Nancy entered the room, Mom opened her eyes wide and a flicker of joy shot through them. Nancy took Mom's hand in hers and planted a big kiss on her cheek while Mike hung back a moment, trying to find his mother in this patient. When he bent to kiss her, I swear she gave him a look that understood and forgave his fear. Then she fell asleep and they stood above her, one on each side of her bed, looking down, absorbing the reality of her condition.

After a few minutes they had seen all they could see, and I asked them to come to the cafeteria with me so I could tell them what I knew before I had to leave for the airport. As soon as we were seated, Mike said that he could not imagine Mom ever leaving the hospital, that this was clearly the end, and that we must make it clear right away that we didn't want the hospital to take any extraordinary measures. He wished, in fact, that they hadn't given her the transfusion of platelets and he suggested we have the transfusions stopped if that was legally possible.

I felt the blood rushing to my head, pounding in my ears.

"Wait a minute," I said. "You've been here twenty minutes and you think you know what is happening. You thought she had twenty-four hours to live a month ago. And in fact she has looked as if she was about to die any minute for weeks now, but she hasn't died. So don't make any decisions to ensure her death until you have spent a few days here." I told him this was the first day Mom had seemed peaceful, and after what she and Dad and I had been through these past weeks, all three of us needed to experience that peace.

The thought of his taking actions that might make her die before I returned made me so mad that I described, graphically, the extremity of our days together. Mike's face paled, then turned green, and he pushed his chair back from the table as if that could put distance between him and my words. Nancy looked ill too, but she leaned forward on the table, and made my words her experience. I stopped my rant, glad that I had made my point but suddenly ashamed that I had made it so harshly. Mike eased his chair back toward the table, and I told him I agreed no heroic measures should be taken, but I asked him please to let her be as long as she was conscious and comfortable.

We went back to the room and watched Mom sleep for another hour, her face fleetingly transfigured by a passing pain every fifteen or twenty minutes. New to this vigil, Mike and Nancy quickly became wild-eyed with tedium, but I was content to witness the closest approximation to peacefulness I had seen in several days. At 2:30 I wakened her to say good-bye. I wish her a few good days, but if she dies before I return, I will find a way to accept that.

I sat in the last row of the plane, with an empty seat between me and a young woman who cried quietly as she turned an engagement ring round and round her finger. I imagined she had just endured a difficult parting, and though I envied the nature of her sorrow, I was glad for her subdued company. For two and a half hours, my mind remained in the hospital room while my body moved east.

Suddenly the plane began its descent into Newark and I panicked; when the plane bumped its wheels against the runway, tears spurted from my eyes and ran down the sides of my nose into my mouth. I had landed safely in another place and it felt horrible. I belonged with her, in danger.

When the plane came to a stop, I hurried into the bathroom and slumped against the locked door, sobbing. They were not wracking sobs, just a steady flow of tears that carried my strength and energy with it. A stewardess knocked on the door to ask if I was sick. I opened the door, and seeing my face, she asked me to sit in the rear galley seat, out of sight, until the other passengers had deplaned. I became quiet as the procession of legs filed slowly by me; when the plane was empty, I gathered my possessions and walked through the gangway into a terminal full of people who were going about the business of living. I felt I belonged to a different species from the purposeful men and women striding past me toward known destinations. We inhabited different planets, breathed a different atmosphere. I no longer belonged among them; I belonged with the dying, with the families on the hospice ward who knew what a day meant, "a good day" or "a bad day."

MANHATTAN

FRIDAY, OCTOBER 10:

By midafternoon today, I too was going about my business, standing in lines at the bank, calling my lawyer, stocking a grocery cart with the implements of housekeeping. My jaw was set with as much purpose as anyone else walking down Columbus Avenue. I had a refrigerator full of black moss to clean. All the fuses in my apartment had blown while I was gone, and the stench that greeted me when I opened the door would have been sufficient grounds for the buyers to break our contract if it had reached their nostrils first.

Yesterday, when I arrived at Milena's apartment to spend the night, I told her I did not want to get too far removed from the situation in Minnesota during my days here; it would only make it harder when I returned. But now it seems I have no choice. I am finding it impossible to stay within the tight vise of Mom's decline once I allow myself any degree of physical distance.

I called the hospital this morning and was told Mom's condition was stable. But this evening, as I packed to head uptown to Charlotte's, where I planned to spend the night before driving to the country with her in the morning, I decided to call again.

Mike answered the phone and told me Mom's condition was "dire." She was developing edema again; there was swelling in her hands and face as well as her legs and Mike suspected complete kidney failure. She was uncomfortable, anxious, and Mike had asked the doctors to stop giving her platelet transfusions. He thought it likely she would not survive the night.

I hung up the receiver angry and confused. Should I catch the next plane to Minneapolis? Was Mike's judgment reliable or would I be succumbing to panic, as I did a month ago when I left my affairs in shambles to rush to Minneapolis at Mike's prediction of an imminent death that never came? If Mom does die tonight, should I spend these hours trying to get my life here in order so I will be ready to handle what comes next? I have been thinking of Mom's death as the end, beyond which there is nothing, but now that it is so close, I have to start thinking about Dad and the very real possibility of his collapse. I am furious at Mike for stopping the transfusions, for trying to hasten Mom's death, for depriving me of these few days to restore order to a life I barely remember but that I desperately need to have waiting for me.

In the taxi, I cry my way from Sixteenth to Eighty-sixth Street. Once at Charlotte's, I become numb with anxiety and indecision. If I leave for the country early in the morning as planned, I might arrive home only to learn that Mom has died and then I will be several hours from an airport. If I delay, it means that much less time to take care of whatever urgencies the country house may have in store for me.

About 1:30 A.M. I fall asleep. All night I am in one of those shallow sleeps in which you dream about being in bed sleeping. This time I dream I am lying in a narrow bed, trying to stay as still as possible, because I don't want to disturb the IV tubes attached to my body. About 6:00 A.M. I wake up long enough to realize that I am indeed sleeping in a narrow bed but there are no IV tubes attached to me. I change beds, hoping that if I have more room, I can shake the dream. It doesn't help.

SATURDAY, OCTOBER 11:

When Charlotte wakened me at 7:00 A.M., I suggested she and Milena leave for the country without me. I would call the hospital at 10:00 A.M. and decide whether to catch a 10:45 A.M. train to Hudson based on what I heard. As soon as she closed the door to my room, I returned to my tube-entangled dreams.

A stranger answered the hospital phone at 10:00 A.M. and told me Mrs. Schreiber had been moved to a private room late last night. I reached Nancy, who told me that Dad had gone home to sleep after spending the night in the hospital. Mom had been uncomfortable and restless, waking him every five minutes for a change of position or a sip of water. Her vital signs are stable; she is neither closer nor farther from death than she had been last night.

I decided to take the 10:45 train, take care of essential business and be prepared to leave at a moment's notice. Milena met me at the Hudson station, and as we drove the twenty miles to Ancram, I felt as if I was seeing the landscape for the first time. A month's exile had made me forget the clean, aquiline profile of the Catskills on a clear day. As we drove east on

Route 82, through hillsides of dairy farms and apple orchards, the sharp angles of the Catskills at our back, the soft curves of the Berkshires ahead, the roadside red and gold with turning leaves, the county seemed too good to be true, too beautiful to be mine.

The house welcomed me with running water, hot and cold, and a well full enough for two showers, several flushings and a dish-washing—more bounty than I've had since moving in. Bob had installed a new hot water heater this morning; Zack had mowed the lawn; Milena had swept away the cobwebs and other signs of desuetude. I walked from room to room, house proud. This is where I lived, where I would live again. I could hardly believe my good fortune.

I spent most of the afternoon sorting through stacks of mail and paying bills. I have never written checks so happily; I felt grateful to the phone company, the electric company, my mortgage holders and auto insurers, each one acknowledging by invoice my right to be here. I was content to be sitting with my ledgers, but Milena was eager to get me out into the soft, warm air.

About 4:00 P.M. we went across the road to the park with a flimsy paper kite I had bought and assembled the last weekend I was here. After three tries, we had it soaring, the string running out so fast it burned my palm. With our backs to the cemetery, we flew it west toward the Hudson, letting out all 1,500 yards of string. We flew it west, our backs to the cemetery, because the wind came from the east. I did not choose the metaphor. It was given me.

When the kite was at its highest, I left it in Milena's hands and went across the road to find Zack and Merc; what good is a high-flying kite without young boys to admire it. Zack spied me before I saw him and came running up to boast of his many accomplishments in my absence—he was getting his license for small-game hunting, he had a coyote in the barn that he was going to skin and, yup, he'd seen the kite and it was flying good but he had flown one east all the way over Winchell Mountain just the other day. I followed Zack to the barn to admire his dead coyote, found last night on Empire Road near Copake. It was small and perfect and showed little damage from its encounter with steel and rubber.

After hauling in the kite, we went back to the house and I called Edina. Dad answered. He said he was exhausted after his sleepless night, but he thought Mom was stronger. His evidence: She was awake more today and she complained more. I told him to tell Mom it was a beautiful day in the country and I was looking at the leaves for her.

About 6:00 P.M. I opened a bottle of Fumé Blanc, which was a mistake. I drank too much, talked too much, ate too little too late and then fell asleep, full of wine, on the sofa. Milena says that when she tried to awaken me, I kept telling her to be careful of my IV tubes. I have no memory of that, but I do know I spent most of the night in a shallow sleep again, dreaming my body was my mother's body and I had to keep it very still or something bad would happen.

ANCRAM, N.Y.
SUNDAY, OCTOBER 12:

When I called Edina at noon, Nancy said Dad was at the hospital, where he had spent the night again, and Mike had flown back to Philadelphia, incurring, she thought, our father's wrath.

Mom has been taken off the IV; the liquid had started to seep through the walls of her minuscule veins and collect in the tissue under her skin. Her only sustenance now is sips of water administered with an eyedropper. Nancy says Mom is very anxious, asking, "Am I okay?" or pleading "Help me" whenever she awakens, which is about every fifteen minutes. She is easily reassured, though, by a squeeze of the hand or an "It's all right, I'm here." Father Mahon visits her every day with communion. Today she asked him if she was going to be all right, and he, apparently thinking she was asking about her soul, answered, "More than all right."

When Mike said good-bye this morning, he became very upset and had to leave the room to avoid breaking down. Dad followed him into the hall while Nancy stayed with Mom, who knew that something unusual was happening and became very frightened. It is not clear to me why Mike left and Nancy stayed. I think he probably couldn't stand his helplessness before her "help me's," but I don't really know and I don't think I should ask.

Nancy also said that she and Mike are at odds with Dad over the issue of medication. Dad accepts the nearness of death, but he wants to keep Mom conscious as much as possible, even if that means her discomfort and his exhaustion. Mike and Nancy think she should be given morphine in higher dosages and with greater frequency. For the last two days she has received half the recommended amount, and only at night.

After talking to Nancy, I decided to drive back to Manhattan tonight, shop tomorrow for clothes to wear to the funeral and then fly on to Minneapolis by evening. Whether I'm in New York or Minneapolis, I have to do this shopping, and whether I'm here or there, I run the risk of my mother dying while I am buying clothes for her funeral. I have come to accept the inevitability of grotesque decisions. And I know that, even on her deathbed, my mother is counting on me to look good at her funeral.

I readied the house for another departure and then took a walk with Milena, camera in hand. Succumbing to territorial lust, I asked her to snap pictures of me in "my Ancram": shoulder leaning against the County Route 7 sign; one foot propped on the railing in front of the post office; hand pointing to the pool under the waterfall where I caught my first Ancram trout. We walked east on Route 82, where a short distance past Pooles Hill Road, I saw a footpath leading into a wooded area. We took it with little expectation that it would lead far from the road, but, to my pleasure, it wended through woods up an incline and into a meadow. I had found the path leading to the broad expanse of hillside I see from my bedroom window.

We climbed the hill through fields of uncut hay, each ten yards yielding ever more sweeping views. At the crest we could see in 360 degrees, west to the Catskills and east to the Berkshires, the Roe/Jan winding in and out of sight through rolling farmland to the north and south, Ancram nestled in the valley below. We walked along the crest of the hill into a woods where the scent of deer was strong. The only sound was the rat-a-tat-tat of woodpecker beaks against birch bark. Gratitude struggled with disbelief. "Why me?" I thought. "Why do I get to live with such beauty?"

After settling into Charlotte's apartment for the night, I called Edina. Nancy answered, exhausted and incredulous. "I just don't understand why she is still alive," Nancy said. "How can she hang on like that?" With new respect for Mom's tenacity, Nancy, like me, is now uncertain how long this can last. Still, it is time to talk about funeral arrangements, and Nancy did. She asked my opinion about embalming (in Edina or Fort Dodge?), about caskets (open or closed?). I did not want to hear these questions, visualize these alternatives.

I slept in Charlotte's double bed to avoid the cramped sensation that had fed into my dreams the last two nights. But I slept the shallow sleep again, this time believing my body was immobilized by morphine. In the morning I felt as if I had in fact been drugged. Milena says that last night, and for the two previous nights, I have shouted in my sleep. She imitated my loud groans and I recognized them as Mom's.

MONDAY, OCTOBER 13:

I bought the clothes I will need at a new shop on Amsterdam and Eighty-fourth, near Charlotte's apartment. I told the owner I wanted something fashionable but conservative, appropriate for a funeral in a small Iowa town. I did not tell him it was for my mother's funeral. The incongruities were too great to expose. I tried on his very chic, very expensive creations, discussing how, with a few slight changes of accessories, I could recycle the outfit for other occasions. I imagined some future self, having fun, looking sexy. I was aware of wanting to model these clothes for my mother, but how can I court her admiration for the clothes I intend to wear to her funeral?

Nancy picked me up at the airport about 10:45 P.M. and we drove straight to the hospital. I walked down the corridor of the hospice ward into a darkened room, where Mom and Dad were both sleeping, he in a reclining chair at her bedside. Awakened by my entrance, he swiveled his sagging head and looked into the doorway with bleary, unfocused eyes. In the dim light from the hallway, it looked as if Mom's eyes were fixed in a half-open stare. Nancy caught my glance and said, "Morphine can do that." I spoke to Mom, told her I was back, but her level of consciousness was beyond fathoming. Earlier in the day, though, she had been perfectly alert and received short visits from several neighbors who had asked if they could "see Bea one more time."

About midnight, Dad agreed to let Nancy spell him for the night and the two of us left the hospital, in two cars, so that I could return later without stranding him. He was so exhausted I had doubts about his ability to drive, but we arrived home safely, and despite his grogginess, he was eager to talk with me about funeral arrangements. Smiling proudly, he led me to the bedroom closet and pulled out two "beautiful silk blouses" he had selected for Mom to wear in her casket. They were threadbare, polyester rags that I cannot believe she ever wore, one a shiny blackish blue, the other a muddy maroon. He must be so tired he literally cannot see.

At 12:15 A.M. Nancy called to say the night nurse had checked Mom's vital signs and felt she would not survive the night, maybe not even the next hour or two. I asked to speak to the nurse to see what grounds she had for her predictions. Dad's fatigue was so extreme it seemed dangerous to subject him to another sleepless night if this were a false alarm sounded by someone who had not witnessed Mom's will.

The nurse told me she had never tended Mom before, but her blood pressure was 78/40, her respiration slow and labored, her kidneys nonfunctional, her eyes fixed open six hours after her last morphine injection—all signs of very impending death. There was, in short, no reason for Mom to survive another night, but that had been true for the past several days. I suggested to Dad that he go straight to sleep and then I returned to the hospital.

Mom was in a deep, open-eyed sleep, her breathing loud and labored but even—twelve breaths a minute, every minute, drawn deep from the diaphragm with the only strength left in her body. Over the phone, the nurse had told me that Mom was beginning to awaken and moan loudly, so I was surprised and disappointed to find her so deeply unconscious. I asked Nancy if they had given her more morphine, and she said, "No, not unless it was while I was out of the room phoning you." I was glad for Mom's peacefulness but sorry I had missed her fifteen minutes of consciousness. I wanted to be sure she knows I am here.

For the next several hours Nancy and I sat on opposite sides of the bed, each holding a hand. Twice, we each got a faint squeeze of hand from Mom, but we weren't sure whether it was voluntary or involuntary movement. Every half hour the nurse came in to check Mom's blood pressure and pulse, which remained steady at 70/50 and 104, indicating her heart was working very hard to keep blood pumping through tiny veins to swollen limbs.

At 3:30 A.M. I suggested Nancy try to sleep on one of the couches in the visitors' lounge, which she did. I remained in the reclining chair on Mom's left side. Every so often I would doze for a few minutes and then wake with a start, panicked if I woke during one of the five-second pauses between breaths. Several times I stood up to stroke Mom's arm or kiss her forehead or tell her I loved her and she wasn't alone. She was toothless, with a tube strapped across her face to help her breathe through her nose; her hands were blue and swollen to twice their size, but her brow was smooth. It was not at all hard for me to look upon her, hour after hour. It was the only sight worth seeing.

By 5:30 A.M. nothing had changed; breathing, pulse, appearance were unwavering. I didn't want to leave, because Dad and Nancy had told me Mom usually regained some consciousness about 7:00 A.M. and I wanted that possibility of contact. But if I stayed, I knew I would be too tired to be of use later in the day. I decided to go home and sleep in case this vigil be required for tomorrow night, when Nancy would be gone and Dad too exhausted to keep it. I wakened Nancy to take my place at Mom's side and drove home at 6:00 A.M., dragging Dad from a deep sleep because I had locked myself out.

I slept till 10:00 A.M., with several interruptions from the telephone. Each time it rang, I expected to hear Mom had died, but all the calls were from neighbors wanting to know how they could be helpful. I didn't know how to tell them the best help was a silent phone.

When I returned to the hospital about 11:00 A.M., Nancy drove home to take a shower. I suggested she stay home and sleep, but she said, "No, I want to come back. It's going to be today."

Mom's breathing was still steady but shallower, faster and more quiet—twenty breaths a minute, the movement visible only in her throat and mouth. Her eyes had been fixed in an open position for fifteen hours and were unrecognizable as living eyes. It was so very sad to see her limpid blue eyes shrivel, turn dry and dull and blind. I asked a nurse if we could do something, and she said, "Yes, I'll get some Liquid Tears." She brought a bottle and squeezed a few drops onto Mom's eyes, but the thirst was too great to be slaked. When the nurse left, I kept trying to bring life back into Mom's eyes, but the Liquid Tears would catch in her lashes and fall to her cheek or roll straight over her unblinking eyes to form pools in the indentation between eye and nose. Her unseeing stare fixed me and I thought, "So this is the hardest, to look at these eyes and still see my mother. How can this be my mother if she doesn't have the most beautiful, all-seeing eyes in the world?"

Dad was in the room, but I barely noticed him. He seemed to be disconnecting. His chair was pushed back farther from the bedside than it had been yesterday, and he wasn't watching every breath as I was. When he left to go to the bathroom, I talked to Mom. I told her I knew she couldn't respond, but I hoped she could hear or understand me in some way. I told her my eyes would see for her, my ears would hear for her, my hands would touch for her. Her heart, I knew, would carry on for itself. I told her the leaves outside the window were turning with her and my eyes would take her to Italy again, soon. I would eat *gelati* for her, even though I was not so fond of it as she was. I told her she was the bravest, strongest, most stubborn woman I had ever known, and I told her she should feel free to die now. Dad and I would be okay.

Then I took my seat at her right side and held her hand, now cold and deep blue. The swelling extended all the way up her arms, ballooning to normal size the sticks I had gotten used to seeing. I lifted the blanket to look at her legs to see if they could be massaged. I accepted that she had been right; her obsession with her legs had not been misplaced. They were the symptoms of her undoing, the sign of kidneys stopping their work, poisoning her body, turning it toxic.

Dad came back and I left to give him the time I had stolen. I went to the nurses' station and asked Barb, the nurse I liked best, if it was conceivable that Mom would live another twenty-four hours. "I don't think so," she said, "but she has amazed me for days."

When I returned to the room, I noticed Mom's breathing was fainter. Her chest was absolutely still and there was only slight movement in her neck. I rummaged in the bureau to find the rain-scented lotion I had brought from home last week and smoothed it into her forehead and cheeks, careful not to disturb the oxygen feed. I massaged it into her arms and hands in an attempt to give her a few, last, good sensations. Dad stroked her cheeks with the back of his hand in a slow, gentle motion she would recognize as his touch among a million others.

We both sat back and watched her breathing. Only her chin and mouth moved. I told Dad I thought these were the last minutes. When only her lips moved, we both stood and placed our hands on her head, my palm curving her right brow, his her left. She stopped breathing. Nothing else changed. It was very peaceful. "Is this death?" I asked. Then I noticed a pulse beating in the left side of the neck. "Look, Dad," I said. "Is it possible for her heart to keep beating after breathing has stopped?" He said he didn't know. We watched as the pulse kept beating in her neck. "Maybe you better get a nurse," Dad said.

I didn't want to leave the room, but I forced myself to walk the long corridor to the nurses' station, where I found Barb. She said the heart beats for a little while after breathing stops, but never for very long, sometimes only for seconds.

I ran down the hallway, with Barb following, and joined Dad on Mom's left side. We watched her neck pulse as if it were the most exquisite sight in the world. "Look at the sun shining on it," Dad said. We were both smiling broadly as if we were watching a baby take its first breaths. I asked Barbara if we could take the oxygen feed off Mom's face. She removed it. Barb was smiling too.

"Can we put her teeth back in?" I asked, exhilarated at the possibility of restoring her to beauty. Barb said, "Sure," took Mom's dentures from their container and began putting them in. It was not easy and the effect was not what I wanted. Still, Mom's neck kept pulsing. It was as if she had the peace of death and yet was still living. We were having it both ways and we were happy. And then the pulse stopped. The color drained from her face, and in that instant, everything changed. Two forty-five P.M., October 14. She was dead. When there was only that pulse, there was still so much. And then there was nothing. Her face was a death mask, and it was horrible, her dentures fixed in a fright-show grin. Dad and I put our arms round each other and I sobbed, as much in shock as grief. I had never known how death looked, how utterly other than life.

I tried to look upon her dead face and see my mother, as I had tried to see her through so many layers of symptoms this past year, but I could not find her.

We left the room and did not return.

Dad seemed strong, calm, relieved, almost elated. "It was so peaceful," he said. "Almost beautiful."

I didn't respond.

"Have you ever seen anyone die before?" I asked him.

"Yes," he said, "my mother. It wasn't peaceful. It often isn't. There was a terrible final waking and struggle, blood. I am so glad that didn't happen."

Yesterday, he said, Mom had her final alertness. She opened her eyes wide, and with more strength and clarity than she had shown since entering the hospital, she said, "I want to get up out of here and walk."

"Isn't that great?" he said. Is it, I wondered. Whatever it is, it is her.

WEDNESDAY, OCTOBER 15:

Yesterday, when Dad and I returned home from the hospital, Nancy was on the phone with Mike. She handed the receiver to Dad and hugged me. There was a wild look in her eye, and she said, "I feel so guilty." I stared at her with incomprehension. "I knew it was going to happen," she said. "That's why I left, that's why I didn't come back. I couldn't do it."

I asked her if she had ever seen anyone die, and she said yes, as if that were the reason she had not returned. I told her, sincerely, that she had no reason to feel guilty, that she had been there during Mom's last conscious days, when there was still comfort to be given, a squeeze of hand, a drop of water.

"I was afraid it would be bad," she said. "That's why I asked the nurse to give her morphine at midnight last night."

Nancy had lied to me about the morphine. If there were any anger left in me, I would have been furious at her for robbing me of my last chance for conscious contact with my mother. But my anger was exhausted. I sighed and realized I would always have wanted one more contact, no matter how much time we had shared. I always will want one more contact. And Nancy was alone in the night, with Mom moaning, and a nurse telling her death was coming. What would I have done?

Today there is no time for such questions. All is business. There are people to be notified. Airplane reservations to be made, cars to be rented, funeral services to arrange in Edina and Fort Dodge. The bell jar is broken and the world is rushing in.

I had my first encounter with the death bureaucracy today. Dad and I chose a casket at Werness Funeral Home in Minneapolis. Then we were asked to choose a vault to enclose the casket. The vaults are hideously ugly and I asked if we absolutely had to have one. "No, not anymore," the young funeral director explained. They used to be required by federal law, as protection in the unlikely case of a cemetery cave-in, but the Reagan administration budget cutters did not want to pay for vaults to enclose the caskets of veterans buried in national cemeteries, so the law was changed.

The funeral director also said he would notify the federal government of Mom's death, so that Dad could apply for "a death benefit." I asked questions and learned that very few people in fact qualify for the $50 death benefit, and the real reason funeral homes notify the government of deaths is to ensure the immediate suspension of social security payments. They don't want any welfare chiseling from the grave.

Today is Mom and Dad's forty-ninth wedding anniversary.

Before we left for the memorial service at Werness today, I was uncertain how I would react to seeing Mom's corpse in the open casket. If the corpse bore close resemblance to Mom as she was before her illness, it might make it harder to accept her loss. If she looked as she did these final months, but at peace, the image might be consoling.

Dad and I arrived at the funeral home forty-five minutes before visitation hours were to begin. The bouquets of flowers we had chosen to surround her looked beautiful, and as we approached the casket, I braced myself for a heart-stopping sight. But when I stood over her corpse, I felt nothing but disappointment. This was not my mother. It looked nothing like her. The mouth was stretched to twice its normal width and they had padded the lower half of her face in a way that had no likeness to her actual facial structure in sickness or in health.

I was outraged at first, then relieved. I would not have to go through the days ahead, here and in Fort Dodge, feeling I was in the presence of a haunting corpse. Nothing of my mother was in that corpse, and nothing had been since the instant of her death. The casket is only a symbol, surrounded by flowers and fabrics and colors that do her honor.

When the visitation hours were over, and Dad was heading toward the parking lot, I pretended I had left something behind so I could spend a few minutes alone in the room with the casket. I looked closely at her corpse, touched her hands and forehead, and confirmed her absence upon my senses. I told her, speaking not to the corpse but to the air in the room, that I knew she wouldn't mind if I did not show the expected reverence toward her corpse. Beginning now, my communications with her will be conducted through whatever medium feels right. She resides more in her pictures, in a color, a breeze, than she does in that cold flesh. She resides in anything that has life far more than she ever could in a corpse.

Dad does not feel as I do. He sees his wife in that casket. He is pleased that "she looks beautiful," that she is restored to the robust youthfulness that was hers before sickness. Mourners like her cousin LaVonne, who had not seen her in these last months, also seem to feel she is her corpse. Standing over the casket, they feel the shock of her death for the first time, they see her as if she had been mysteriously struck down in the pink of good health. They are shaken, cry, and I comfort them.

SUNDAY, OCTOBER 19:

The wake at Laufersweiler's funeral home in Fort Dodge lasted from 2:00 to 8:00 P.M. She is too long above ground, too long on display. Sisters, cousins, grade-school and high-school class-mates stand over her casket and say, "Doesn't she look beauti-ful." I feel a conspiracy to deny the time of sickness and suffering. "No, she didn't really suffer in the last four months," Dad tells them. "The Chinese doctor took care of her pain." Denial does not end with death. I am made to feel my memories are obscene. One of my cousins says of her own mother's sickness and death, "You have to forget the last year." I am supposed to start for-getting, now.

MONDAY, OCTOBER 20:

Last night I dreamt I was a corpse. There was no plot to the dream, just an intimation of nonbeing, and a sensation of cold-ness. When I awoke I felt my right arm with my left hand to make sure there was warm flesh in the bed with me.

Before the funeral we all gathered at Laufersweiler's to be led in the interminable telling of a rosary. Then we were asked to file by the open casket one more time. Mom's sisters are steeled against grief. This is the fifth time in two years they have contributed their sons as pallbearers to their brothers and sisters. "I've no more tears," Veronica said. Only Katherine cried, and Nancy.

The funeral Mass is held in the chapel of the Catholic nursing home where my grandmother spent the last three of her ninety-nine years, and where ninety-year-old Father McElroy, who buried the other four "Meyer children" and their mother, now resides. His assistant at Mass is a ninety-six-year-old priest, also a resident of The Marion Home. Relatives entirely fill the pews of the small chapel, but a partition dividing the chapel from the recreation room has been opened and a dozen rows of folding chairs face the altar. They are filled by residents of the home, who clutch their canes in anticipation of the show. Others maneuver their wheelchairs for a better view. This is Grand Guignol, but I approve. These elderly strangers know what sickness is, and loss. I feel closer to them than to the proceedings.

After Mass, the funeral cortege drives to the outskirts of town, where Corpus Christi Cemetery sits on the only hill for miles around, flanked by flat fields of unharvested corn. It's a glorious fall day, Indian summer; white light and the warmth of the midday sun take some of the sting out of leaving her body here. As we leave the cemetery, I notice the dates on her father's headstone. He died October 14, 1944, preceding his adoring daughter forty-two years to the day.

Driving back to Edina with Dad, I see a full harvest moon rising orange over the flat horizon. It makes me sad that Mom cannot see it, sadder by far than the sight of her corpse.

THURSDAY, OCTOBER 23:

Yesterday I took Dad to Highland Park and we walked the trails together. The soft browns and grays of this wan autumn are a solace. Today I took him to the Isaac Walton preserve on the Mississippi. He found oyster mushrooms growing on the trunk of an enormous cottonwood near the river's edge. I took a picture of him reaching for the mushrooms, which he cooked for dinner tonight. He looked so very small against the great girth of bark.

FRIDAY, OCTOBER 24:

I'm midair, between his home and mine. It is less than a half hour since I said good-bye to Dad at the airport, and suddenly I feel the strain of these past ten days, the strain of having to participate in the obliteration of memory that seems so essential to everyone else's recovery. I thought death would end denial, but it just ushers in a new phase of it. First we deny that death is coming, and then, when it's arrived, we pretend the coming was peaceful.

My mother died toothless, blind, her limbs blue and swollen with edema, an oxygen feed strapped to her face. My trial was to keep seeing her, to find her amid the grotesque distortions of disease. It was the hardest thing I've ever done, and it is being taken from me. Her four days as a prettified corpse are being used to cancel out the reality of the previous fifteen months, robbing her of her courage, and me of mine. The lie that she didn't suffer much is taking hold. Forgetting may help Dad but it leaves me isolated, my experience nullified except in the pages of this journal, which come to seem an obscenity. Do I violate my mother by recording what I've recorded here? Would she wish it buried with her? Must my communications always be to myself?

DREAMS

ANCRAM, N.Y.

SUNDAY, OCTOBER 26:

Every night since the night before the funeral, I have dreamt
that I was in the presence of a corpse, perhaps hers, perhaps my
own. Last night the dream changed. I wasn't with cold flesh, but
I was aware of the state of death in an ethereal way. The image
was of my mother's body, more as a form than a solid reality,
and I was more clearly the witness than the object.

WEDNESDAY, OCTOBER 29:

Last night I dreamt of the periwinkles Freya sent to Mom, and
somehow they seemed an image of her in death and I was happy.
Then the image changed—a black snake slithered across black
earth—and I awoke with dread, my eyes open in a fixed stare
like hers in the last twenty-four hours before death.

THURSDAY, OCTOBER 30:

All night I kept being awakened by the sudden image of my mother's corpse as pure fact. It was as if someone kept awakening me to say, "She's dead. Don't forget it. She's dead." The words formed in my mind as if they were spoken by a voice over in the dream. "Voice" isn't the right word, though, for what delivered the message. The words were absolute, disembodied, more incontrovertible than anything spoken. "She's dead" was the message. She, not me, was one part of it. Dead was the other part.

MONDAY, NOVEMBER 3:

Bruno and Gwen came today, armed with machetes and sickles to help me carve paths through the jungle out back. We hacked our way in at the upper north corner of the yard, where the lawn meets a thicket of blackberry bushes, then worked our way toward the back boundary of the property by creating a series of wide switchback curves. We decided to spare most of the wild honeysuckle and stands of sumac trees but to be merciless with anything that pricks or stings. When we could make progress only by cutting through honeysuckle, we left the uppermost branches intact as an overhead archway.

After two hours and about fifty yards of pathbreaking, we were rewarded by the discovery of a relatively open area with clear views of the hills to the east and the Lutheran church steeple to the south. We laid down our machetes and began swinging long-handled, sawtoothed blades though waist-high weeds to make an oval clearing. An apple tree and a small stand of white pines formed a natural boundary for one segment of the oval. As I paused, sweaty and exhausted, to imagine a hammock slung from apple tree to pine, I noticed that Bruno and Gwen were swinging their blades at angles that threatened dismemberment. We agreed to call it a day, but before we backtracked, we thought we would just take a few minutes to see what stood between us and the back boundary.

An hour later we reached the surveyor's stake, pounded into the ground under one of the biggest apple trees I've ever seen. The lowest branches were several feet overhead, providing a natural canopy nearly thirty feet in diameter. I would have my choice of clearings, a shady circle or a sunny oval, connected by the back and forth of bird calls. Today, we heard only squawks of disapproval from creatures loath to share their sanctuary.

SATURDAY, NOVEMBER 8:

Last night I dreamt that Dad and I were in a cemetery where Mom was buried. There was no plot to the dream, just a climate, strange to say, of contentedness. The cemetery was green and leafy and it seemed a fine place to be. Dad and I were smiling. There was a vivid sense of Mom's presence there, and of her contentment with her new home. In fact, the mood was almost what it would be if one of us were showing the other two the new house we had bought and everyone was pleased with the choice. In this case, the new home was hers, a dream reversal of my frustrated wish to show her mine.

MONDAY, NOVEMBER 10:

Last night and the night before, Mom was alive in my dreams for the first time since her death. Saturday night, I dreamed it was three weeks before her death; she was thin and sick but still walking. We—Mom, Dad and I—were trying to arrange for a Christmas celebration in the three weeks we had left together, because, in this dream, we had the hindsight we now have in real time.

Sunday night, I again dreamt it was three weeks before her death. Mom was sick but she was not thin and she had no trouble walking. I was preparing a dinner party for friends and I expected

Mom to be able to join us. As I cooked and greeted guests, Dad was sitting with Mom and one or two others in another room. Suddenly I heard sounds of distress from the other room and instinctively knew that Dad, in his desire to have Mom behave as if she were well, had given her hors d'oeuvres and liquor. She, in her desire to please him and to trust his judgment, had nibbled, sipped and become nauseated.

I rushed into the room as if I were her savior, the only one clearheaded enough to realize how stupid we had been to expect her to attend a party. Filled with both righteousness and remorse, I put my arm around her shoulders and led her to the bathroom, where she and I both vomited. The sickness, hers and mine, was not violent or painful; neither of us was distressed now that we were alone together. We knew her illness was fatal, but we didn't seem to mind as long as we didn't have to pretend otherwise.

WEDNESDAY, NOVEMBER 13:

Today I picked up a UPS parcel that Dad sent me with a few items of Mom's clothes and a bag of dahlia bulbs. I wanted the dahlias; they are third-generation bulbs, progeny of flowers that bloomed forty years ago in Grandma Schreiber's garden in Indianola, Iowa. I didn't want the clothes, which only make me sad, but since Dad had told me they were coming, I was braced for the sight and smell of them. What I wasn't prepared for was the small box of keepsakes he included in the parcel. Size o silk baby shoes in their original wrapping, baby lockets and rings, a letter I wrote Santa Claus when I was seven years old asking for "a cowboy—not a cowgirl—outfit please." It made me feel I had lost the one person in the world who cherished me enough to safeguard these mementos; from now on they would only be trinkets of self-love. I've taken mother love so much for granted that I didn't realize what an underpinning it was until I felt it knocked out from under me when I opened that box.

The well diggers removed their rig this afternoon, leaving me with a four-hundred-foot hole in the ground and unconvincing assurances that water would fill it. They say the well will produce a gallon a minute and top off within eighty feet of the surface, but when I asked for proof, the twenty-year-old crew boss simply dropped a pebble down the well and let me hear its splash. "If you can hear the splash," he said, "it means the water is within one hundred feet of the surface." I asked if there wasn't some more precise means of measuring the water level, and he insisted there wasn't. When I pressed him further, pointing out that the well was an echo chamber that could probably carry the sound of a splash from only a few feet of water in the bottom of the well, he became nasty. "Look, lady," he said, "if you want us to leave the rig here overnight, it'll cost you another three hundred dollars for keeping us from the next job, plus ten dollars a foot for the digging." I told him to get his rig out of my sight. His parting words were a warning not to drop or lower anything into the well because I might damage the pipe or contaminate the water.

As soon as he left I began devising my own, organic methods of sounding the depths. First I dropped a peanut down the well, with stopwatch in hand to measure the seconds before splash-down. I planned to apply the formula for the acceleration of a falling object in feet/per second/per second; but when I heard the peanut ricochet against the sides of the six-inch-wide pipe a dozen times before hitting water, I realized I would never be able to achieve the necessary free fall. I would have to improvise a plumb line.

I poked a hole through the middle of a lemon, threaded one end of a one-hundred-foot length of clothesline through the lemon, tied it off and lowered it down the well. It came up dry. Maybe lemons don't show water very well, I thought. Maybe most of the water drips right off its waxy surface and the rest evaporates in the time it takes me to pull the lemon back up through one hundred feet of air. I tied a strip of cloth, a piece of kite tail actually, to the rope around the lemon and lowered it again. Lemon and kite tail both came up dry. There is definitely no water within one hundred feet of the surface. Tomorrow I will fashion a longer plumb line.

FRIDAY, DECEMBER 4:

Last night I dreamt that I discovered the ruins of an ancient Etruscan bath in the basement and made plans to excavate the site. The bath was made of beautiful colored stones, laid in geometric patterns with great precision. The overall form was of two T-bars, placed crossbar to crossbar. When I awoke I realized it was a dream pun: a well in the form of a double cross.

A prophetic pun. This morning, I attached my kite-tailed lemon to a 450-foot length of heavy twine wrapped around a wine bottle. I lowered the lemon down the well, letting its weight spin the line off the bottle until I heard a loud splash. I tied a loop to mark the distance and reeled in 220 feet of twine. I called the well-digging company and told its owner what I thought of his crew's pebble-drop test. He advised me to stay calm; sometimes, he said, it takes a well several days to reach its head. Then how could they assure me of a gallon-a-minute flow rate, I asked. He admitted that flow rates for "low-producing" wells were very difficult to estimate.

WEDNESDAY, DECEMBER 11:

I've got a whole new set of wrist muscles from lowering and raising that soggy lemon several hundred feet a day. The water level, which is now within one hundred feet of the surface, seems to rise twenty feet every twelve hours, which is closer to a gallon an hour than a gallon a minute. The way I figure it, the well will hold about three hundred gallons when it is full, which is far more than I will use in any given day. That's good. But it will only refill itself with about forty gallons a day, which is less than I will use most days. That's not good. Unless I conserve water very strictly, I will run dry every couple of weeks. So be it. I've asked another company to install a pump next week. At least I'll have water for Christmas.

MALVERN, PA.
WEDNESDAY, DECEMBER 24:

I drove the bleak New Jersey and Pennsylvania turnpikes through rain and arrived at Mike's about four in the afternoon. Dad, who arrived yesterday, was the only one home to greet me. He looked fine, as hale as his voice over the phone these last weeks. Mike, Nancy and the kids arrived not too long afterward and so we were gathered as a family for the first time since the funeral. Nothing marked the occasion. It was as if someone was missing, but she might just be arriving late, on the next train maybe.

It wasn't until many hours later, when we all went to church and took our places in the pew that it hit. We filled the pew, but there was a great emptiness in the church. This was her place. I had no place there without her. I was sitting next to Dad and presumed he felt the same weight of loss, the same displacement, but it was hard to tell.

At the offertory, when the priest asked that the sick of the parish be remembered in our prayers and listed them by name, I felt a pang, not of remembrance but of empathy for the families who had members on that list. God's hit list. I thought of all the times I had heard priests rattle off the names of the sick, other people's sick, and been untouched. I wondered how many people in that church care about those names the way I now do, how many had cared when Mom's name was on the list. More, I'm sure now, than I ever suspected.

I had decided to receive communion in her memory, but wondered what Dad would do. Throughout Mass Dad sat and stood on cue, but he didn't kneel with the rest. Mom was convinced that Dad had become a believer during her illness, but I was never sure whether he was receiving communion for her peace of mind or his, out of graciousness or belief. Without her as a witness, would he receive? Dad was sitting at the head of our pew and when the usher indicated it was our turn to file out for communion, he stood and without hesitation walked down the aisle.

I followed, conscious that the past year had removed all guilt from this act. As I placed my left palm in my right to receive the host, I remembered my displays of bad form at those first hopeful Masses for Mom's health. Returning up the aisle to our pew, I felt an impending sense of communion. I knew that as soon as Dad and I knelt side by side the host would dissolve into a strong sense of Mom's presence. She would feel alive in us. I reached our pew with a growing sense of excitement; then, as I headed to my place, Nancy tapped me on the shoulder and said, "We're leaving now, before the kids go stir-crazy."

I felt robbed, angry, but I passed the request onto Dad and we all filed out into a downpour. We spent the next fifteen minutes sitting wet and cold in the car because our exit from the church parking lot was blocked by parishioners who were staying until the end of Mass.

THURSDAY, DECEMBER 25:

When we gathered around the Christmas tree this morning, Dad and I found a much larger pile of gifts from Mike and Nancy than we received on previous Christmases. We were being treated as orphans, which was the only overt acknowledgment of Mom's absence. Several of Dad's presents were items of Mom's. He gave me a watch that had been hers and Susanne a coral necklace and matching earrings that had been hers. It made me glum, but Dad would never have guessed. About 2:00 P.M., Nancy's parents, Matt and Vivian, arrived with arms full of presents. Again, Dad and I received more than our usual share for the same unspoken reasons. Everyone remarked on how well Dad was doing, with both relief and puzzlement in their eyes. Matt is recovering from surgery and radiation for kidney cancer, and his quiet, subdued manner was a comfort, an implicit acknowledgment of shared reality that made me want to be around him.

FRIDAY, DECEMBER 26:

We attended a party tonight at the home of Mike and Nancy's best friends. I had not seen Carol or Mick in several years, and both of them remarked how much I now looked like my mother, which I liked hearing. Several of my cousins in Fort Dodge had made the same observation. Even Freya, who thought I looked like my father, suddenly decided I looked like my mother the first time she saw me after her death. I wonder if my appearance has changed or whether people who knew Mom now need to see her in someone else.

SATURDAY, DECEMBER 27:

Nancy, Susie and I spent the day shopping at a "home store." Late in the afternoon, after dropping Susie off at her gymnastics class, Nancy and I were together alone for the first time of this visit. As we pulled into the parking lot of yet another shopping mall, she paused before getting out of the car and said she had been thinking a lot about how she would respond to the death of her mother or father. "How are you doing?" she asked. I told her I was doing fine, that Mom's suffering was still so much on my mind that it overwhelmed or postponed the fact of her loss to me, and that I didn't know how or when I would react to the finality of her loss. I told her about Dad's sending me the box with my baby shoes and how it made me feel. When I stopped talking, she said, "I'm so relieved." She said that whenever she tries to ask Mike how he is doing, he looks angry and says, "I don't want to talk about it." She had been afraid I might respond the same way. She interprets Mike's silence as anger at her for having urged him to leave his mother's deathbed. One of them needed to return home to their children and Nancy thought at the time it should be Mike. Now she feels terribly guilty, and terribly blamed.

It was a short talk, dispatched while the motor was still running, but we both felt better for it. It was the first and last opportunity we had to talk alone, but back home, we developed a shorthand. If, for instance, Susie asked what we were having for dinner, one of us would look at the other and say, "I don't want to talk about it."

ANCRAM, N.Y.

WEDNESDAY, DECEMBER 31:

I left Dad home alone for several hours when I went to Hudson to run errands for the party I'm giving tomorrow. On my return, he greeted me at the kitchen door with a guilty look on his face. He confessed that while cleaning the stove in my absence, he had polished the numbers off the oven dial. He was trying to fix it by etching numbers back on it with his knife, but the result was too faint to read.

We had been invited to a New Year's Eve party, but I didn't even mention it to Dad, because I didn't feel like going out. We spent a very quiet evening at home watching TV rock-'n'-roll parties broadcast from New York and L.A. We were both bored and seemingly without the means to animate ourselves. By 9:30 I was wondering how we could last till midnight. By 11:00 I felt an overwhelming fatigue. By 11:30 I was in a depression so deep and unexpected it frightened me. I resented the new year. It seemed wrong, unjust for a new year to start without Mom in it. I felt I was being urged to move on, to leave her behind, to consign her to 1911–1986. I would not have been surprised by this sadness on Christmas; in fact, I was ready to welcome sadness on that day but it never came. I had not expected to feel this way today.

TUESDAY, MARCH 10, 1987:

Last night I dreamt that my mother appeared to me when I was sad. I don't remember the context of my sadness, just a vague sense of feeling orphaned and sorry for myself. She appeared out of nowhere, looking healthy and vital, and said, almost as if she were upbraiding me, "Don't forget you have a mother, and a grandmother."

I woke up immediately and wanted to seize upon the dream as a good sign. If the figure in the dream is my mother before her death telling me I have a mother, the dream is no consolation. It is outdated, untrue. But if the figure is my mother appearing from beyond death, then I can take heart from it. I decided the reference to my grandmother means that she is addressing me from beyond death and so her message is that I still have a mother. Happy, I fall back asleep. This morning, I still feel good about the dream, even though it did not have an aura about it the way certain, very significant dreams do. It's the best image I've had so far, and I'll take it, thank you.

TUESDAY, MARCH 17:

A chipmunk joined the birds under the feeder today for the first time this year. Green shoots are making an appearance in the flower beds. Yesterday's snow left a thin, white carpet over the ground but by noon today it had melted, leaving only those few stubborn patches that survived the seventy-five-degree weather of the weekend before last. It is the time of year when it is hardest to believe that spring will ever come. While a foot of clean snow covered the landscape, one could imagine spring; winter beauty implied the possibility of other beauties. But how can one imagine beauty emerging from this half-thawed shabbiness? Will leaves really return to these dry, dead sticks? Do I care?

Yes.

EPILOGUE

MONTEVARCHI, ITALY
JUNE 1987:

I am sitting in the open arch of the loggia looking down onto
the patio, where Dad is sunning himself in a lounge chair. He
is looking tan and fit, clad only in the madras swimming trunks
we bought at the market in Florence on Sunday. A white handkerchief is draped over the crown of his head as protection from
intense morning heat. He is unaware of my gaze, just as my
mother was two summers ago when I snapped a picture of her
sunning in exactly the same spot, her head covered with one of
Dad's handkerchiefs. When I took that picture from this same
perch, I thought I was capturing the image of my mother in a
state of perfect repose and unself-conscious enjoyment. It was
not a rare state for her, but it was a rare setting, one that matched
her capacity for quiet pleasures.

I am surprised, though, to see my usually restless father so at
ease in postures that were once hers. During this week we have

spent together, he has not paced or interrupted. He is calmer, more attuned to my needs for quiet and solitude. For the first time in my adult life, I feel in his company something close to the bedrock of well-being I always felt in my mother's presence. We spend active, sightseeing days together, but most evenings he reads the books that would have been in Mom's hands two years ago. On this visit, his third to Tuscany and my seventh, we have forsaken the heady enticements of the High Renaissance for the more subdued pleasures of Etruscan ruins.

When I proposed this trip to my father and brother several months ago, I imagined it, without saying so, as a time when we would come together to take comfort in the places where my mother had last been happy. I think they accepted my invitation in the spirit it was offered, but things have changed in the short time since then. Mike and Nancy, who arrive next week, desperately need this vacation, their first in Europe, as an escape. Last month, Nancy's father, Matt, who seemed so well at Christmas time, died of the cancer they all thought had been cured. Dad has come with a different need. He is using this time to let his children know how important the companionship of a new friend has become to him.

He has expressed himself so forthrightly that it is impossible to object, even if I had the heart to wish him loneliness as well as loss. The first night he arrived at the villa, he proudly showed me pictures of his "new girlfriend" and her family. Alice's adult children have welcomed my father into their widowed mother's life, and as difficult as it is for me to hear him speak another woman's name with such pride and tenderness, I am, above all, relieved. He will never again be as forlorn as he was on the fall day we walked along the Mississippi together one week after my mother's death. The pictures I took on that day, portraits of him dwarfed by a cottonwood tree that seemed to possess all the strength and endurance he had spent, are not final images. He is not spent. He is insisting on more life, as she did; I accept this fierce attachment as their legacy.

I feel relieved but alone. Each of us experienced the time of my mother's illness so differently that we were seldom able to take comfort in our shared sorrow. I hoped that the time of mourning might be less isolating. Without the confusion sowed by medical misinformation and mismatched periods of denial, I thought we might be united in a mutual need for remembrance. But we three—father, daughter, son—are as diverse in our needs now as we ever were. Why, I wonder, did I ever expect it to be otherwise? Why do I even want a merging of desires now, when I know perfectly well that we have survived as a family all these years by respecting our differences? Maybe I fear that the only thing that ever united us was the deep pleasure we took in my mother's existence and love. Without erecting an icon of her at the center of our disparate lives, we three survivors may splinter like schismatics, suffer the willful isolation of heretics.

I proselytize in subtle ways, make the Etruscans my co-conspirators. I take my father to the Archaeological Museum in Florence, where we spend hours walking from room to room, everywhere encountering evidence of the honor Etruscans lavished upon their dead. Almost all the artifacts of this ancient civilization have been found in their necropoli, miniature cities of the departed carved into hillsides or raised upon flowering meadows. Each tomb was built as a home, in which the most valuable possessions of the departed were placed for their continued pleasure and use. Remains of the dead were placed in cinerary urns shaped like houses, whether simple huts or pillared mansions. In later, more affluent centuries, they were placed in sarcophagi of alabaster or terra-cotta. Often the lid of a sarcophagus bears a sculpture of a husband and wife reclining together in a smiling embrace. The equality that existed between Etruscan men and women was, scholars say, the scandal of pre-Roman times.

My father becomes fascinated with all things Etruscan, gives over long evenings to reading what is known of their civilization's rise and fall, but finally, after a five-hour drive to Volterra, where we view another dozen rooms of urns and sarcophagi, he says, "Please, no more bone boxes." I laugh and relent, which it is within my power to do, because here in Italy, I am in control. I am the one who speaks the language, reads the maps, sets the agenda. I exert his kind of authority, cordial, considerate, but unchallenged. Since the time of my parents' first visit to Italy, I have been impressed by the gracefulness with which he relinquishes control to his more-traveled daughter. He places himself in my hands with complete trust and never questions my judgment, a concession which for two summers had the side effect of making him and my mother equals during their visits here. This, I think, was part of the pleasure she took in Italy.

One evening, after putting a veal roast in the oven for our dinner, I decide to take a walk through the vineyards toward a distant ridge where my parents and I once explored the crumbling remains of an abandoned villa. A gentle breeze stirs the poppies and sends waves through the rye fields as I follow a tractor path in soft, late light. Suddenly I feel inexpressibly happy, and I remember this is why I returned to Italy, to take a walk for her. There is nothing sad, elegiac, in this moment. I feel as if I am walking with her, not for her. I expel a great sigh and feel a grin spread over my face, parting my lips and tugging at the corners of my eyes. I want to walk this path forever, but there is a veal roast cooking for my father, so I turn back, promising to return at the same hour another day.

When Mike and Nancy arrive, they immediately fall under the spell of Italy. Everything is so foreign, so engrossing and welcoming, so perfect a setting for escape; for their sake, my father and I return our interest to the High Renaissance, to towns and cathedrals so dazzling that they compel total attention, leaving none to spare for the sad spectacles of last year, last month. At the villa, Mike and Nancy are the perfect, appreciative guests, but by the end of a week, I see my brother chafing under the double yoke of sister and father. He does not like me speaking for him, ordering his food and negotiating his purchases. And he does not like his father telling him what to notice in places that are new to him, old acquaintances to Dad. The problem is, we three are too much alike. Each of us wants to be in control. We need a peacekeeper, but she is gone.

We find our own way. I learn to keep my mouth shut when Mike tries to communicate with Italian waiters by speaking a loud, slow English. Mike learns to laugh at himself when his attempts at assertion backfire. Dad keeps his pointing finger curled toward his palm. Keeping quiet, laughing, deferring, we incorporate parts of her into us. It's a useful kind of remembering.

When we say our good-byes at the Rome airport on July 4, no one mentions it is her birthday. I return to the villa, where I will pay for that silence. That night I dream that my teeth loosen and crumble; it's a classic dream, the kind one finds listed and decoded in pocketbook Freud, but this time the dream has a plot twist; I dream that my father is still at the villa, and I can't bring myself to leave my room, because I'm afraid the shock of seeing me toothless will kill my father. Two days later I develop a painfully abscessed tooth and submit to the skills of an Italian dentist. He prescribes drugs that make me groggy and listless; an allergic reaction causes my legs to swell with a hot, red rash.

Without the energy to travel, I stay close to the villa. One afternoon, to relieve my boredom, I walk down the road to visit the Pabbis, a family of *contadini* who have tended vineyards on this hill for countless generations. Their oldest son, Moreno, became a friend during my previous summers here, but I have not spoken with him since my arrival. When I enter their court-yard, Signora Pabbi greets me with tears in her eyes; without saying a word, she ushers me into a small room, where Moreno sits on the edge of his father's bed. Moreno's father is yellow, shriveled; Moreno is trying to wash his father's face with a damp cloth, but the father angrily waves a stick arm in the air toward Moreno as if dismissing him. Moreno and I exchange glances before I retreat from this room where I do not belong.

The next morning Moreno comes with the news that his father has died. "Cancro," he says, pointing to his throat. I nod my understanding of the diagnosis, and we sit together for a while. Several times, he says, "Dio, non c'e." God doesn't exist.

A few days later, Moreno's sister calls me on the telephone at the villa to say there is a woman waiting for me to pick her up at the train station in Montevarchi. I think we are having a language problem, because I am not expecting a visitor, certainly not anybody who would know the Pabbis' phone number and call them instead of me to announce her arrival. But Maria is emphatic; a lady is waiting for me. I drive to the train station, find no one and return to the villa, where I receive another call from Maria. The lady has called again, she says; I must go back to the station immediately, because the lady is angry after waiting so long. Maria asked the woman her name, but all she remembers is that it begins with a B. I return to the station, mostly to appease Maria, who is near tears because the lady accused her of not giving me the message.

There is, of course, no lady waiting at the station, but for the next two days, the phone rings at inconvenient hours. I answer, early in the morning, in the middle of the night, and listen to the wordless caller hang up. What have I done to deserve a crank caller? Is Maria, distraught by the death of her father, the caller? Moreno says no.

I begin to think the hill is cursed, but by whom and why? Then I remember I am here to fulfill a deathbed promise and I haven't done it. I promised my eyes would see for her, my ears hear for her. Except for that one, truncated, evening walk through the vineyards, I have not kept my promise. My energies have gone into being my father's daughter, my brother's sister; certainly she, wife and mother, would understand. Wouldn't she? I entertain the thought that my mother is angry, that she is punishing me. The thought is frightening at first, as if I'd conjured up a witch who had stolen my mother's soft-spoken soul. Then it occurs to me that it would be entirely natural for her to be angry. Now that she's free of the earthbound need to be good, free of her constraints as wife and mother, there's no reason for her to hide her anger. And no reason for me to hide mine.

I apologize and promise to make amends. I take an evening walk through the vineyards to the abandoned villa, but this time she is not borne on the breeze that stirs the poppies. Later that night, though, a full moon shines on the hill and I feel my mother's presence, benign and forgiving, sent to me on the beams of light that enter my bedroom window. I leave the shutters open even though the moonlight is so bright it makes sleep impossible. Death is making a pagan of me.

I have my answer, at least for now. I don't find the living presence of my mother in memory, in photographs or anecdotes; I find her instead in moonlight and breezes. On August nights, I pretend shooting stars are signals sent from her to me. I am not talking about belief but the experience of consolation. Certain, unexpected sights or sensations console me the way the feel of familiar beads passing through thumb and forefinger might console someone else. I am thankful that my discovery of death coincided with my discovery of a new setting, thankful that death found me midstream, where the play of light on water makes me feel blessed.

The last time I entered the stream, fly rod in hand, I heard a loud crashing and looked upstream to see a buck highstep across the riffles from one bank to the other, neck arched to hold his heavy rack erect. I thought of cardinals, of Bede's sparrow, and I thought of my father. I wished him the pleasure of the sighting. And I knew that when the time came, I would remember the splendor of that crossing. The stream is generous; someday, I'm sure, it will give me the image of my own life's completion.

FOR THE BEST IN PAPERBACKS, LOOK FOR THE

In every corner of the world, on every subject under the sun, Penguin represents quality and variety—the very best in publishing today.

For complete information about books available from Penguin—including Pelicans, Puffins, Peregrines, and Penguin Classics—and how to order them, write to us at the appropriate address below. Please note that for copyright reasons the selection of books varies from country to country.

In the United Kingdom: For a complete list of books available from Penguin in the U.K., please write to *Dept E.P., Penguin Books Ltd, Harmondsworth, Middlesex, UB7 0DA*.

In the United States: For a complete list of books available from Penguin in the U.S., please write to *Dept BA, Penguin*, Box 120, Bergenfield, New Jersey 07621-0120.

In Canada: For a complete list of books available from Penguin in Canada, please write to *Penguin Books Ltd, 2801 John Street, Markham, Ontario L3R 1B4*.

In Australia: For a complete list of books available from Penguin in Australia, please write to the *Marketing Department, Penguin Books Ltd, P.O. Box 257, Ringwood, Victoria 3134*.

In New Zealand: For a complete list of books available from Penguin in New Zealand, please write to the *Marketing Department, Penguin Books (NZ) Ltd, Private Bag, Takapuna, Auckland 9*.

In India: For a complete list of books available from Penguin, please write to *Penguin Overseas Ltd, 706 Eros Apartments, 56 Nehru Place, New Delhi, 110019*.

In Holland: For a complete list of books available from Penguin in Holland, please write to *Penguin Books Nederland B.V., Postbus 195, NL-1380AD Weesp, Netherlands*.

In Germany: For a complete list of books available from Penguin, please write to *Penguin Books Ltd, Friedrichstrasse 10-12, D-6000 Frankfurt Main I, Federal Republic of Germany*.

In Spain: For a complete list of books available from Penguin in Spain, please write to *Longman, Penguin España, Calle San Nicolas 15, E-28013 Madrid, Spain*.

In Japan: For a complete list of books available from Penguin in Japan, please write to *Longman Penguin Japan Co Ltd, Yamaguchi Building, 2-12-9 Kanda Jimbocho, Chiyoda-Ku, Tokyo 101, Japan*.